IN STITCHES

IN STITCHES

A Memoir

ANTHONY YOUN, M.D.

WITH ALAN EISENSTOCK

GALLERY BOOKS

New York London Toronto Sydney

Gallery Books
A Division of Simon & Schuster, Inc.
1230 Avenue of the Americas
New York, NY 10020

First Gallery Books hardcover edition April 2011

GALLERY BOOKS and colophon are trademarks of Simon & Schuster, Inc.

For information about special discounts for bulk purchases, please contact Simon & Schuster Special Sales at 1-866-506-1949 or business@simonandschuster.com.

The Simon & Schuster Speakers Bureau can bring authors to your live event. For more information or to book an event contact the Simon & Schuster Speakers Bureau at 1-866-248-3049 or visit our website at www.simonspeakers.com.

Designed by Renato Stanisic

Manufactured in the United States of America

10 9 8 7 6 5 4 3 2

Library of Congress Cataloging-in-Publication Data

Youn, Anthony.
   In stitches / Anthony Youn with Alan Eisenstock.
      p. cm.
   1. Youn, Anthony. 2. Plastic surgeons—United States—Biography. I. Eisenstock, Alan. II. Title.
      RD27.35.Y68A3 2011
      617.9'5092—dc22
      [B]

                                                         2010044106

ISBN 978-1-4516-0844-1
ISBN 978-1-4516-0883-0 (ebook)

Author's Note

This work is a memoir. I have changed names and some identifying details of many characters portrayed in this book—including all the doctors and patients—and a few individuals are composites. In some instances, the precise details or timing of events have been changed or compressed to assist with the flow of the narrative, and some comedic license has been taken. Nevertheless, I believe this book provides an accurate portrait of my journey to become the doctor (and man) that I am today. I hope you enjoy it.

For Amy, the love of my life.

Contents

IN STITCHES

Prologue: The Face in the Ceiling

What a pair. Double D's. Poking up at me like twin peaks. Pam Anderson, eat your heart out.

Too bad they're attached to a fourteen-year-old boy.

I ease the black marker out of my lab coat pocket and start drawing on my first surgery patient of the day. Phil. An overweight African-American boy. Phil has severe gynecomastia—in layperson's language, ginormous man boobs. Poor Phil. Bad enough being fourteen, awkward, and a nonathlete in a tough urban Detroit school. Now he has to deal with *breasts*?

Two weeks ago.

I sit in my office with Phil and Mrs. Grier, his grandmother. Phil lives with his grandma, who's raised him since he was ten, when his mom died. He's never known his dad. Mrs. Grier sits on a chair in front of my desk, her hands folded in her lap. She's a large woman, nervous, well dressed in a light blue dress and matching shawl. Phil, wearing what looks like a toga, sits on a chair next to her. He stares at the floor.

"It happened fast," Mrs. Grier says. "He shot up, his voice got deeper, he started to shave."

She speaks in a low rumble. She looks at her grandson, tries to catch his eye. He can't see her. He keeps his head down, eyes boring into the floor.

"Then he became quiet. Withdrawn. He would spend more and more time in his room alone, listening to music. He would walk around all day wearing his headphones. Seemed like he was trying to shut out the world."

Mrs. Grier slowly shakes her head. "Phil's a good student. But his grades have gone downhill. He doesn't want to go to school. Says he's sick. I tried to talk to him, tried to find out what was wrong. He would just say, 'Leave me alone, Nana.' That's all he would say."

Phil clears his throat. He keeps looking at the floor.

Mrs. Grier shifts in her chair. "One day I accidentally walked in on him when he was drying off after a shower. That's when I saw . . . you know . . . *them*."

Phil flinches. Mrs. Grier reaches over and touches his arm. After a moment, he swallows and says in a near whimper, "Can you help me?"

"Yes," I say.

I say this one word with such confidence that Phil lifts his head and finds my eyes. He blinks through tears.

"Please," he says.

THE NIGHT BEFORE Phil's procedure.

I can't sleep. I lean over and squint at the clock on the nightstand.

3:13 A.M.

I twist my head and look at my wife, deep asleep, her back arched slightly, her breath humming like a tiny engine. I exhale and study the ceiling.

A shaft of light blinds me like the flash from a camera. My mind hits rewind, and I'm thrown backward into a shock of memory. One by one, as if sifting through photographs, I flip through other sleepless nights, a string of them, a lifetime ago in medical school, some locked in the student lounge studying, some a function of falling into bed too tired or too worked up for sleep. Often I would find myself staring at the ceiling then, the way I am now, talking to myself, feeling lost, fumbling to find my way, wondering who I was and what I was doing. The memory hits me like a wave, and for a second, just as in medical school, I feel as if I am drowning.

My eyes flutter and I'm back in our bedroom, staring blurrily at the ceiling. I see Phil's breasts, pendulous fleshy torpedoes that have left him and his grandmother heartsick and desperate. I know that his emotional life is at stake and I am their hope. I know also that isn't why I can't sleep. I blink and see Phil's face, and then I see my own.

I was Phil—the outsider, the outcast, the deformed. I was fourteen-year-old Phil.

I grew up one of two Asian-American kids in a small town of near-wall-to-wall whiteness. In elementary and middle school, I was short, shy, and nerdy. Then I shot up in high school. I became tall, too tall, too thin. I wore thick Coke-bottle glasses, braces, a stereotypical Asian bowl-cut hairdo, and then, to my horror, watched helplessly as my jaw began to grow, unstoppable, defying all restraint and correction, expanding Pinocchio-like, protruding to an unthinkable, monstrous size. I loved comic books, collected them, obsessed over them, and as if in recognition of this, my jaw extended to a cartoon size. I *was* Phil. Except I grew a comic-book jaw while he grew *National Geographic* breasts. Like Phil, I only wanted to look and feel normal. I just wanted to fit in.

It hits me then.

My calling—my fate—was written that summer between high school and college, the Summer of the Jaw. My own makeover foreshadowed my life's work. Reconstructing my jaw showed me how changing your appearance can profoundly affect your life. Now, years later, I am devoted to making over others—helping them, beautifying them, changing them. I have discovered that plastic surgery goes beyond how others see you; it changes how you see yourself. On occasion, I have performed procedures that have saved lives. I believe that I will save Phil.

My mind sifts through my days in medical school, and in a kind of hallucinogenic blaze, I conjure up every triumph, every flub, every angst-filled moment. I remember each pulse-pounding second of the first two years of nonstop studying and test-taking, interrupted by intermittent bouts of off-the-hook partying. I see myself in years three and four, wearing my short white coat, wandering through hospital corridors trying to overcome my fear that someone—an administrator, a nurse, or God forbid, a patient—would confuse me for a doctor and ask for medical attention. I teetered a hair's width away from those moments that might mean life and death, facing the deepest truth in the pit of my stomach: that I had absolutely no idea what I was doing. And neither did any of my medical-school classmates, those doctors in training who stumbled around me.

But things changed. Thanks to my small circle of close friends, my focus, work ethic, and drive to succeed, I slowly grew up. I entered medical school a shy, skinny, awkward nerd with no confidence, no game, and no clue. I came out, four years later, a man.

A smile creeps across my face. My eyelids quiver. I catch a last glimpse of the face of my younger self in the ceiling as it shimmies and pulls away. Sleep comes at last.

Phil's surgery goes well. Ninety minutes, no complications. I lop off his breasts with a scalpel, slice off the nipples, then suture them back onto his now flat chest. I nod at his new areolas. They have decreased in diameter from the size of pie plates to quarters. I leave Phil stitched up and covered with gauze, a normal-looking high school freshman. Good news, Phil. You will not break new ground and become the first male waiter at Hooters.

I once saw an episode of *Grey's Anatomy* in which a character suggested that she—and every doctor—experienced an "aha moment" when she realized she had become a doctor.

That never happened to me. I experienced an accumulation of many moments. Some walloped me, left me reeling. Others flickered and rolled past like a shadow. They involved teachers, classmates, room-mates, friends, family, actors playing patients, nurses, the family of patients, and patients themselves, patients who touched me and who troubled me, patients whose courage changed my life and who taught me how to live as they faced death, and of course, doctors—doctors who were kind, doctors who were clueless, doctors who were burned out, doctors who inspired me and doctors whom I aspired to be, doc-tors who sought my opinion and doctors who shut me down.

Thinking about all these people and moments, I see no pattern. Each moment feels singular and powerful. They stunned me, envel-oped me, awed me, but more often flew right by me unnoticed until days, weeks, months, years later. Until now.

This is my Book of Moments.

I Premed

1

Karate Kid

November 2, 1972.

Detroit.

I am two days old.

My father stops the car outside of our apartment. My mother waits for the engine to cut out and for my father to haul up the emergency brake. She leans into the back, lifts me out of my car seat, swaddles me inside her coat, and carries me to their bedroom, where she lowers me gently into my bassinet at the foot of their bed. My dad trails, wearing a suit, hands clasped in front of him as if in prayer. He looks down at me, and his heart fills up. He fights a grin, keeps his face tight as leather. He would never allow his feelings to spill over and make an unscheduled appearance. That's not his way. Still, he can't keep his eyes off of me.

"Anthony," my mother whispers. "Good name. Strong."

My father nods. "A doctor. Surgeon. Vascular. Big money."

My mother blows out a sigh, tips her head onto my father's shoulder. "Don't rush him. Wait until he's at least a week old."

"You're right." He smiles, curls an arm around my mother's shoulders. "Transplant surgery. That the *big* money. You not believe what they get. One surgery. Ten thousand dollah. For one *hour*. Early retirement. Mercedes-Benz. Condo in Florida—"

She lifts her head, knocks him back with a stare.

My father blinks at her. A prisoner of her eyes. "What?"

"Why don't you tell him he has to marry a nice Korean girl, too?"

"No. Come on. He's two days old."

My mother rolls her eyes, nudges her head back onto my father's padded pin-striped shoulder.

"That he already knows," my father says.

GREENVILLE, MICHIGAN. POPULATION 7,945.

I am six years old.

I'm learning English. I've picked up most of it from watching *Sesame Street* and spending my days at my friend Chris's house. My father doesn't know. Or if he knows, he doesn't let on. I'm sure he wants me to learn English, even though he and my mom are heavily into their Korean roots. We do live in America, and I am going to be a doctor, so it would be helpful if I knew English, even though I'd rather not be a doctor. I'd rather be a superhero or own a toy store.

My father casts a huge shadow in our house, in my life, although when I think about it, I see him only once a day for about an hour. He works long hours, often leaves when I'm asleep. He always comes home for dinner. When we hear his car grind into the driveway, my older brother, Mike, and I stop whatever we're doing and race to the front door to greet him. Sometimes I get lost playing with my toys or flipping through a book, and I zone out. Takes me a minute to come back to earth, to regroup. But the instant that front door opens, I snap out of my trance, scramble to my feet, and race Mike to the door.

Something happens in the house when my father walks in. The atmosphere shifts. The air feels heavier. My father changes the energy in the room, too. Slows it down. Makes you more careful. And I know this. You do not want to get him mad. I'm never sure what will upset him. He's like the weather. Cloudy with a chance of rain and occasional thunderstorm.

"Good evening," my father says in Korean to my brother and me at the door. Sometimes I feel less like his son and more like his employee.

"Good evening, Father." We answer in Korean, and then we bow. He doesn't give us a full bow back. He bends slightly. He's the authority. That's all he has to do.

"How was your day?" I ask him.

"Fine."

Mike, a year and a half older, grunts, avoids eye contact. I can feel my father staring at him.

"Anything interesting happen?" I ask, trying to deflect, trying to avoid any imminent storm on the horizon.

Eyes first on Mike, then sweeping back over me like a prison searchlight, my father says, his voice weary, "Rake the leaves" or "Sweep out the garage."

My father doesn't believe that his sons should be idle for a minute. When you finish a job, there is always more work to be done. Banished to the backyard or en route to the garage, I turn back for a moment and catch my father smiling at my mother, a knowing, familiar smile, the closest they ever come to intimacy in front of us. He'll then make his way into the family room, plop down in his La-Z-Boy recliner, wriggle out of his shoes, put his feet up, and open the evening paper. Soon my mother will arrive with a drink, orange juice or tea, then return to the kitchen and finish preparing dinner. My father will flip on the TV, lay the newspaper on his lap, and stare at the evening news.

Outside, my brother and I alternate stretches of working hard with slacking off. The leader, he'll lean on his rake or broom, make cracks at me, or fool around and attack me, turning his rake or broom into a weapon. But no way will we go inside for dinner with the leaves not raked or the garage not swept. I'm not sure what my father will do, but

I know that he'll punish us, and I'd rather not find out how. Even at this young age, I've learned certain survival skills. Top of the list, I avoid confrontation at all costs.

My parents, both Korean émigrés, try to retain some of their native traditions. My mother has decorated our walls with traditional Korean art. She reads me popular Korean children's stories, sings Korean children's songs, and recites Korean folk tales. And she cooks traditional Korean food. Seafood, mostly. Scary seafood. I walk casually into the kitchen and find myself facing the dead eyes of a two-foot-long fish flopped across the kitchen table, which, steaming in its own succulent juices, we will pick apart later with chopsticks. More often my mother will serve us tureens of sizzling squid and octopus soup, tentacles and snouts bobbing, attached to, I swear, half-alive mini–sea monsters, devil fish that we have to batter and subdue before we choke down the slimy morsels with mouthfuls of sticky rice. Recently, on the sly, Chris and his family have introduced me to McDonald's, Pizza Hut, and KFC, and I have fallen hard, beginning a hot and heavy love affair with American fast food.

When dinner is ready, my mother calls to us or rings the dinner bell. Mike and I finish raking or sweeping and dart inside. I wash my hands, then head into the family room and tell my father in Korean that it is time for dinner. At dinner, we speak little and only in Korean.

Tucking me in at night, my mother brings the covers up to my chin. I turn to her and whisper, "Why do we always have to work when Daddy comes home?"

"Your father believes in hard work. That's how he was raised."

"On the farm."

"Yes. On the farm. He believes you have to get your hands dirty."

"He never does."

My mother's eyes bore into mine.

"Well, he doesn't," I say. "Mike and I do all the work. And you."

My mother's lip quivers. I can't tell if she's about to yell or laugh.

"He works very hard. At night when you're sleeping, he gets calls, all the time, to deliver babies. He has to go out in the middle of the night. He's the only baby doctor in town. That's why he's so tired all the time. He works all day and all night."

I hadn't realized this.

"Hard work being a baby doctor," I say.

"Very hard work," my mother says. "But there are all kinds of doctors. Family doctors, eye doctors, nose doctors, hand doctors, foot doctors—"

"That's good," I say. "Because I'm never going to be a baby doctor."

A RELATIVE SETS them up. I'm sure someone from my father's side. That's the only way this beautiful daughter of a high school principal would meet, much less date, the son of a poor farmer, the oldest of nine children. He has potential, true, and they have at least one thing in common—he has been accepted to medical school, and she is studying to be a nurse. She likes him right away. When he talks, he speaks with a quiet confidence. And passion. He has big dreams. After completing medical school in Korea, he plans to move to America and do his residency and become rich. He vows to send money home every month, and when he becomes a trained American doctor, he will return to Korea and pull his family out of poverty. She falls for his steely determination and the touch of his strong hands. Soon after they are a couple, he brings her home to meet the rest of his family and see the farm. Smart move. Because if she'd seen the farm *before* she fell in love with him, she might have had second thoughts. Her mom—my grandma—certainly does. She voices early and frequent objections about him, his poor background and his religion—he was raised Buddhist and not Christian—and his crazy future plans.

Good thing she doesn't take her mom with her to the farm. That would clinch it.

A small patch of land. A balding rice patty. A few humped and crooked rows of radishes and onions. A teetering shell of a farmhouse.

Rotting, patched, sweltering walls. Paper-thin floors that buckle and creak. Three tiny rooms. Nine kids. No plumbing. A pot in each room to piss in. A pot in the last room to shit in. A large basin sits near the back wall of the middle room. My grandmother fills the basin with buckets of cold water she pulls from the corroded well outside so each of the nine kids can occasionally bathe. The farmhouse has no stove, just a mound of kindling under a small grate. Chickens roam everywhere. The hens drop eggs that the kids pick up for breakfast. The older chickens become lunch, dinner, and part-time pets.

I wonder how my father could have lived this way. Before bedtime, I ask my mother.

"You make do," she says. "You play the hand God deals you."

I'm too young to understand. My father's former life seems unreal, impossible, invented, a figment of some Korean folk tale. That appalling, crumbling farmhouse bears no resemblance to our sturdy, spread-out ranch house on a wide plot of land in a small town in Michigan.

"Day and night," my mother says as if reading my mind. "Your father came from nothing. Now look. All because of hard work. And faith. You become resourceful."

I don't know what she means. She tells me a story. I pop my thumb in my mouth, nuzzle against her cheek, and close my eyes to her words.

During the war, when my father is my age, soldiers descend on the farm. They see it as a safe house, a place to spend the night, an opportunity for a home-cooked meal. My grandmother sees the soldiers as predators. If she feeds them, she will have no food left to feed her family. She's afraid that her family will starve. To preserve her food supply, she buries all of the rice she has in the backyard. When the soldiers arrive, she tells them that she has no rice to feed them. They don't believe her. They crash through the tiny rickety farmhouse, overturning pots, upending the meager furniture, smashing dishes, searching for the rice stash. They give up and move on.

"Your grandmother took care of her family," my mother says. "Your father takes care of ours."

. . . .

DAD COMES TO America. A Korean right off the boat. Steve. That's his new name. The name he calls himself. I imagine some racist encounter drove him to Steve. His actual name, his given name, the name he changed, is Suck. In Korea, parents often give their oldest child the same middle and last names. Technically, then, my father's name is Suck Youn Youn. Pretty bad, but not as bad as his brother's name. His middle name is Bum, sticking him with the unfortunate handle: Suck Bum Youn.

Let's face it. Suck Youn and Suck Bum both suck.

Steve is better.

Newly arrived, my father's residencies take him and my mother on a rock band–like road trip of the Midwest, moving them from Pittsburgh to Detroit to Dayton, Ohio, finally planting them down just outside of Grand Rapids, Michigan. There my dad struggles to find his place, struggles to fit in. He feels like an outcast. He doesn't make friends easily because of his long hours and difficulties learning English. One time some doctors invite him to a barbecue. They ask him to bring the beer. The word is new to him, the beverage unfamiliar. Confused, unsure, he brings two six-packs of *root* beer. The rest of the barbecue does not go well. The doctors don't ask him to socialize with them again.

In Grand Rapids, he takes out a loan and starts his own practice. The people in the area shut him out. They refuse to embrace a foreign ob-gyn who speaks broken English. He makes them uncomfortable. The practice fails. Desperate, my father scans medical journals for other opportunities. He finds one in Greenville, about forty-five minutes away. Their one and only ob-gyn has retired, leaving an opening. My father shuts down the Grand Rapids practice and sets up shop in this tiny blue-collar factory town. These people don't care that my dad is Korean and that he speaks broken English. They're having babies and they need a doctor. His practice booms. His English improves. He purchases a ranch-style house, a big-screen TV, a fancy car. He and my mom raise a family of their own.

And that brings us here, to Greenville, where I live, population 7,945, 7,941 of whom are Caucasian.

I'M PUSHING SEVEN. Thanks to my best friend, Chris, *Sesame Street*, and school, I speak fluent, impeccable, American elementary school English complete with midwestern twang. Close your eyes and you'd never know I looked Asian. To be honest, there are times I wish I were white, like everybody else in my class. I have a lot of friends, but some of the tougher, dumber kids call me names and make fun of the way I look and my Korean heritage. Eating our traditional dinners every night doesn't help. We sit at the table using the blunt end of our chopsticks to bash in the skulls of half-dead crustaceans who circle the surface of our sizzling, crackling soup. I grimace and hold my nose as I chew. My father pops pieces of the things into his mouth like candy.

My mother, squirming in her chair to find a comfortable position, pregnant with my sister, says in Korean to my father, "How was your day?"

He swallows, and a smile climbs up his face like a sunrise. "Good day at the office. Daddy worked hard. Two C-sections!" The words burst from his lips at a volume needled up with excitement.

"Daddy making big money so Daddy can retire early. Play golf five days a week." He winks at me, his co-conspirator. "Daddy want to leave you kids a lot of money when he dies."

I say nothing. At this point in my life, halfway through second grade, I'm having some doubts about becoming a doctor.

My father giggles. "Yesterday. I do laparoscopy. Fifteen minutes. One thousand dollah. Fifteen minutes, one *thousand* dollah!"

He shakes his head. Then I feel his eyes on me. I slink into my chair, try to disappear inside the soup.

"Tony, you become transplant surgeon. One transplant, five thousand dollah. That's what they pay. One proceejah, five thousand dollah."

"Wow. Great. The only thing is sometimes I wonder if, you know, I should *be* a doctor when I grow up."

Time stops. Silence like a tomb. Crickets chirping. A bomb ticking . . .

Did I just *question* my father?

Not the brightest thing to do.

My mother looks off, pats her belly to soothe her suddenly kicking unborn child, then pokes through her soup with her chopsticks. My brother stares at me, his lips locked in a stunned, frozen circle. He lifts his eyebrows. He says something, but I can't make it out because of the loud thumping of my heart, which has traveled into my head and drowned out every other thought and sound.

"You *what*?" My father stares at me, his eyes filmy with incomprehension. He looks as if he's been slapped.

I have to fix this. At least make an attempt. "It's nothing definite. I'm just saying that I'd like to keep my options open. I'm only seven. I'm still relatively young."

"But what . . . what you *do*?"

I'm regretting every second of this meal. Wishing I had never opened my mouth. Wishing I could evaporate into the steam.

"Daddy doesn't understand. You want to become *salesman*?"

He spits the word out. The equivalent of *garbage collector* or *drug dealer*.

"Or maybe you work at factory? Assembly line? Make fan belts? Make boxes? Become unhappy drunk?"

I look down into my soup bowl. I feel as small and defenseless as the half-dead squid staring back at me.

"Look across street. Poor Chris father. He not doctor, he get fired. Doctor never get fired. Daddy has best job. Daddy has best boss. Daddy." My father shakes his head slowly. He begins absently rearranging the silverware. "You have to *think*, Tony. How you gonna pay your bills? How you live? You gonna live on street? Or worse—live at home when you're thirty-five?"

"No, I—"

"Doctor is the only thing. Every other job is no good for you. You have to make Daddy proud."

I glance at my mother and my brother. They shake their heads in a sad chorus, twin windshield wipers. My father picks up his bowl with both red hands, pinkies extended, and slurps his soup. Conversation over.

And that's how I decide to become a doctor.

FIFTH GRADE. I now have a sister. Lisa. She's cute and playful, kind of like a puppy. I like to tickle her, get her laughing. She's easy. She waddles after me, which I like. She occupies a lot of my mother's time. Fine with me. Lisa can't do that much, and I have a lot on my mind.

The thing is, I wish I weren't different. I wish I looked like everybody else. I don't want to stick out. I don't want to be special. Special means weird. I want to be cool. But that's out. That's impossible. Asians are not cool. Think about it. Rank the cool cultures. Which people are cool? Black people are cool. Latin people are cool. Australians. Italians. Spanish people. Irish people. All cool.

Asians?

Forget it.

When you think of an Asian guy, what comes to mind?

A short, skinny, brainy supernerd with thick glasses, buckteeth, braces, a bowl haircut, and a Nikon camera strapped around his neck.

By fifth grade, I've hit every one of those marks. Except the camera. But some days my mother makes me wear my cloth chin guard to school in addition to my braces. I look like an eleven-year-old Hannibal Lecter. That trumps the camera.

What makes things even worse is the new kid. Kirby.

Kirby—heavily Korean—transfers to our school in fifth grade. Naturally, because I'm the only other Asian kid within miles, every teacher and kid in the school assumes that Kirby and I will become instant best friends, or that we already know each other because all Asians know each other.

The morning of Kirby's first day, our teacher assigns him the desk next to mine. Kirby is Korean, all right, but he's tall and athletic and belligerent and wears a buzz cut. He talks out in class, earns glares from teachers and kids, and when one particularly annoying redneck hillbilly kid makes fun of him, Kirby shoots him the bird.

"See you on the playground . . . *Chink*," says hillbilly redneck.

At recess, hillbilly redneck shows up with ten of his closest hillbilly redneck friends. I'm standing next to Kirby. The teacher has asked me to show Kirby around, give him a tour of the playground—as if this dusty asphalt blacktop is a local tourist attraction—and introduce him to my friends. I do. Grunts. Kicking of dirt. Muttered hellos. Can't say I see much chemistry there.

With the redneck horde now descending, Kirby looks at me and nods. I think he assumes we're in this together, as if we're the leads in the Baldwin Heights Elementary School production of *Rush Hour*. This couldn't be further from the truth. Not only am I not bosom buddies with Kirby, but I am also not into fighting. A few months ago my mother enrolled me in karate class. I made it to yellow belt. Yellow belt is the grade up from white belt. Everyone gets a white belt. You join the class, you pay the fee, you get a white belt. Yellow belt means you've advanced to the point where you can put on your *gi* properly and get into your fighting stance without falling over. Almost everybody earns a yellow belt. I got mine. Barely. I recently announced at dinner that I hate karate and want to quit. My mother, after a short, passionate exchange in Korean with my father, agreed but insisted that I replace karate with another after-school activity. Something less violent, I pleaded.

Which is how I joined the church choir.

As hillbilly redneck and his army surround us, I decide this is probably not a good time to explain to Kirby that even if I were his trusted ally, which I'm not, I am no longer even a yellow belt. I am a tenor.

I needn't have worried. Kirby is a junior Bruce Lee. He kicks, chops, punches, and wipes out the entire fifth grade.

Karate, I know, is an Asian stereotype.

Wiping out a swarm of fifth-grade douche bags, though, is cool.

And since I'm standing next to Kirby when he does it, I, too, have become cool.

For the moment.

2

Jawzilla

Cool, I discover, has a short shelf life.

Sixth grade.

My jaw is growing. Subtly and steadily it advances, protruding *Alien*-like, a beast inching, crunching forward, unchecked, unstoppable. My mother and I attend countless consultations with dentists, orthodontists, oral surgeons, and jaw specialists. She bombards them with questions. *Why is this happening? What did he do? What did he not do? Can you make it stop?* In return, we receive a cacophony of theories and explanations accompanied by elaborate charts, milky X-rays, medical mumbo jumbo, and flailing rubber-tipped pointers. The theories include:

- My constant and passionate thumb sucking mangled my bite, causing what dental journals will soon hail as the world's all-time number one most extreme underbite.
- My thumb sucking played absolutely no part whatsoever. My dentist simply didn't alert my orthodontist soon enough.
- My dentist alerted my orthodontist in plenty of time. My orthodontist didn't fit my braces properly.
- My dentist and my orthodontist both screwed up.

And my favorite theory and the one I believe:

- *I don't know.* It's just nature. Nature decided to mess me up. It happens. That's why we have dwarfs and giants and Siamese twins and people with cleft lips and webbed feet and three breasts and girls born with penises and . . . *twelve-year-old kids with jaws that won't stop growing!*

My mother puts her faith in the last guy we see, mainly because he's convincing and we're exhausted. He decides, bottom line, that my orthodontist, at the very least, put the pressure in the wrong place. He will have to reset the braces, fit me again, and I will have to wear my chin cup and headgear all night and all day. Every day. Twenty-four/seven. At home and at school. We have to pull the front teeth forward and push the back teeth back. We have to correct the correction. Or else—

I can't envision the *or else.* I picture a cartoon kid with a massive, jutting Jay Leno jaw. A chiseled chin sticking out like a front porch. Grotesque. Deformed. And I imagine my friends pointing at me and snickering and laughing out loud and making faces, sticking out their chins in comic exaggeration of my own. It's not bad enough that I'm saddled with thick, goofy glasses, a bowl-cut haircut, Kmart wardrobe, and Korean features with no karate to back me up. I now have to deal with Jawzilla?

As my jaw thrusts forward, my inner nerd rides out with it. I enter middle school and promptly retreat into my room, losing myself in comic books and video games. I discover a knack for drawing. I fill up notebook after notebook with sketches of cartoon characters I copy from my comic books and create on my own. To appease my parents, who want me out of my room, I take up the cello and join the school orchestra. While I play classical music at school, at home I listen secretly to the Carpenters, Olivia Newton-John, and John Denver, whose maudlin sentimentality mirrors my own. Might as well slam the exclamation point after my name—Tony Youn, *nerd!* In my room, my sanctuary, I devour each new issue of *Spider-Man* and watch *The Karate Kid* over and over, memorizing every scene, every line, every inflection, every moment. Both resonate with the same theme: skinny loser nerd overcomes hideous looks, beats up jock bad guy and his stupid jock friends, and of course, gets the cute strawberry-blond girl.

Yes, I'm noticing girls. I differentiate now between those who cause my heart to seize up as they walk by and those I want as science-fair partners. One fateful morning I notice that a small cluster of facial hairs have unmistakably popped up on each cheek. I look as if my cheeks have begun to sprout pathetic minuscule Brillo pads.

At school, as my nerd identity expands along with my jaw, the few authentic Greenville nerds attach themselves to me like magnets. We form our own little nerd fraternity, committing ourselves to the most uncool, socially depressing Saturday nights imaginable. We gather in our finished basements and play marathon games of Risk, Axis & Allies, and Ultima, or watch each other fight monsters, battle armies, and maneuver through mazes in the latest and greatest video game. In our recently deep voices that occasionally crack, we lament that the girls we ogle in the hall ignore us, snub us, or body-check us. No surprise. We are the original Geek Squad. We lob Cheetos at each other and try to catch them in our mouths. We exchange glasses, compare astigmatisms. We make the guys in *Big Bang Theory* seem like studs.

And then everything flips upside down.

SUMMER BEFORE HIGH school. My parents pack me up and send me to Phillips Exeter Academy in New Hampshire to attend a six-week summer session so I can get a jump on my classes and begin studying for the SATs. Yes, I know I won't be taking my SATs for *two years*. Have I mentioned that my parents are Korean?

At Exeter I gravitate first to the Caucasian kids. To my shock, they won't have anything to do with me. Why? Because I'm Asian.

I'm devastated and indescribably lonely. I escape to my dorm room, wriggle my headphones over my ears, and listen to Olivia soothingly croon some sappy melody that brings me to tears. A few days later, as I wait in the cafeteria line for the sullen hairnetted cafeteria worker to scoop some brown glop onto a plate, three Korean-American kids behind me introduce themselves. Two things about this stun me. First, they look sharp. They wear buzz cuts, pilot glasses, and tragically hip clothes that you'd see in a music video. Second, they ask me to hang out with them.

My life changes on the spot. My new friends introduce me to new-wave music by bands like Erasure and Depeche Mode. I like it, although I still prefer my beloved Olivia Newton-John, John Denver, and the Carpenters. I don't tell my new buddies, though. I'm too busy pretending to be cool.

At night, unable to sleep, eyes tracking the shadow of a lone fly crossing the ceiling, I wrestle with this sudden and violent cultural shift: in the crazy new universe of elite East Coast high schools, Asians—even Koreans—are *cool*.

What am I supposed to do with this beautiful, mind-blowing, everything-that-was-down-is-up new world order?

I have only one choice.

I bring the cool back to Greenville.

SEPTEMBER.

I walk into school a new man. To start with, I've grown. I'm still thin, but I'm no longer short, dumpy, and mousy. I've shot up past six feet and I'm still going. I also show up with a new haircut, a new wardrobe, new designer glasses, and new music that I share. I abandon the cello and try out for the tennis team. I don't abandon my nerd fraternity. Rather, I bring them with me. Or try to. They follow clumsily. But I am clearly their leader, their role model. My kindness to them only adds to my appeal. The cute, popular girls view me as sensitive and accessible and want me around. The jocks, rulers of the school, the ones who didn't notice me a year ago or wrote me off as a hopeless nerd, now embrace me. I make the tennis team, which adds to my cred. After school, I float in a pack with the in crowd.

Weekends, by decree, I reserve for homework and family. My father declares it his time to relax, to bond, to exercise, and we—in particular, his sons—must relax, bond, and exercise along with him. Whether or not we want to or have plans of our own remains beside the point.

My father prefers individual sports, tennis, golf, and skiing, sports that we can play with or against him. As I become more entrenched with my new group of friends, they accept, reluctantly, that I will run with them during the week and abandon them on weekends. At the same time, as I allow myself the perception, imagined or real, that certain girls I find attractive might—*might*—find me semi-attractive as well, and could—*could*—possibly accompany me to maybe a movie or miniature golf or out for a milk shake, if I mustered the courage to ask them, I find my father's decree to hang out with him on weekends increasingly intrusive. Typically, teenagers choose not to hang out with their parents on weekends. It's not fair. It's not right. And it's way not cool. I begin to resent having to go off and bang tennis balls around or whack golf balls down hard public fairways while schlepping my clubs in the heat. It's not as if my father and I have *fun*. At least not my sixteen-year-old self-absorbed version of fun. I begin to resent having to commit this time to him. I don't say anything. We engage in these weekend exercises mostly in solemn silence.

One Saturday morning at breakfast, my father hits me with a knowing half-smile. "How about we go skiing in Grand Rapids."

It's not a question.

I hesitate. "When?"

He dabs his mouth with a napkin. "Right now. Let's get early start."

After a second of staring at my hands, I lift my head and allow these words to exit my mouth. "I don't know if I want to go. I may have plans with my friends."

My father's face pulses purple. He stands up, leans his fists into the table, and glowers at me. He has to look up. I have grown taller than he is. It does not feel that way. It feels as if he looms over me, a giant. His voice trembles. "Who you think you are?" He holds, inhales, blows out a tiny torrent of air, then—

"You telling me you're not gonna GO? You are SON! You get your skis and get into the car. We are GOING SKIING!"

He storms out.

We leave for Grand Rapids fifteen minutes later.

Humiliated, angry, my father seethes. He drives in silence. We ski in silence. We return to Greenville in silence. He refuses to speak to me for two straight days. I am the good son, the accommodator, the one who never rocks the boat, and it occurs to me that by questioning him, I have not just made him angry, I have broken his heart.

I never question him again.

I STEAM TOWARD graduation. I apply to a handful of colleges, receive several acceptances and scholarships, including one to Kalamazoo College, the best small liberal-arts college in Michigan. Weighing my choices, among them a large local university and an Ivy League college in New England, I ask my parents what I should do. To my shock, they back off. My father tells me that this is my decision.

"Consider all factors—location, size, amount of scholarship they give you, and which one prepares you best for medical school. Then decide. Your decision. Up to you."

If it were up to me, I'd choose to become a rock star or cartoonist, but since I've already taken on my father over skiing and seen how well that went, I opt to stick with the default position—medical school. Ticking off my father once in my lifetime is more than enough.

Ultimately, I choose Kalamazoo because of the hefty scholarship they offer and the school's manageable size. I worry that I'll get lost at a large school. I'm a small-town kid at heart and a homebody. Kalamazoo is far enough for me to go away to college and come home for weekends when I feel homesick. Or when I run out of clean clothes.

I end senior year at Greenville High in a blaze of glory. I achieve the highest GPA in the history of the school and earn the honor of class valedictorian. My classmates vote me "Smartest" and "Most Likely to Succeed." Both great. But nothing compared to the award I worked hardest to achieve: "Best Dressed—Runner-up."

Thank you, Greenville High Class of 1990.

SUMMER OF THE Jaw.

School ends with a flurry of graduation parties and drunken send-offs. For months I've been trying to distract myself from the painful and obvious fact that my jaw has started to jut out more than ever; I look hideously deformed. When I'm hanging out with friends, I try to hold my jaw in tight, the way a heavy guy might hold in his bulging stomach. I know, though, that as mightily as I attempt to impede my jaw's dreadful progression, nothing can stop it. My jaw continues to grow, millimeter by terrifying millimeter. Finally, my mother and I agree that the week after my last graduation party, I will go under the oral surgeon's knife.

I don't fight this at all. I want to have the surgery. I can't stand my ugly underbite and monstrous chin. I can't wait to put an end to ten years of braces. I long to shred that bizarre cloth chin-cup contraption I strap over my head every night like a leatherhead football player. I want to start college with a clean slate and a brand-new jaw.

Of course, like most patients, I focus on the result of the surgery and allow my mind to skip over the details of the procedure itself. One example: when Dr. Schwarzman, my oral surgeon, says that he will have to break my jaw, it doesn't register somehow that he means he is going to *break my jaw.*

Do you know what happens when someone breaks your jaw?

I'll tell you.

It fucking *hurts.*

It hurts beyond any pain you can imagine. We're talking Guantánamo-type pain. I would've given away state secrets, ratted out friends, given Dr. Schwarzman all of my father's account numbers. That kind of pain. And it isn't enough for Dr. Schwarzman to break my jaw once. Because he's a cackling sadist—that's how I imagine him in my drugged-out stupor—he breaks my jaw twice, in two places, sets it back into its original position, and then wires it shut . . . *for six weeks.* No solid food—nothing but liquids and mush—for a month and a half. I drop from a rail-thin 135 pounds to a 120-pound stick. After the surgery, I pop pain pills like PEZ and guzzle milk shakes. Mostly, I crave pizza. I stock up on frozen pizzas, microwave them, shove one nuked slice at a time into the blender, liquefy, and drink. *Yum.*

I HAVE A girlfriend. Sort of. I call Janine my girlfriend. She calls me her—

Not sure what she calls me. I probably shouldn't go there because it will only hurt. Not to mention that my parents have no idea about Janine. I've chosen not to tell them because my father has a unique, rather old-school perspective about dating in high school: "No time for girlfriend, Tony. Time only for study. You have girlfriend later, after medical school."

Sure, Dad, no problem. I can wait eight years.

I meet Janine at the beginning of junior year. I see her and immediately go into heat. Blond, blue-eyed, dimpled cheeks, slight overbite. A strand of hair covering one eye. A cheerleader. Dating the quarterback. Janine finds me smart, funny, cool. She invites me to become her friend. Her confidant. Her designated driver. I'm tripping all over myself with joy. And I have a plan. The quarterback is an idiot. Janine will tire of him soon. She will realize that we are meant to be, and we will launch into a passionate, hot, sweaty love match. We will become Greenville High's Top Couple. I'll have to move in with her and her parents because my father will have a shit fit and disown me, but I'll jump off that bridge when I come to it.

I'm on the money. She tires of the quarterback before the second game. She breaks up with him and begins dating the middle linebacker. No worries. He's even dumber than the quarterback. I'm right again. She drops this dope and takes up with the starting center on the basketball team. Meanwhile, I'm like Morgan Freeman in *Driving Miss Daisy*, driving her ass everywhere and listening to all her problems.

At some party senior year, after Janine has run through pretty much every guy at Greenville with a varsity letter jacket, I pop open a beer for her, open one for myself, and listen attentively as she tearfully recounts the sad details of her wanton love life. I nod sympathetically, truly not giving a shit about any of these hicks, when all of a sudden I'm aware of her lips on mine. Or mine on hers. I have no idea who makes the first move, but this is what I've been dreaming about for over a year.

So now we're friends with benefits. Or call me her driver who gets an extra-nice tip. Not sure what we are, exactly, but I'm saying she's my girlfriend. We never do anything more than kiss, but that's okay. I don't see her as that type of girl. I see her whole person. I see her heart and, okay, her breasts. But only because they're located right over her heart. Janine may be a cheerleader, and some of my friends may call her shallow or whatever, but I see beyond all that. And when I get my jaw surgery, Janine is there for me, meeting me at her house while her parents are at work, making out with me on the living room couch, even when my jaw is wired shut. Now, that is love. That is devotion. That is a girlfriend. Of course, my parents have no idea that when I say I'm going out for a milk shake, I'm actually going out for a milk shake and a make-out session.

A few days after Dr. Schwarzman unwires my jaw and pronounces it fit for solid food, Janine dumps me.

I take it hard.

I choke up.

"You're never gonna find anyone like me again," I tell her.

I shout this. We're at a party, pressed into a corner. People bang into us as they slam-dance to deafening, throbbing hard rock, which I'm starting to despise.

"I know," she admits. "You're wonderful."

"Don't say that. It only makes me feel worse."

"I'm sorry."

"*Why?*" I scream, a plea. I am both heartbroken and deaf in one ear.

"We're going separate ways. You're going off to school."

"So are you."

"I'm going to beauty school. It's different."

"We could see each other every weekend. I'll come home."

Janine shakes her head sadly and kisses me on the cheek.

I drive home alone, feeling as if I've been kicked in the stomach. For a week I lie in bed, drawing cartoons of men in pain, pining over lost or stolen lovers. I pull myself together enough to pack up my room and shove everything into the pint-sized trunk of my used Ford Tempo, a present from my parents. A few days before I leave for Kalamazoo, I gather enough strength to attend one last party. It's a party like any other—townies and college-bound seniors dancing pathetically, smashing potato chips into their absent parents' carpeting, beer cans popping, beer spilling over, Guns N' Roses wailing their guts out, the bass knob flipped to red line. I lean against a back wall, thinking, *I won't miss this.*

"Hi."

I whip around, nearly spill my beer.

Janine.

Looking really fine. I try to see her whole person, but honestly, I see only her mouth, her eyes, her breasts.

"When do you leave?"

My voice cracks. "Couple days."

She rolls her mouth into a pout and says, "I have a confession." I lean in. Close. Her hair brushes my lips. "I miss you."

I nod. It's the best I can do. I'm struck mute. My knees clang into each other so loudly, they threaten to drown out Axl Rose.

"I was hoping we could still be friends," she says.

"That would be, you know, excellent."

So smooth.

"Maybe we could spend some time tonight and talk. Or."

She touches her finger to my mouth. She squeezes past me. I want to reach out, bar her moving by me with my arm, but I don't think of that move until about two hours later. I run a hand over my chin, my newly minted jaw, and feel its smooth, freshly chiseled surface. I like how it feels. It feels like the hood of a brand-new Porsche.

I begin to fantasize. I imagine a whole new start for Janine and me. I'll bust ass home after Friday classes, pick her up at beauty college, and we'll shack up for the rest of the weekend, living on cold beer, pretzels, and the heat of our passion. At some point, in, say, seven years, I'll break the news to my father. First he'll have to get over that she's not Korean. No. First he'll have to get over that I have a girlfriend. No. First he'll have to get over that I kept Janine's existence from him. Wait, wait. I have to get my father out of my head . . .

Maybe we could spend some time tonight and talk. Or.

She means what I think she means, right? It's the *or* that got my attention. I need to track her down. Now.

I can't find her. I search the house. I go from room to room. I check all the bathrooms. I ask people if they've seen her. I look in the closets. No sign of her. I guess she'll call me. Or I'll call her. I slide my nearly full beer can onto a hall table and leave.

And there in the driveway, sitting in the passenger seat of a battered old Impala, making out with the driver, is Janine.

The guy looks familiar. I think he once worked construction on our street. Or snaked our toilet. Or bagged my groceries. Now he's bagging my girlfriend. Ex. My ex-girlfriend. Then a light goes off in my head. A cloud bubble appears, the word *duh* dancing inside. News flash.

"Reporting for CNN, I'm Tony Youn from Greenville, Michigan. In breaking news, I'm the only guy in town who *hasn't* screwed my girlfriend. Anderson?"

3

Zero for Four Years

Freshman year.

I live in a dorm in a suite, a common room and two bedrooms. My roommate, Ross—pale, wispy thin, a loner—and I stack our beds into a bunk bed to free up space in our tiny bedroom. I offer to flip a coin, but Ross insists on taking the top bunk. We catch a meal or two together at the dining hall, but basically, Ross prefers to keep to himself.

I enter college determined to put high school, my ugly stage, and Janine all behind me. I commit myself to bulking up, begin a boot camp–like regimen of hitting the weights at the gym. This amps up my appetite. No more liquid pizza for me. I'm into the real stuff. Domino's delivers right to my dorm and within thirty minutes or it's free. I share nightly midnight pizzas with my other two suite-mates and occasionally Ross, although he's an early riser and is usually already asleep.

By the end of first semester, I'm pumped up and filled out. I retire my glasses into the back of a drawer and start wearing contacts. Best of all, my jaw remains stationary. No sign of sneaky chin movement in the middle of the night.

Academically, I'm a stud. I'm premed, which means mostly science classes. Those come easy to me. I work hard, but not as hard as I'd expected, and pull all A's. I get all my work done with plenty of time left for an active college social life.

That is, if I had a social life.

Despite my new ripped body, nonspectacled face, and steady jaw, I have slipped through the cracks socially. Small, exclusive Kalamazoo College feels like a small, exclusive town made up of cliques and clubs, none of which I'm invited to join. The athletes, who, as always, seem to host and have the run of all the best parties, keep to their own. I succeeded in tennis at tiny Greenville High, but I can't play at this level. While I hung with the jocks in high school, no way I can crash their circle here. I'm forced to party with my own, the friends I make in my classes—biology, chemistry, physics, and calculus. Let's be honest. These classes don't attract flocks of smoking-hot women and cool guys who throw great parties. We're talking awkward, horny science geeks. Of which I am one.

I don't look like one, damn it! I've worked so hard to be cool. In high school I was voted "Best Dressed—Runner-up," remember?

The jocks don't care. My roommates, all liberal-arts majors, none of them into science and none of them geeks, don't care. They all manage to attend class, study, and date. They have lives outside of the classroom. They ask girls out. Girls say yes. Laughing, drinking, and sex follow. For everyone. Except me.

I refuse to let a little thing like being frozen out of the best parties stop me. I see girls everywhere—walking across campus, in the library, in the cafeteria, and in all my classes. I need a new tactic. I create a dating strategy designed to get my feet wet. I'll select a likely candidate, someone attainable, and ask her out. Someone not too cute. Someone who's clearly eager for companionship. A safety date.

I ask out Magda, a girl in my organic chemistry class. She replies with a bored "I don't think so." I can't believe it. Rejected by my safety date. All the way back to my dorm, I mutter aloud, "I just got shot down by a girl in my *organic chemistry class*." It had taken me two weeks to confirm that Magda was a *girl*.

I shake it off. I have to find another candidate. In biology, I start absently sketching in my notebook. I feel someone looking at me. I look up. A girl across from me is watching me draw. She smiles. She has beautiful, arresting eyes. She blushes and turns away, clearly embarrassed that I caught her staring. I wait for her after class. She comes out of the classroom, sees me, ducks her head, grins. Close up, she's even prettier than I thought.

"Hi," I say.

"Hi."

She half-smiles, walks faster.

I catch up to her. We say nothing for about thirty seconds.

"I was wondering," I say finally. "Would you mind if I gave you a call? Maybe we could go out to dinner sometime."

"I guess so," she says.

In my head, I scream, *"Score!"*

"Nice," I say.

I don't want to appear too eager, so I wait an hour and then I call her. She doesn't answer. I leave a message on her answering machine. I identify myself, mention dinner. I call her again two days later. She doesn't answer. I leave another message. *Play it nonchalant*, I tell myself. *You are not desperate. Well, you are, but don't show it. Be cool.*

I call her twice the next night. Leave two messages.

She doesn't call me back.

I keep calling. All told, I leave her nine messages.

She never calls me back. Not once.

I make a decision.

I'll give her one more chance.

I call her for the tenth time. Phone in hand, waiting for her recorded voice to finish telling me to leave a message and she'll call me back as soon as possible, I hang up.

I'm starting to pick up a vibe.

It's possible that she's not interested in me.

. . . .

EARLY DECEMBER. FINALS loom, then home for Christmas break. I assess my first semester.

Academics. No problem. Unless I tank every final, I see not a B in sight.

Living situation. So-so. Ross slinks in and out of the suite like a tenant who's ducking the landlord. He's pleasant enough but rarely interacts with the rest of us. The other two guys are fine. They don't study much. Or go to many classes. They spearhead a series of all-night poker games in the student lounge, culminating in a winner-take-all Texas Hold'em tournament. They're decent guys, and since they come in for the night at the same time as I leave in the morning, it works out.

Social life. Nonexistent. I've made several friends in my classes, but they remind me of the first group of nerds I hung out with in high school—socially inept and repellent to women. One day, while eating lunch with them, I notice a cute girl sitting alone, reading. I excuse myself, walk over to her table. I say hello, make clumsy small talk leading up to asking her out. Suddenly, her eyes fill with panic. Sure. I'm about to ask a girl out, and her immediate reaction is horror. *Loser*, I think. That's what I am. *Lose-her.* And that's what I do. Every time. I lose her. I don't know why no one will go out with me. Even the girls I wouldn't be caught dead with in public turn me down.

I feel a presence behind me, hot smelly breath fouling my neck. I whirl around and see that the whole group of geeks I've just left— all six of them—have gathered behind me. Why are they here? What are they doing? My role-playing, video-gaming, motherboard-loving so-called friends have advanced upon the girl I'm trying to ask out as if they are the children of the corn and she is the corn. They guffaw maniacally at something. I shush them and turn back to the girl. She's gone. I catch a glimpse of her back as she bolts through the door and sprints into the quad.

I need new friends. These guys could scare away a horde of zombies.

At the very least, I need to keep them far, far away from any girl with potential. Damn, I need to go out on a date. I'm horny, yes, but my confidence feels as if it has totally disappeared. I can feel my hands shaking, my bottom lip trembling. I start checking myself in the mirror. Everything is where it's supposed to be. I can't call myself handsome, but I'm not fugly, either.

Two nights later, I meet a girl in the checkout line at Kmart. I'm buying CDs, and she's purchasing a large bottle of lighter fluid. We start talking. She's hot. Long jet-black hair with occasional streaks of red. Dark gray eyes. Smoky. Curvy lips that look as if they've been drawn on. Exotic. She's sexy enough to pose for an album cover. I ask her out. Right on the spot. In freaking Kmart. When she says yes, I feel like breaking into a victory dance.

We meet Friday night for dinner at the Olive Garden. Driving over in my Ford Tempo, which has developed a sudden hacking cough, I start to freak out. I have a *date*. An actual date. With a real live girl. What the *hell*.

It occurs to me then that I have never been on an actual date. What do I do? What do we talk about? And what is the point? I buy her dinner and then . . . what? I take her home? We're meeting at the restaurant. Dumb move. I should've picked her up. In this? In my tubercular Ford Tempo? I'm a wreck.

I pull into the restaurant parking lot and start to sweat. Perspiration gushes from my armpits as if they're faucets, sopping my shirt. Nothing I can do. I'm already ten minutes late. I dash inside and locate my date, seated at a corner table. She's done something to her hair. Braided it like a challah. Killer. And she's done something to her lips. Applied dark Goth lipstick, the color of licorice. Murderous. She stands when I approach and, to my shock, gives me a *hug*. She rubs her palms in a slow circle on my back.

"You're warm," she says. "And your shirt is kind of . . . moist."

"Yeah. The AC in my car conked out."

"Ah."

37

We sit. I fumble my menu. It flies out of my hand, lands at the foot of a woman two tables away.

"We can share," she says.

I laugh like a hyena.

I need to chill. I need to calm the hell down. She slaps her laminated menu on the table, folds her hands, and laps me up with her eyes.

"So," she says.

"Yeah," I say.

"What do you want to know about me?"

"Oh." I clear my throat. "Everything. I mean, okay . . . do you have a job?"

"No," she says.

"Ah," I say.

"I have a career."

"Oh. Nice. What field?"

"Entertainment."

"Wow."

"I'm a fire-eater."

"Interesting." I pause. Stutter. "So . . . you eat . . . f-f-f-fire. Where?"

"In a carnival. We move around a lot."

Perfect. I'm dating a carnie. The hits just keep on coming.

"Do you enjoy eating, you know, fire?"

"Love it. I don't want to brag, but they call me the Human Candle."

Mom, Dad, I'd like you to meet my new girlfriend. As you can see, she's not Korean. But if our pilot light ever goes out, we're sitting on gold.

"Tony, you look pale. You all right?"

"No, no, yeah, I'm fine."

"Why don't you tell me about you."

"Sure. Well, let's see. I'm Korean. Korean-American. When I'm not in college, I live with my parents. My mother and father."

"Those would be your parents."

"My father is strict, hard-line, tyrannical. But in a good way. My mother is just great. Everyone loves her. She's a wonderful cook. She makes these amazing native dishes. Delicious. A lot of shellfish. Steamed in their own juices. Very fresh. Still alive, basically. You kind of poke them with your chopsticks. Crustaceans swimming around with their little beady eyes. If you're squeamish, you might be nauseated the first time . . ."

I'm off and running. I can't stop myself. I speak in whole paragraphs. Pages. Chapters. Volumes. *Tomes.* I cannot shut up about my mother and her delicious Korean cooking. I spew forth nonstop as if I have some form of Tourette's. At some point, I glimpse a stricken look on the carnie's face. She glances nervously from side to side like a spy who suspects she's been followed. I pause to catch my breath, and she plunks both of her hands on top of mine, pinning them to the table. I scan the backs of her hands for burn marks.

"Tony."

"Yes?"

"I have to call it a night."

"What? Why? We haven't even ordered yet."

"My stomach is acting up. Shooting pains. I have a very sensitive stomach. Feels like it's on fire."

"Well, sure, your line of work. I'll drive you home—"

"No. I have my car." She shoots to her feet, extends her hand. I shake it. Feels as if she's concluding an unsuccessful job interview. "This was lovely."

"Totally. Maybe we can do anoth—"

Before I finish, she burns out of there.

My first Christmas home from college.

The Christmas from hell.

First semester, over and done. I can't wait to chill out at home. See friends. Go to parties. I even entertain thoughts of hooking up with Janine. Desperate men do desperate things.

My brother came home from Northwestern a day earlier. When I walk into the dining room and see Mike's face, I know we've got a problem.

"Dad wants to talk to us."

"About what?"

He shrugs, drums his fingers on the oak tabletop. If he knows, he's not saying. I don't press him. We sit without speaking for ten achingly long minutes until my parents arrive in the dining room. My father nods at my mother, steps farther into the room, leaves her framed in the doorway. "Your brother," my father says to me.

A lump rises into my throat. Mike must be sick. I look at him. He looks down. I turn to my father. "What's wrong?"

"Look." My father slides a sheet of paper toward me. It flutters against my outstretched hand.

I pick up the paper and start to read: *Northwestern University Official Transcript.* I hand the paper back to my father. "This is none of my business. These are Mike's grades."

"No. Read. Please."

I hesitate, then reluctantly scan the transcripts. One A, the rest B's. I look helplessly at Mike. I don't know why I'm here, why I've been included in what should be a private conversation between Mike and my father. Mike stares straight ahead. He looks numb.

"Your brother," my father says, "has shamed the family." He lowers his voice, speaks solemnly. "How can he become a doctor with grades like these? No way. Impossible."

Normally, at this point, my brother would stand up to my father. But today, a week before Christmas, he doesn't fight at all. He seems defeated.

"Michael, *how?*" My father leans back, then shoots up both hands in surrender. "How you get into med school? You need to study. Both of you."

I blink, not understanding.

"You don't study?" my father says, his voice rising. "You can't become a doctor. You end up bum on the street. You have to study every day. Christmas, too."

"I'm sorry," I say. "I'm not sure what's happening here. We finished school. Took our finals. We don't have anything to study."

My father pulls out a chair. On the seat, he has placed a stack of MCAT-prep books. Each one weighs in at three hundred pages, minimum. "You study these. MCAT prep." My father holds, waiting for the fight in Mike to come out.

Mike shakes his head, amazed, stunned. I try a tiny laugh to soften the moment. "You mean a couple hours a day—"

"No, *no*," my father says. "All day, every day. Otherwise—" A massive helpless shrug aimed at my mother. She nods sadly from the doorway.

None of this is making sense. I look at my mother to get my bearings. She stares back, her mouth flat-lined in compliance. I look back at my father. "I thought we were going to L.A. for Christmas to see Grandma. We have plans, plane tickets—"

"No more," my father says. "Not going to L.A. Not this year. This year you boys study. Very important. This year Daddy cancel Christmas."

Mike swears under his breath. He jerks a book out from the middle of the pile, causing the rest of the stack to topple and crash onto the floor. My father flinches slightly but shows no other reaction. Mike opens his book in slow motion, drops his chin an inch above the page, and starts to read, moving his lips. My father pivots and walks out of the room, my mother at his heels. Mike and I look at each other and then, the dutiful sons, now prisoners, begin silently reading, studying for the MCAT.

Every morning after breakfast, Mike and I return to our bedroom and hit the books. Or so my father thinks. We alternate standing watch, two-hour shifts each, while the other lies in bed dozing, reading comic books, or listening to music. In reality, we study not at all. At times when my father surprises us with a random check-in, I force myself awake, spin the book around on my chest, hoping it's not upside down, and pretend to be glued to the page. We take half-hour breaks for lunch and dinner, then "study" into the night until my father dismisses us. My mother and sister do fly to L.A. for a shortened Christmas holiday. On Christmas Day, my father goes to a friend's for dinner. Mike and I microwave hot dogs and sneak some TV until we hear my father's car in the driveway. We shut off the set, shove the dogs in the trash, and hustle upstairs, taking our positions in our beds, eyes trained on our MCAT books.

In those two weeks, during the moments when I daydream—and I daydream a lot—I think about my father on the farm in Korea. I imagine how hard he must have worked and how disciplined he must have been to escape from that dirt-poor farm overrun with eight brothers and sisters, not an inch of space for privacy or study, and while I want to hate him for killing my Christmas, ruining my winter break, and humiliating my brother, I can't. It's crazy, but I feel a rush of respect for him. I'm also royally pissed and so antsy that I'm jumping out of my skin and embarrassed beyond words to tell my friends the truth, that I'm stuck home studying because my brother bombed his grades and my dad freaked out.

But what the hell. Here I am. I have no other choice. I might as well accept my fate and embrace it. Yes, I'm locked away. But you can't really call this prison. I'm in my room, all the snacks and soda I want, hanging out with my brother, whom I love, and with whom I'll laugh about this someday. It could be worse. For my father, it was worse.

The afternoon of New Year's Eve, my father releases us from our room. I quickly patch together a sketchy New Year's Eve plan and head off for some party in hopes of finding Janine, which doesn't happen. My brother, sullen, vague, talks about attending a party with some friends, but he doesn't really seem into it and stays home.

Three days later, my backpack riding shotgun in the fussy Ford Tempo, I return to Kalamazoo College to my dorm, my suite-mates, my group of nerd friends, and no women, no women at all.

Before I leave, my father announces that he has transferred my brother to Kalamazoo College and moved him into a dorm not far from mine. What I know in my heart but dare not utter is that no matter how many MCAT books my father forces him to study and how many Christmases my father cancels, my brother will never become a doctor.

. . . .

JANUARY.

I am a second-semester freshman. And I am horny.

Winter hits, and my dating life goes ice-cold. We're talking frozen-tundra cold. Maybe I'm simply shooting too high. Maybe I should lower my standards, scrape the bottom of the female species. Consider convicted felons. The certifiably insane. The terminally ugly. Open myself to any woman with a pulse. No. All I have left are my standards. I have to refine my approach. I read how-to books. I flirt. I hint. I ask direct questions. I send out good vibes and sincere compliments and promise a good time or your money back. Ha-ha-*ha*. Nothing. Blank stares. I study my face in the mirror. Am I that unattractive, unlikable, undesirable? What is my problem? Maybe hiding somewhere in the folds of my skin lies a nasty invisible zit field that appears only when I ask a girl out. I'm at a loss and sinking fast.

One night my suite-mates, minus Ross, invite me to a party. They warn me that it involves alcohol and poker with only a slight possibility of women. Slight possibility? Score! As we dress for the party, one of the guys, Gary, begins banging around the room, searching for a watch he's misplaced. He flings open drawers at random, thinking that maybe someone stuck it into their stuff by mistake. Suddenly, he goes quiet and pulls something from Ross's desk.

"Whoa."

The urgency in his voice pulls us around him. I look over his shoulder. In his trembling hands, he holds a gay porn magazine.

"Ross?" Gary's roommate says. "Is that his?"

"No, you moron, it's mine," Gary says.

Gary swats him with the magazine, then rolls it up and holds it in front of him like a giant undulating dildo. He chases us both into the common room, screaming, lisping, wagging his magazine dick. I join in the fun, flapping my arms and squealing effeminately. Our romp quickly fades, because in fact we are all freaked out, not sure what happens now.

"I wish I hadn't found this," Gary says.

"I have to live with the guy," I say.

"You share a bed with him," Gary says.

"It's a *bunk* bed."

"Hey, whatever you guys do is your business. I just don't want to know."

I don't answer him because I want this conversation to end. We all know that everything in our suite has forever changed. In silence, we finish getting ready for the party. As we go out the door, Gary tosses the magazine onto Ross's bed.

Which is how we push Ross out of the closet.

I CAN'T SLEEP in my room. I call my brother and, for the next three nights, crash on his floor in a sleeping bag. When I finally return to my room, I strip my bed and wash the sheets. Ross, outed, starts keeping even weirder hours. He disappears for days at a time, then shows up at four one morning, gathers up his bedding, and leaves. I rarely see him, and when I do, we barely acknowledge each other.

One Saturday night a couple of weeks later, my friends, the science nerds, of which I am one, dateless, hold court at a corner table of our favorite off-campus Burger King. Other than a potential video-game marathon and eating more fast food later, we have no plans. It won't take another of these Saturday nights to confirm that I have absolutely no life. This night, a bracing February freezer, we chomp our burgers, slurp our drinks, and sit morosely in our booth. A typical fun Saturday night.

In the distance, I hear a familiar voice ordering food. I stop in mid-bite and listen. I recognize that voice. Ross. I turn and verify. I notice that he has grown his hair longer. He dips a knee, flicks a wrist. It seems that he's making a point to appear more effeminate. Then the jokes start.

"Ross, what are you doing at Burger King? Shouldn't you be at Dairy *Queen*?"

"Have it your way, Ross. You know which way I'm talking about. In the butt."

"I didn't know you liked burgers. I thought you liked *hot dogs*!"

Then things get crude.

I want to say that I refuse to participate. I want to say that I come to Ross's defense, storm out, outraged. I want to say all of this, but I can't, because it's not the truth. We crack vulgar, hurtful, stupid jokes.

Ross doesn't wait for his food. He yanks up his coat collar and runs out of the restaurant.

Most of my friends laugh. I don't. Almost immediately, I'm filled with shame. I see Ross's face—stunned, hurt, helpless—and I can't believe that I have contributed to this act of cruelty. I excuse myself. I go into the bathroom and slap cold water on my face. Then I look into the filthy mirror.

A stranger stares back.

Who is he?

Who am I?

I don't know anymore.

GREENVILLE, MICHIGAN. POPULATION 7,945. Minus the number of homosexuals—7,945.

No homosexuals live in Greenville. No black people, no Hispanic people, no Jews, no Muslims, and after Kirby and his family move away, five Korean-Americans. Us. My family. People here come in three colors: white, whiter, whitest. The whitest go to my church.

My father, a reluctant and infrequent churchgoer, cedes everything religious to my mother. I attend services presided over by an evangelical preacher, a road-company Jerry Falwell who screams fire-and-brimstone sermons that, on more than one occasion, he peppers with bigotry and hate. One Sunday he attacks gay people.

Gay people destroy families. Gay people ruin our culture. Gay people corrupt us and seduce our children. God blew up Sodom and killed the Sodomites! Gay people are going to hell!

I'm a child. I'm impressionable. I may look different, but I see myself the same as everyone else in the pew around me. I fervently want to be accepted. I guess some would say that I want to be white. By the time I get to high school, I've assimilated. I'm known and accepted and included. And like all my friends—like everyone I know in Greenville—I distrust gay people. When a guy in our social circle does something weak or shows signs of sensitivity or displays indifference to manly pursuits such as cars, sports, or war, we call him a "fag." I grow up believing in the fiery words of that third-rate preacher: gay people have it in for me, gay people want to do unspeakable things to me, gay people want to marry me. Never having met one single gay person, I have an aversion to all of them. But if pressed, I would admit the secret truth: I am afraid of them.

In the weeks following our encounter with Ross at Burger King, I retreat to my brother's place, where I now essentially live. Between episodes of debilitating self-pity and bouts of loneliness that leave me bedridden, I think about Ross. I think about how he must feel. Before I found out he was gay, I had no problem with him. He was a fine roommate, quiet, respectful, courteous. Now that I know he's gay, am I supposed to hate him? It doesn't make sense. Of course, nothing in college makes sense to me except my work ethic. I bust ass in the classroom, study like a convict on death row looking for loopholes. I don't just learn my textbooks well; I memorize them. My insanity pays off. I score A's with ease.

It's only everything else that sucks.

Not only am I second-guessing my choice of college—this was *my* decision, remember?—I have doubts about my faith. I have doubts about pretty much everything in my life. I have doubts about *me*. Actually, I have no doubts about that preacher from my childhood when it comes to gay people. I know he is wrong. Most of all, I know I am wrong.

I begin to read. I start with the Bible. I follow that up with scholars' interpretations of the Bible. I read history. I read philosophy and books about religion. I read books about culture and sociology. I read self-help books. I read memoirs. I read about gay people and their struggles to find acceptance in society. I read how they come to grips with their identity, how they fight to fit in, and how they learn to accept themselves. I start to see myself in them. I begin to reform my faith. I study the teachings of Jesus. I reject my former Bible-thumping, "our way is the only way" brand of Christianity. I find a church in Kalamazoo whose pastor preaches tolerance and acceptance. I think about the nature of sin. Jesus hung out with sinners, spoke to them, embraced them. Everyone has value and everyone sins. No matter who you are or what you have done, I am no better than you. I have committed at least as many sins, maybe more. I am not a better person than Ross. In fact, based on how I acted, I am a worse person.

I have plenty of time to think and read because I spend most of my time alone. I pull away from the friends who seem intolerant and toxic. Sophomore year, I move into an apartment with Mike. It feels safe and familiar, but living off campus isolates me. My social life, if possible, falls even deeper into the void. Occasionally, Mike invites me to join him at a party or a movie, but I feel awkward, a hanger-on, a pity case. I prefer to stay home and wallow.

I use my free time to take up the guitar. I practice for hours and become accomplished enough to copy chords from songs by Poison and Tom Petty. Sometimes friends show up unannounced at my apartment, drag me away from my guitar or my books, and force me to go with them to the latest supposedly hot party. My friends mean well, but without fail, these parties turn out to be loud, raucous, boring, and stag. I inevitably leave early, stop at the local all-night Kmart, and browse the CD aisles. At around two A.M. I treat myself to an A&W root beer on the way home. Life in the Kalamazoo fast lane.

The next two years flick by in a blink—I guess time flies when you're having no fun—and suddenly, I'm a senior. My scorecard reads like a pitcher's dream: no runs, no hits, nothing across. "Dateless in Kalamazoo." That's how my final chapter in college should read.

And then I meet Gloria.

MY FRIEND FELICE, fellow science nerd and premed, invites me to dinner at her apartment with her boyfriend, Stan, and Gloria, an exchange student from Spain who is living there for three months. I make a thousand lame excuses—I need to practice my guitar, catch up on my reading, do a load of wash, floss—but Felice says if I don't get right in my car and haul ass to her apartment, she'll send Stan to take me by force. Stan, a former hockey player who had a tryout with the Boston Bruins, misses checking people into the boards and tearing off their heads. He'd love to stuff me into the trunk of his car and drive me to the dinner party, his captive.

I shower, throw on a fresh shirt, stop at Kroger on the way, and pick up a limp bouquet of flowers. I'm not really up for a social evening—I haven't been for three years—so I expect nothing except a good meal. Felice, a compact woman with broad shoulders, is a gourmet cook who loves to throw dinner parties with a color theme. She greets me at the door with a hug that would crack the ribs of a wrestler. Tonight, Felice says when she releases me, the theme is green.

"You shouldn't have," I say. "I'm fine with a bucket of KFC and a Coke."

"I went all out for Gloria, not you. Lettuce salad, spinach pasta with peas and broccoli, green tea, and for dessert, homemade peppermint ice cream."

"I bet it's not easy being green."

"Ha-*ha*. Hey, let me introduce you. Tony, Gloria."

She moves aside to reveal a young woman with wavy brown hair, mountainous-high cheekbones, snow-white skin, olive-green eyes, and full lips that partially conceal a slight overbite. Gloria sips red wine out of a water glass and uncrosses her dancer's legs. She extends a long pale arm, tinkles her fingers toward me, and smiles. My knees buckle. I feel as if I'm tumbling down into a warm, bottomless pit.

"Nice to meet you," Gloria says. Perfect English. Touch of an accent.

"Likewise," I say, extending to her my fistful of sagging flowers.

"So beautiful," she says, holds, and laughs. Deeply. Then, the topper, Gloria shakes the flowers lightly, pretending they are my hand.

Has any man fallen in love so quickly, so completely?

"Vase," Felice says, noticing that my mind has left my body.

"I'll get it," Gloria says.

"I'll help."

I'm about to vault over the dining room table and hurdle anything else in my way—furniture, Felice, Stan—when Felice clamps her fingers onto my wrist, hard.

"Dial it down, Casanova. P.S., she has a boyfriend."

I nod like a bobblehead, take a couple of cleansing breaths, and land at Gloria's side. In the apartment's galley kitchen, we locate a vase and fill it with water out of the faucet. Well, she does. I stare.

Felice appears with a plate of guacamole encircled by rings of green potato chips. I follow Gloria to Felice's reupholstered thrift-store couch and sink in. I swig half a beer—yes, *green*, and not as gross as it sounds—and within a minute I'm able to calm myself down. We talk about Spain and bullfighting and Gloria's boyfriend and her classes and how Kalamazoo differs slightly from Madrid. Eventually, Felice herds us to the table and brings out our green dinner, which, to nobody's surprise, is both insane and delicious. We ooh and ahh over every course, dab our green napkins to our lips, linger over our peppermint ice cream and spearmint cookies. I'm tipsy and tripping and, for the first time in literally years, indescribably happy.

"Tomorrow's Saturday," Felice says. "I want to take a drive to the lake. Supposed to be a nice day."

"Great idea," I say. Silence. I feel everyone's eyes on me. "What?"

"We don't have a car."

"I have a car."

Big laugh. Followed by applause.

"So that's why you invited me here. For my *car.*"

"We all have a purpose, Youn," Felice says. "Now you know yours."

"I feel so touched. Used. But touched."

Of course, I'm overjoyed to chauffeur Gloria, Felice, and Stan to the lake. And Sunday I volunteer to schlep everyone to a nearby park for a picnic. Monday I cut a class and take Gloria to the store. Let me repeat that. *I cut a class!*

By week's end, I'm driving Gloria all over Kalamazoo and back—to class, home, the movies, clothes shopping, the Laundromat—everywhere. I know this sounds like high school and my doomed relationship with Janine the sequel, but this is much different. With Janine, I wanted sex. With Gloria, I want something else. Her.

WE QUICKLY BECOME a foursome. It appears that way to everyone we know, and most of all to me. Gloria and I feel like a couple, except for one small detail that prevents us from actually being a couple—the boyfriend back in Spain. Time and again, watching Stan and Felice snuggling in the overstuffed armchair, Gloria invites me to stay overnight.

"There's really no place for me to sleep."

"We can find a place, Tony."

"No, no, no, no. That's okay. I'll go back to my apartment. Better that way."

"You sure? I can make up the couch. It's really comfortable."

Stay! The hell with the boyfriend. He's in freaking SPAIN. Go for it. Go, for, it!

"Nah, I'm good. Well, good night. See you guys tomorrow. Gloria, I'll pick you up at nine sharp. You can't be late for history."

A peck on the cheek. A squeeze of the arm. Her hand landing on my back just below my neck, absently circling, massaging the base of my neck slowly . . . sensuously . . .

AHHHH!

In my room at two A.M. I lie awake, stare at my ceiling, and beg sleep to take me away, to remove Gloria from my mind. I climb out of bed, pace, strum my guitar, turn on the radio, find a sad song, crash back onto my bed, and shout to the dark empty room. "This *sucks!*"

With pulse-pounding dread, my heart heavy as an anvil, I tick off the days until Gloria will be leaving, returning to Spain and rejoining . . . him. If anything, during these final days, we see more of each other. I arrange my schedule around hers. I remain her sidekick, her driver, her companion, her more than willing wingman. Everything but her lover. It's not easy to restrain myself. A hundred times I fight the urge to take her in my arms and lock my ravenous lips on her full and—I can only imagine—supple mouth. I remain the poster boy for restraint. The dutiful and lovesick friend. The perfect gentleman. I never disrespect her, never cross a line, never make a move. Every night I go to bed a lovesick mess. But I wake up every morning pure, my honor—and hers—intact.

Gloria has to respect that, right? Although I'm sure I feel her eyes trolling over mine, searching, widening, wondering, What if? What would happen *if* . . . ? I sure do.

Sadly, I never find out. Two days before she is to leave, I overhear her in loud and angry conversation with Pau, my rival, my nemesis. When she comes out of her room and joins the rest of us in the living room, she swipes at one creamy cheek, sighs, and sniffs.

The bastard made her cry! I ought to get on a plane, fly to Spain, and kick his skinny Spanish ass!

Or—second choice—ask her to stay.

Declare your love, Tony. Tell her right now that the two of you are meant to be. Stop being a wuss! Go for it! Claim her!

Of course, noble gentleman that I am, I say nothing. I reach out my arms and hold her stiffly while she sniffles and tries to compose herself.

"I'm going to miss you, Tony," she says. Low. Smoky.

I'm trembling.

It's raining the day I drive her to the airport. Classic heartbreak drop-off weather right out of a movie. Bogart and Bacall in *Casablanca*. Tony and Gloria in Kalamazoo. We hardly speak on the way. And when I lug her suitcase out of the Tempo's trunk, I fight back the urge rising up in my throat like a fire to say, "Gloria, don't go!" Instead I say, "This was really great. I'm so glad we got to hang out."

She places a hand over her heart. "Oh, Tony, thank you for everything. I'm overwhelmed by your kindness. You are very special. I love you so much."

A kiss on one cheek, then the other, European-style. The rain picking up, she sweeps her suitcase out of my hand and runs into the terminal, her raincoat slapping against the backs of her bare legs. She stops before the terminal's revolving doors, whips around, waves, and blows me a kiss. Then she is gone.

I stand still as a rock, the rain pounding, my eyes locked on the revolving terminal doors, knowing that in a matter of seconds Gloria will reappear and run into my arms. I wait, losing all sense of time, watching and listening to the doors whap around.

I stagger back to my car. Tears mixed with rain slosh down my cheeks. I fling open the clanking door of the Tempo and squish down into the driver's seat. I let out a moan. How could I let her go? How could I drive her to the airport without telling her how I feel? With open palms, I punish the steering wheel. I'm exhausted; my head throbs. I turn on the ignition and, with the back of my hand, wipe the mist that covers the inside of the windshield like a fog. I click on the radio. Harry Nilsson's nasal crooning, "I can't live if living is without you . . ." floats out of the radio. I lose it. My sobs ransack me.

Leaving me for dead.

. . . .

I write Gloria a letter. Five pages, longhand. On a legal pad. The words flow out of me hot and urgent. I lay it all out on the page. I tell her how much I love her. I say it's obvious she feels the same way about me. I know that she probably expected me to make a move, but I couldn't. I had too much respect for her and her relationship with her boyfriend to step out of bounds. I believed she would think less of me, and if I lost her respect, I could never live with myself. I tell her that what we built in a mere three months was extraordinary and that it is only the beginning. I plan to go to medical school, and even though she will be living in Spain for a few more years, she indicated that she is interested in traveling, pursuing a career as an interpreter. Perfect. I can travel with her during summers and holidays, and she can come here for extended periods. We can make our relationship work long-distance. And when we marry and have kids—

I strike that. Too far.

I tell Gloria that geographical distance is irrelevant when two hearts are as linked as ours. Our hearts beat as one.

I underline that.

I tell her each second will feel like an eternity until I hear from her.

I sign it, *Love Always and Forever, Tony.*

I mail it at the post office the next day.

I give the letter a week to arrive and another few days for her to respond. Two weeks conservatively.

I don't hear from her in two weeks.

I rush home every day and practically rip the door off my mailbox in search of her letter.

Two and a half weeks. No letter from Gloria.

Three weeks. Nothing.

Four weeks. No letter.

Five weeks. *Nada.* Which is Spanish for *nothing.*

Six weeks. *Cero.* Which is Spanish for *zero.*

I've become a useless lump of flesh. And then I realize—

She never got the letter.

Of course. Stupid crappy inept U.S. mail!

I call her.

She answers on the third ring. Softly. Hint of annoyance. As if she expects someone doing a survey.

"Hello?"

"Gloria. It's Tony."

Silence.

"Tony. Tony *Youn.*"

"I know, Tony, oh my God!"

"How are you?"

"Fine. I'm fine." She clears her throat. "How are you?"

"Great."

"Good. Oh, Tony. My God!"

"I know, right? Hey, you know, I sent you this letter and stuff, and I was wondering, you know, kinda, what's going on? I mean, um, what are you thinking about what I said? Did you get the letter?"

"I did. I got the letter."

Dead silence. A hole you could drive a truck through.

"So." I twist the phone cord around my wrist. I toy with the idea of knotting it into a noose. "The letter."

"The letter," Gloria says.

"Yeah."

"It means so *much.*"

Oh, no. Here it comes.

But.

"But I have a boyfriend. I'm *so* sorry. You're *so* sweet, Tony. And *so* special. I want to be friends. Truly. I wrote you back."

"Really," I say.

"I did."

"Oh. Good. Great."

Moron. I am a total moron. I want to vanish. I want to change my identity, alter my appearance, and go someplace far away where nobody will find me, ever.

"Tony, I left Pau waiting in the other room—"

Pau. She left Pau. No, Gloria, you left *me*. You left me standing in the rain. Sobbing over you. Losing my mind over you. I tore my guts out, put it all on the line, and wrote you that stupid fucking five-page letter. I wasted five months of my life pining over you. I am such an idiot.

In a heartbeat, I have gone from heartsick to mad as hell.

"Tony—"

"I have to go. Goodbye, Gloria."

The phone slips and I slam it down.

Two days later, Gloria's letter, thin as a blade, appears in my mailbox. I tear it open and read on light blue stationery, flimsy as tissue paper, smelling of her intoxicating perfume, these four cursive handwritten sentences.

Dearest Tony, Your letter touched me so. I will always be your cherished friend. I have a serious boyfriend so more is impossible. I will never forget our time together. With love, Gloria.

With love.

I sign letters to relatives from Korea whom I've never met *With love*.

I don't really remember the exact words she wrote. Because after I read her letter, I tear it up and flush the pieces down the toilet. Right next to my ego. Ripped up and swirling in the crapper.

I'M IN! I'M going to medical school! I have choices, among them Wayne State University and Michigan State. I prefer Michigan State's kinder, gentler, more hands-on approach over Wayne State's highly pressurized, academic approach, which appeals to all my science-geek friends who got in to both. They will descend on Wayne State in a pack and pick right up where they left off here. I can't think of a bigger turnoff or a more compelling reason to attend Michigan State. I want a clean slate. Most people call college the best four years of their lives. Me? No. I call college the *worst* four years of my life. After the fire-eater, and getting shot down by every girl I ever asked out, including the ones I didn't want, and the months I wasted on Gloria, I need to find available and interested women. I'm not saying I'm going to med school to get laid—

Screw it. I'm saying it. Chicks love doctors. *I'm going to med school to get laid.* Sure, I want to care for the sick, and contribute to society, maybe do some research to help find a cure for a dread disease, and be a good provider for my eventual family, and make my parents proud, and carry on my father's tradition. Absolutely. I said all that stuff at my med-school interviews.

Mainly, I want to get laid.

I haven't come close in four years. Ponder that. Zero for four *years*. A goose egg for college. Do you know how hard that is to do?

I'm going to medical school, why?

I, want, to, get, *laid*.

GRADUATION WEEK. WE party, pick up our caps and gowns, and pack up. I meet for coffee and drinks with friends whom I will not see for a while and maybe never again. I look up Gary, my freshman suite-mate, and meet him for drinks at an off-campus dive. As we nurse our beers, I mention Ross. Since we outed him, Ross has become famous, openly and flamboyantly gay. A theater major, he often appears on campus dressed as a woman.

"Maybe we did him a favor," Gary says.

I suppose that's possible, in a twisted way. But among the low moments I experienced in college, including the many moments of anxiety and loneliness and depression, my absolute lowest moment remains the night my friends and I taunted Ross at Burger King. Over three years later, I still feel ashamed. I finish my beer, shake hands with Gary, wish him luck, and wander in a loop around campus. I think about the reading

I've done, the church I now attend, and how I've changed. I've grown more open-minded, less judgmental. I'm a different person than the immature, clueless, prejudiced guy who made fun of Ross. As soon as I get back to my apartment, I decide to look up Ross's number and call him.

I enter the quad and walk by the student union. The front door opens and Ross comes out, dressed in creased jeans, polo shirt, loafers, no socks. He looks like a model out of a J. Crew catalog.

"Ross."

"Tony."

"This is so weird. I was going home to call you."

"Yeah?"

"I really was. I wanted to tell you—" I stop. Standing with him, I'm momentarily struck dumb.

"Tony, you all right?"

I nod. Squint into the sun. I face him. I need to tell him. "Ross, that time. At Burger King."

I realize why this is so hard. I want *him* to forgive *me*. I can't expect that. All I can do is apologize and accept his reaction. *I was an asshole, Ross.* Start there.

I try again. "That night."

"It was a long time ago," Ross says. "We were freshmen."

"I was a jerk. I was an asshole. Ross, I apologize." I swallow. "I was stupid. And hurtful. And not at all funny. I'm very sorry."

To my utter shock, Ross smiles. A soft, kind smile, as if he does know how hard this is for me. "It's fine. Honest."

He extends his hand. I look at it as if it's a foreign object, as if I don't know what to do with it. After a moment, I reach out and shake it.

"I really appreciate this, Tony. It means a lot."

Briefly, we hug.

"Good luck, Ross."

"You, too, Tony."

Bathed in a shaft of hot sun, I stand in front of the student union and watch him walk away.

II First Year

4

Little Asia

My new life.

Day one.

I drive to East Lansing in my clattering Ford Tempo, the trunk bulging with suitcase and duffel, boxes of books, my guitar, a case of ramen noodles, and a shiny new five-speed road bike, a Huffy purchased at Toys R Us. Nobody—*ever*—has felt so eager to move on from college. At commencement, when our college president proclaimed at the podium erected in the quad, "Congratulations, graduates, class of 1994!" and we flung our caps into the air, I watched mine sail above me in slow motion, believing that mine and only mine would disappear into the clouds and never return, a fluttering symbol of freedom. I was riding a rocket ship out of Kalamazoo (okay, a used Ford Tempo, but still) and never looking back. Michigan State College of Human Medicine, lock up your ladies!

My cap shot back down. I missed the catch, and the spinning razor edge became a chakram and nearly sliced my head off. I refused to acknowledge *that* symbol. I would not accept the remote possibility that, while college sucked, medical school could turn out worse.

. . . .

My dorm, Owen Hall, looms before me. Or is that a parking structure? No, that's my dorm. For the next year, home. I sling my guitar over my back and lug suitcase and duffel to my room, which is roughly the size of a veal pen with none of the charm—four bare walls, a slit in one impersonating a window, and a dull overhead fluorescent light that flickers and chatters. I drop my stuff on the floor, squeeze past, and squint out the window. If I stand on tiptoe and pretzel my neck, I can make out the parking structure next door, which looks exactly like my dorm. The only reason I know it's a parking structure and not a dorm is cars keep driving into it. I exit my room to grab the rest of my stuff, and I'm assaulted by a smell. Pungent, sharp, brutal. Hits me like tear gas. Nostril-ripping. Eyeball-bending. Sinks me to my knees. One more second in this hallway and I'll name names, rat out my friends.

I know that smell—

Thai food.

Someone's cooking Thai food. No. *Everyone's* cooking Thai food.

That's when I notice the students.

Asians.

Every one of them.

They see me and smile happily, welcoming me like I'm their long-lost cousin.

What kind of place is this?

I prowl the halls in search of Caucasians. I see none. Not one. I'm only asking for one lousy non-Asian. *One.* I know I look like I belong. I look like I fit in. But I don't! I am an American in a Korean person's body!

Wait, wait. Two Hispanic women walk by. Two rocking-hot Hispanic women!

"Hey," I say. Cool. Suave. Killer. The new Tony. Superhero Tony.

"*Hola,*" one mumbles. They both giggle and sprint down the hall.

"Nice meeting you," I shout after them. "It's Tony!"

"Hi."

I look down. Hand extended, face grinning behind huge glasses that make her look like a welder. A dwarfish Asian girl.

"Hello," I say.

"You want to get some dinner?"

"Oh, thank you, no, I have to move in."

"Stuck-up, huh? You don't like me? I'm too short? Too *Asian*?"

"No, no, no, I have all this stuff I have to do—"

"Screw *you*."

Where am I?

An hour later, my belongings crammed into my ten-by-ten cell, I lay my guitar down on the threadbare couch that will tonight unfold into my bed. I stack a pile of books high enough to make a night table, then stack two more piles and shove them together to create a precarious stand for my minuscule TV. I'm officially unpacked and settled in. Tomorrow I'll buy my textbooks, tour the campus, and—

I have nothing else to do for two more days until orientation. Suddenly, I feel unbearably lonely. I hadn't expected this. It has to be this place. This dorm. This room. All the warmth of a tomb. I feel like an unwanted stranger.

I have to fix this. I need to change the energy. I'm going to go next door and meet my neighbor. I'll knock on his door and introduce myself. Seems only right, since the two of us share a bathroom.

Outside his door, I hesitate. I feel awkward. Pushy. *Get over it, Tony.* I ball up my fist and knock cheerfully. The door opens slowly. A rotund Asian man roughly my age—Chinese, I'd guess—stands in the doorway in a half-squat. Eyeglasses dangle from two plump fingers. He pinches his nose, returns his glasses to his face, and nods.

"How you doing," I say. "I live next door."

He nods and exhales, his breath coming fast and sour against my cheek. Thai food. The guy's been eating Thai food. I want to retch, but I stifle a cough.

"I just finished moving in," I say.

He nods.

"I'm Tony, by the way."

I offer my hand. He looks at me, confused, then grips it with a hand so wet it feels as if he's pulled it out of a bucket of water. He nods again and bows.

"Oh. Sorry." I bow in return. I wave my hand in the general direction of nowhere. "So. Wow. This is exciting. A little nerve-racking. I'm a med student. Not sure what to expect. My father's a doctor, so I have a vague idea. He's an ob-gyn. I don't think that's for me, though. Not my style. Long hours. It seems like every baby in the world is born at three o'clock in the morning. Ha-*ha*. I'm kidding. What about you? What program are you in?"

"Goodbye, sir," he says, and shuts the door in my face.

Am I in *hell*?

An hour later, I turn in for the night. Eight-forty-five. I haven't gone to bed this early since third grade. Screw it. I have nothing else to do. I'll read, maybe watch some TV, second-guess coming here, that sort of thing. I strip down to T-shirt and boxers, tuck a comic book under my arm, stick a toothbrush into the corner of my mouth, and hit the head. I fling open the door and nearly swallow my toothbrush. Shirtless, revealing a mountain range of hairless flab, my Chinese neighbor sits on the toilet, his pants bunched at his knees.

"Whoa! Sorry."

He smiles, nods.

Like an idiot, I nod back and bow.

"So, okay, I'll come back. Hey, a thought. You might want to lock the door."

He nods. "Goodbye, sir."

I dash the hell out of there. I give him a half hour, then slink into the bathroom. I open the door an inch. The smell smokes me. Rocks me back like a shove. "Freaking Thai food," I say.

64

I hold my breath and go in. I discover that the bathroom door has no lock. What a treat. We can walk in on each other at any time. Sweet. Privacy is overrated. My father never had any privacy as a kid, and he survived, although no wonder he spends almost no time in the bathroom. I imagine that Korean farm. Nine kids living almost literally on top of one another. You crapped in a pot in the corner in front of everyone. At least we have a door.

By eleven-thirty, I'm not close to falling asleep. Nothing but negative thoughts jostle around in my brain. I'm officially in need of a sedative or a kick in the head, whichever will do the trick. On my foldout couch with a foam mattress not quite as thick as cardboard, I toss, turn, and stare cross-eyed at the ceiling, my entire body an electrified nerve ending about to snap. *Breathe, Tony. Slow, deep breaths. Tomorrow is another day. New start. Breathe—*

Bang.

"Ohhhh."

Bang, bang, *bang.*

The ceiling grumbles. The room shivers. My joke of a window throbs.

"What is that?"

I sit up, poised to flee what I'm convinced is a tornado tearing up East Lansing. Although my gut tells me to stay put and not to worry— Owen Hall would kick the shit out of any tornado. A stage-five tornado would hit this building, bounce off, and land in the middle of Chicago.

"Ohhhh."

Wait.

That's a woman. Moaning. Having . . . sex. Right above my head. Threatening to fall through the ceiling. That would be par for this course.

"Oh. *Yeah.*"

A man. Moaning. Yep. We've got us some sex. Some loud, frantic sex.

"SHELDON!" the woman screams. "SLAP MY ASS!"

Sheldon, slap my ass?

That really annoys me. Not the *slap my ass* part. The *Sheldon* part. Somebody named Sheldon is getting laid, and I can't?

"Ow! Yes! Harder!"

"This I need," I say.

Then the Chinese guy groans, followed by a vicious flush.

DAY TWO. I force my butt out of bed after getting exactly no sleep, shower, shave, and stagger out of my room. I need to shake off day one. Put it behind me. Especially Sheldon. I'll grab some breakfast, then spend a leisurely day getting familiar with the campus, buying supplies, textbooks, a few staples. I need to nest.

I come off the elevator and practically run over the dwarfish Asian girl.

"Hi, you," she says.

"Oh, hi there."

"I'm Peggy."

"Tony."

"Want to get some breakfast?"

"Oh, no thanks, I'm going to the bookstore."

"Liar!"

"Excuse me?"

"The bookstore doesn't open until nine. You *are* stuck-up."

"Okay, look, I had a rough night. I got no sleep. I need to regroup. I kind of want to be alone."

"No problem. I get it. You're prejudiced against short Asian women. That's fine. Screw *you*."

Is this all a dream?

Day three. I spend the day doing laundry, ducking into the bathroom when my neighbor allows me a five-minute window of opportunity, and dodging Peggy, whose dogged determination to share a meal with me is starting to creep me out. I have a hard time picturing her as a doctor.

"Doctor, are you sure I should have the operation?"

"You don't want to? Fine. Screw YOU."

I call it a night before eleven. Tomorrow it truly begins. All of the first-years will convene at ten for orientation. I want to be fresh and alert.

Not in the cards. Around midnight Sheldon goes at it again. More moaning. More ass slapping. Even less sleeping. I had such high hopes going in, and I'm already freaking out. What have I done? Have I made a wrong turn? I lie on my back, jam my eyes shut, and attempt to fight off a debilitating attack of what-ifs.

What if the smell of Thai food never goes away?

What if the image of Sheldon having sex never goes away?

What if I never make a single friend in medical school? So far, I've met two people—my neighbor, a large Chinese man who speaks no English and spends all night on the can, and Peggy, a nasty Asian dwarf stalker.

What if my entire class consists of losers from foreign lands? What if everyone else is worse than the Chinese guy and Peggy?

What if I should have gone to Wayne State with my friends?

What if I never should have gone to medical school at all?

Yes, *what if* . . . I've made the biggest mistake of my life?

5

Master of the Shopping Cart

Main lecture hall, administration building.

First day of orientation.

9:27 A.M.

I arrive thirty-three minutes early.

I'm not close to the first one here.

I walk into the auditorium and count twenty-three other obsessively early nut jobs. They're way ahead of me, settled in, sipping coffee, checking me out. I claim a seat, right side, middle back. I want to establish a strong lookout point, in military terms—okay, in military videogame terms—the clearing on the hill overlooking the action. I want to position myself so I can observe the people coming in. I want to size up the competition and assess my peers, but mainly, I want to determine possible friends and women who might go out with me. I said *might*.

I start by scoping out the walk. The women who walk with purpose—those who stride in as if they own the place—scare me. I cross them off. I realize almost immediately that every woman strides in. I have to lower my standards. I'm down to homely women who seem nervous or confused and who aren't towing a boyfriend or cradling a baby.

Within fifteen minutes the auditorium is full, and I identify every conceivable type of student—freaks, geeks, nerds, stoners, mathletes, punks, weirdos, jocks, preppies, and surfers. Asians represent, along with a rainbow coalition of international students from other countries and cultures, many of whom I recognize as residents of Owen Hall. All of us gathered in one lecture hall, my class feels comfortably diverse.

As we settle in, a low din thrums through the room, punctuated by the intermittent whacking of wooden seats and the occasional shrill laugh. The nervousness builds, and the volume rises. The auditorium floor vibrates beneath the bounce of shaky legs, mine among them. I begin to sense fear coursing through the room. Fear of the first day. Fear of not fitting in. Fear of the unknown. Most of all, fear of failure.

We heard it all at our interviews. Medical students never flunk out. We all make it through somehow. Some of us will excel, some will squeak by, most of us will land right in the middle. In the end, unless we can't take it and quit, we will all become doctors. But few of us will become the doctors we hoped to be. Maybe that's what fuels our fear. We're afraid that we won't live up to our expectations, that we'll fall short of our own dreams.

A group of semi-decrepit white-haired men and women enter the hall and slowly make their way to the front of the auditorium. Nobody seems younger than eighty. As they walk, the din flattens into a hush. For some reason, I decide to do a quick count of the class. I count 102 of us, half women. How many eligible women? Maybe half of the half. Realistically, I have to whittle that number down, even beyond the confident ones who scare me. I eliminate a few because of age. A surprising number of women seem to be well past thirty, closing in on middle age. A few are *old*, grandmother-old. Even if they're sort of cute, I cross them off. I also eliminate a few on physical appearance. I have a problem with nose rings, lip rings, eyebrow spears, earlobe piercings, tongue studs, and multiple ear hoops—all in the same person. And I have to remove from contention a three-hundred-pound woman in the far right corner who takes up three seats, one for a case of Mountain Dew, the other two for her ass.

The first of a succession of white-haired deans—this one a six-nine scarecrow—steps forward and, towering over a podium, grips both sides to manage his trembling hands, welcomes us. Voice cracking, he cackles into the microphone, causing ear-bleeding feedback. "Say goodbye to the next eleven years of your lives."

I want to join the polite, scared-shitless laughter that results, but I refrain because I don't think he's joking. He follows up this opening remark with a disclaimer: "Medical school isn't that bad." Then he paints a gulag-like picture of endless hours of study, indifference to hygiene, mind-numbing and brain-teasing examinations ("If you flunk, we won't kick you out; you'll just keep taking your exams over and over again until you pass—takes some of you years"), lack of communication with, well, everyone, and—just what I need to hear—involuntary chastity. After Old Dean Happy frightens the hell out of us, a numb, pale second-year student named Mandi gives us an overview of first year from the student perspective, ending with this tearful summary: "I didn't return any phone calls or e-mails during my entire first year. And I'll never forgive myself because I missed my nana's funeral." Mandi gives way to a series of cadaverous deans who repeat pretty much the same cheery message of Old Dean Happy. Then three speakers in a row send me into shock.

First, we endure a convoluted rambling from a flint-eyed financial-aid officer who glumly reports that we will all leave medical school in debt up to our eyes, most of us owing in excess of $100,000 in student loans. He offers no solution to this problem but suggests we set up an appointment to see if we qualify for a low-interest student loan. Is he serious? He must be serious. It's too early in the morning to be trashed.

Second, a lawyer wearing a goop-slicked toupee that threatens to slide off assures us, "It's not a question *if* you'll be sued for malpractice, it's *when* and *how often*. Let me put it another way. Don't worry about screwing up. You will. But what will it cost you? Will you go bankrupt? Doctors do all the time." He waits for us outside the lecture hall, morosely handing out his business card.

Finally, a dark-complexioned man in a dull blue suit, his round, kind face bookmarked by two furry sideburns in need of pruning, implores us not to lose hope even when we think the world is caving in on us and when all we see is darkness and when we believe that our lives are meaningless.

"Who is this guy?" I say to the preppie next to me.

"The chaplain," the preppie says.

"The chaplain? This is gonna be so bad that we need a *priest*?"

One more uplifting speech, this one from the med-school shrink who suggests we begin each day by giving ourselves a hug. Even the chaplain's hairy eyebrows rise at that suggestion. Then Mandi returns to the podium, assures us that we'll all make it through, and ends with a joke: "What do you call the med student who finishes last in his medical-school class? *Doctor.*" To tepid laughter, she thanks everyone who spoke and announces that we will spend the rest of orientation week in small groups of seven. Our names and group leaders—second-year students, who seem godlike to me simply because they've survived first year without becoming drooling idiots or throwing themselves in front of a train—have been posted outside the lecture hall.

I wish the preppie next to me good luck, swim out of my row and into the mass of students surging up the aisle. I find my name on one of the lists and locate the classroom for my group. Outside the door, three guys lean against the wall. We shake hands all around and introduce ourselves—James, a pretty boy in a cutoff Duke sweatshirt; Ricky, slight, hyper, Hawaiian shirt, not just gay but *La Cage aux Folles* gay; and Tim, fast-talking, confident, from Penn and Owen Hall, a floor below me.

I don't know it then, but the four of us—as unlikely a foursome as you could imagine—will soon become best friends for life.

BILLY, OUR GROUP leader, long hair, pouty rock-star aura, waits in the doorway for the last member of our group to show. Every time a cute female passes, Billy hits on her. "Hey there, where you going? Your group's right here. You're number one on my list. Come back! Can I get your number?"

"So, second-year, you want to lead an orientation group because it's a good way to meet women," Tim says.

"Depends on the group," Billy mutters. At the moment our group contains only two women, a white-haired grandma and a brunette with a wedding ring. "We're missing one. Let her please be female."

"I'm not loving Owen Hall," Tim says to me.

"It sucks," I say. "Too many Asians."

This breaks up Tim, James, and Ricky.

"What? I'm not Asian. I'm American. I was born in Detroit."

"You could pass," James says.

"Maybe we should start," Billy says. He looks longingly at a woman in tight jeans who seems lost. "You're in this group. Yes, you are. There she goes. Dissed. Screw it. One more minute and I'm closing the door."

Tim lowers his voice so only I can hear. "One positive thing about Owen Hall. The girls are *fast*."

I'm stunned. "Really?"

"This chick, borderline looks, short—as in tiny, circus tiny—keeps asking me to have dinner with her. Last night I finally did to shut her up. Plus, I was curious about maybe getting some Cirque du Soleil action—"

I stare at him. "Peggy? You slept with Peggy?"

"I'm not very picky, but no, thank you. In the middle of the meal, she starts mashing my crotch with her foot and goes, 'I'm having *this* for dessert.' I ran like hell."

"She's a stalker."

"The official term is 'crazy lunatic psycho stalker.' I'm gonna be a shrink."

"*Woo.*" A throaty voice at the door. Followed by heavy pornographic breathing. "I made it. Sorry."

The three-hundred-pound woman who sat in the corner of the lecture hall stands huffing in the doorway, the case of Mountain Dew tucked under her arm like a football. She coughs, her sumo shoulders heave, her face flames. She shuffles into the room on sandals the size of skis. I notice a pack of Virginia Slims rolled up inside her shirtsleeve, against her WWE-size biceps. I don't want to be judgmental, but this woman is going to be a doctor?

"This building's like a maze," she says.

"Very glad you found us," Billy says in a wobbly voice that tells me he's not at all glad. "Welcome."

"Gail," the woman says, thrusting out an arm the size of an alligator. "My friends call me Gail the Whale. I can't imagine why." She barks out a laugh that goes on forever and alone.

Billy throws on a truly fake smile, then sneaks a look at Tim and me in what I can only call terror. I've never been able to read lips, but I'm pretty sure he mouths, "She-*eeeet*."

MOMENTS LATER, BILLY drops his *I'm only in this to meet women* facade and morphs into the weighty role of second-year medical student and group leader. He asks us to give our name, hometown, college we attended, and share one fun fact, something you'd never guess. I say that I play the guitar and my favorite singer-songwriter is Jimmy Buffett. This elicits a round of groans, undeserved, in my opinion, and one uncalled-for "Were you dropped on your head as a child?" from Tim.

After we've all shared our information, Billy pauses, looks us over, and says, "Now I'm going to ask you a question. But I don't want you to answer until the end of the week. It's an obvious question, *the* obvious question, but we don't trust each other yet to answer the question truthfully."

He holds for a beat.

"Why do you want to be a doctor?"

We actually laugh.

"How about a trial run? For fun. Let me ask one of you now, and we'll see how the answer differs at the end of the week."

He's going to pick me. Guaranteed. Never fails.

"Tony?"

"Pass."

A big laugh. I'm serious, but Billy's look tells me he's not letting me off the hook.

"Okay," I say. "I'll tell you the truth. I don't care. I'm going to say the same thing now and at the end of the week." I pause. "I want to help people."

Even bigger laugh. Followed by applause.

"This isn't your med-school interview," Billy says. "You're already in."

"Fine. I'll get back to you guys in a week."

"Trust each other," Billy says. "That's what we're going for. Okay, everybody up."

"Allow us," Tim says. "You took one for the team." He and James pull me to my feet.

"Cute answer," Ricky says, pushing me from behind. "I would've said I have a constant ache to heal the world."

"All right," Billy says. "We call this exercise the trust fall."

He grabs a folding table that's pressed against a wall and carries it to the center of the room. He vaults up onto the table. "Here's how it works. You climb up here, cross your hands on your chest, close your eyes, take a deep breath, and let yourself fall. We will catch you. All of us. Like I said, it's about trust."

A couple of uncomfortable laughs cut through nervous murmuring.

I have no problem catching a total stranger hurtling backward through space. But *falling*—

I look at James, Ricky, and Tim, and even though I've known them for under an hour, I know instinctively that I can trust these guys, that they will catch me.

"So," Billy says, cupping his hands and blowing on them as if he's warming them over a campfire, "do I have a volunteer?"

What the hell.

I'm ready to trust.

I step forward.

"Ah, whatever."

Gail. Voice jagged as a saw. She shoves past me, waddles to the desk, and reaches two fists the size of basketballs toward Billy, whose mouth has sprung open and flopped to the floor like a puppet's. Billy latches on to Gail's wrists while Tim and James rush over and shove her from behind. Gail rolls onto the table. Panting, she climbs to her feet and stands over us, her tree-stump legs quivering. The seven of us rush toward the table, our arms extended as if we're weekend volunteer firefighters.

Gail looks down at us and, her massive body swaying, shakes her head.

"You may want to get another group in here," she says.

HAVING OUR WHOLE group flattened by a three-hundred-pound medical student is by far the highlight of orientation.

After dismissing us early the first day, Billy cruises the other groups and determines that the other fourteen contain at least two, sometimes three pretty women, while he's stuck with a wife, a grandma, and Gail the Whale. By the second day, he loses interest in our group altogether and tries to switch with a friend, with no luck. Every morning he shows up late and every afternoon he ends our orientation sessions early, earlier each day, to the point that days three and four, we finish before lunch. Billy's abandonment does give us a leg up. Tim, James, Ricky, and I are so bored and eager to begin classes that any pre-med-school jitters we had have evaporated.

We celebrate the stultifying finale to orientation week with a first-year bash at the USA Café, a kitschy diner by day—colorful maps of the states on the walls, laminated place mats and paper napkins of presidential faces on the tables—that converts to a dance club and med-school hangout by night. I meet Tim in his room an hour before the party.

"What if the party sucks?" he says.

"It could definitely suck."

"That's why we should get wasted now." He jiggles a six-pack of Molson at me, tears off three cans, underhands them to me. We pound them.

Allow me to destroy a cliché. At least a cliché that seems to follow me everywhere. Which is—

Med students party like rap stars and drink like Irish poets.

No.

We like to *think* we party hard. We like to portray ourselves as debauched, out-of-control frat boys with stethoscopes. But we're not. No matter how we appear or act, even if we're great-looking and smooth, we are, at our core, nerds and lightweights. Sure, I can think of exceptions. A few. They all become orthopedic surgeons.

This night with Tim, I don't know this yet. As I polish off my third beer and crush the can into my forehead and follow that up with an impressive belch, I picture certain college friends who, on a typical Saturday night, could—and did—drain an entire case of beer alone. I don't strive to be them. Who would? It's just that Tim and I don't know each other well yet, and we overcompensate right out of the box. We assume the role of big-drinking, hard-partying med students. For one night—the first of our many nights together—we become the cliché. As soon as classes start—tomorrow!—we'll find out that the intensity of medical school will fry our brains, leaving us sufficiently fuzzy-headed and bleary-eyed without any need to amp it up with excessive alcohol.

But after three beers, I'm shouting "Woo!" at everything Tim says, and he's laughing at everything I say as if I'm Chris Rock. Slinging jackets over our shoulders, we windmill down the stairwell of Owen Hall, ricocheting off the walls, until we arrive in the parking lot by the bike rack, where we have tethered our twin Huffys. My head feels underwater. I stare at the bikes. His, blood-red, pulsates. Mine, baby-blue, shimmers.

"Identical-twin bikes," Tim says. "Ridiculous."

"'They did not know each other when they bought them,'" I say, going all voice-over-documentary narrator. "'They had no idea they were buying the *same exact bike*. Coincidence? I think not.'"

"You are trashed," Tim says.

"On three beers? Hahahahaha."

"Lightweight. You have to learn to hold your beer. I will train you." Tim fiddles with the lock on his bike, yanks it, slams it, opens his hand as if freeing a bird, and lets the horseshoe-shaped contraption swing and clang unopened against the metal rack. "I need a new lock. You wouldn't happen to have a hacksaw on you, would you?"

"That's my bike, dipshit."

"Well, I'll be. How do you like that?"

"Who's the lightweight?"

"You. By a wide margin."

He laughs, a scary hyena keen, then with a magician's flourish, he springs the lock on his red Huffy, swings his leg over the handlebars like a cowboy, salutes, pedals off, and plows right into the bike rack.

He folds into the pavement like a cartoon.

I RULE THE dance floor. In line-dance-style—thirty of us, our fingertips resting on strangers' hips—we sway, we slide, we shimmy, we reach for imaginary items from imaginary shelves and place them in our imaginary shopping carts, then we shake-shake-shake down the grocery-store aisle. This dance—"the shopping cart"—comes straight out of Greenville by way of Kalamazoo, bouncing its way here to the unlikely USA Café in East Lansing, where tonight, snaking through the entire restaurant, I lead the line. Head and neck bobbing to Duran Duran whining through a bank of tinny speakers, I am the undisputed master of the shopping cart. Sweat puddles up on my forehead. I mop my brow with a napkin someone hands me featuring President William McKinley's nearly forgotten face.

Twenty minutes later, seven sweaty veterans of the shopping cart sit jammed into a booth for four—Tim, Ricky, James; Daisy, a sexy dirty-blond first-year who snuggles up to James between slugs of her beer; Shelly, a dark and edgy beauty with a hive of crow-black hair; and Daisy's boyfriend, Clark, a refrigerator repairman built like a refrigerator himself, who is either blind-drunk or literally blind because he doesn't seem to notice Daisy nuzzling James five feet away. Behind us, a DJ dressed as Uncle Sam spins a series of disco hits. Tim, as he will for the next four years, plays host. He refills our glasses from a recently landed pitcher.

"But Clark," Ricky says, patting a beer bubble dry on his lip with his index finger extended from a ridiculously long brown European cigarette, "how do you *know* if you need to clean out your motor or replace your fan? Or, God forbid, replace your whole *fridge*."

"Oh, you would be shocked how many people do that. They're ignorant. All you gotta do is vacuum out the dust. Takes you five minutes. But some less reputable servicepeople will try to talk you into buying a brand-new unit."

"That's obscene." Ricky slurps his beer, shoots a starlet eyelash flicker across the table. "If you blew the dust off my unit, I would not complain."

Tim chokes. I cough. I glance at Daisy.

"So how long have you two been going out?" Tim says.

"About a year." Clark leans forward. Tim, Ricky, and I lean in to hear him, nearly knock heads. "Tonight's the night."

"For what?" I say.

Clark slides a small velvety box over to me. He raises an eyebrow, a conspirator's signal.

"Open it," Shelly says. Husky voice. Vampira looks. I think I'm in love. I pop open the lid on the purple box. A sparkly engagement ring twinkles at us.

"Man," Tim says.

"Wow," I say.

"Balls," Shelly says.

"You're asking Tony to marry you?" Ricky says, circling his lips into a hurt pout.

"You might be better off," Tim mutters as James and Daisy start snuggling again.

"I'm so jealous," Ricky says.

"We worked out a plan," Clark says. "I'm gonna support her through medical school. Once she's a doctor and in her own practice and whatnot, I'll take care of the kids. Stay-at-home dad and all that. Fine by me."

"You've given this a lot of thought," Tim says, then under his breath, into his glass, "How long you give this marriage?"

I shrug. "A week."

"So, guys, about tomorrow," Shelly says, done with Daisy and her thick-as-an-icecap refrigerator repairman. She swivels her body toward me. We're close enough for a kiss. Our knees touch. One more drink and I might snatch Clark's ring and propose to *her*. "I'm freaking. I've been reading ahead in anatomy—"

"Wait, I didn't quite catch that, loud in here," Ricky says. "Did you say you've been reading ahead?"

"Well, *yeah*," Shelly says, her face flushing the color of Tim's bike. "It's medical school, it's *competitive*? By the way, did you guys take biochemistry?"

"When you talk that way, you make Tony hot," Tim says.

"I'm serious. Tony, did you?"

Not sure how to play this. I want her. I want her bad. I want her now. The four beers have made me horny and bold and hopeful and *horny*. What I say to Shelly in the next five seconds will determine our entire future.

When in doubt, lie. *Lie*. Lie if you want to get off the bench and into the game.

I can't.

"Biochem? Let me think. *Bio*chem. Yes. Yes, I did."

"Damn it."

Lips an inch from mine, withdrawn. Knees formerly brushing mine, gone.

"*Crap.* Everybody's taken biochem but me. My idiot counselor gave me the worst advice. What a moron. He told me to take p-chem instead. How is that gonna help me in medical school? I'm so fucked. You guys have all had biochem, so you'll coast through first year. I'll have to study twice as hard, which puts me at a total disadvantage for honors. It is so unfair."

Our booth goes silent. Clark pokes the inside of his beer glass with his plastic stirrer. Even Daisy and James unclench to listen to Shelly rant.

"I don't really remember anything from biochem," I say, trying to reconnect my knees to Shelly's. I stretch my legs so far under the table that my chin is practically resting on my plate. "You'll be fine, Shelly."

"Yeah, right." She catches James and Daisy staring at her. "Did you two take biochem?"

In unison, they nod.

"*Fuck.*" She flies from the booth, her black hair bouncing as she streaks out of the diner.

"Beware of that species, my friends," James says. "We call her and the rest of her kind gunners. They live to shoot you down and kill you."

"I thought she was hot," I say.

Ricky flicks the ash from his European cigarette into Shelly's abandoned glass. "Don't despair, Anthony, there are so many more where she came from."

"That was a perfect example of my luck with women over the period of time I call my so-called life."

"That's about to change," Ricky says. "Trust us."

"Really? I look at you two, and I don't know why, but I'm doubtful."

"That's hurtful," Tim says. "You are going to be deluged. First of all, I have a way with women. James and I have a gift."

I roll my eyes.

"Second, Ricky gets tons of great women. Most of them he doesn't want."

"He's gay. You're gay," I say to Ricky.

"I am."

"What am I missing?"

"I'm a chick magnet," Ricky says, lighting another foot-long ciga-rette. "I attract crowds of smart, funny, hot women. They assume I'm safe. They assume wrong. I will cross over. I will slum. If I can't find a warm bed with a penis, I'll take a chance in the Bermuda Triangle. As a last resort."

"Not your default position."

"No. I close my eyes and pretend. I say a boy's name to myself. Oh, Tony. *Oh.*"

Tim and I lose it. Ricky flicks his ash into the dregs of the pitcher, which, for some reason, breaks us up even more. The three of us are laughing so hard that we never see Clark make his way toward the center of the dance floor.

"Excuse me. May I have your attention, please."

"Oh, God." Daisy. Who at the moment is latched onto James. She springs back, lands on the vinyl booth with a loud smack. The room goes silent as a midterm.

"I know classes start tomorrow, so tonight feels like the perfect time for something special," Clark says.

He lowers his freezer-sized frame to one knee, the velvet box cupped in his palm.

"Babe, I know we talked about holding off for a while, maybe until winter break, but hell, sometimes love can't wait. Daisy? Where are you? Will you marry me?"

We all gasp. I feel as if I'm watching the shower scene in *Psycho* for the first time. My throat seizes up.

"Shit," Daisy says.

"Timing, huh?" James says.

Fingers grip my forearm. Ricky's.

"I'm light-headed," he says, fanning himself with his napkin. "The vapors. Bring me the vapors."

"Shit," Daisy says again.

I can't watch. I lower my head into the laminated eyes of Calvin Coolidge.

The rustling of our tablecloth. Footsteps. An even louder communal gasp. An "Awww." Tentative, scared applause. A slurred drunken "Yeah!" The applause grows more confident and builds. I lift my head. Daisy, hands clasped behind her back like a little girl, curtsies slightly in front of Clark and says, "Yes, Clark, I will marry you."

He rises to his feet and they hug. He twirls her around. Her high-beam stare hits our table like a floodlight to the face.

AT TWO A.M., beneath a soft drizzle, Tim and I, our heads spinning as much from the loopy night as from our five beers each, lock up our bikes and jog for shelter in the monastic gray lobby of Owen Hall. Because of the tapping of the slight rain mixing with the whirring inside my head, I've kept quiet for the last half hour. In fact, I feel overwhelmed. In eight hours, my new life will begin. A new life that feels as if it belongs to someone else. This night has whirled around me. I have known Tim, James, and Ricky for a week. Impossible. I have known them forever. They're godsends, angels, family.

"We never got to answer the question," I say to Tim a step away from the elevator.

"What question?"

"From orientation. Why do you want to be a doctor?"

Tim yawns, elbows the up button.

"Well?" I say.

"What?"

"Why do you want to be a doctor?"

"You really want to know?" Tim taps his fingers on the outside of the elevator door. "All the clichéd reasons. I want job security. I want to meet women. Doctors are cool. Chicks like cool guys. I become a doctor, I have a better chance of meeting someone hotter than if I work at Subway. I don't want to end up in a completely soulless job, like stockbroker. I wouldn't mind a nice house, a good car, and money in the bank. I want my parents to be proud of me. And, strange as it seems, I actually like helping people."

The elevator bangs to the floor; the doors sigh, rattle, and pull apart. We get in, and I thumb separate buttons to deliver us to our separate floors. We ride up in silence. The elevator opens at the second floor. Tim slouches out, mumbles over his shoulder, "Meet you for breakfast. We'll go over to biochem together."

"Deal. 'Night."

"'Night."

The doors vibrate, grunt, begin to close. Before they bang together, Tim's fist punches into the narrow space between them, forcing them open. He stands in front of me. "What about you?"

"I want to contribute to society and heal the sick."

"Ha-*ha*." Tim doesn't crack a smile. "Now the truth."

I kick at something imaginary in the elevator carpet. I'm stalling. "Okay." I pick my head up and fix my eyes on him. I'm overcome with a surge of sadness.

"The truth is, Tim," I say, "I don't know."

6

—

A Show of Hands

I see dead people.

Eighteen bodies covered with plastic, lying on gurneys. An occasional toe protrudes to verify that beneath the shiny black tarp, a dead person lies.

I smell dead people, too.

Or at least the thick chemical stench of formaldehyde, tearing at my eyes and packing my nose, enough liquid preservative in here to float a yacht. The smell rises from the bodies and from a dozen large clear plastic bins—similar to the type you find at IKEA—lining the back wall of the lab, some stacked on top of each other. The bins contain body parts and organs, all of them cataloged, numbered, and labeled.

We sit at desks in an adjacent classroom, the eighteen bodies lurking behind us, lying in wait. In my lab coat I feel like Igor, the mad scientist's assistant, but in reality I'm sitting in anatomy class, by reputation the most furiously intense class we will take in first year, maybe in all of medical school, especially since our section is taught by the infamous Dr. Gaw, the most ruthless, unforgiving professor who has ever lived. If you believe in reincarnation, Dr. Gaw has returned from her previous life as Attila the Hun in the form of an eighty-five-year-old nightmare who lives to terrorize *us*. She walks as erect as a pencil, her skeletal face a frozen fanged scowl resting atop one throbbing purple vein. According to our school catalog, Dr. Gaw has won awards, a trophy case full. To this day I can't imagine how.

According to Billy, our go-to second-year consultant, who hooked up with a first-year from another orientation group and is now all smiles and helpful when we see him, anatomy is even more of a bear than biochemistry, which, even though I aced it going away at Kalamazoo, is right now kicking my ass. I try to explain this to Shelly. I tell her that med-school biochem is a lot different than college biochem, and I'm happy to share my notes or study with her—my one final feeble attempt to get us alone, where we might resume rubbing our knees together in the hope of progressing upward—but she turns out to be not only a gunner but a first-class ass kisser as well, a lethal double threat, the kind of medical student who takes no prisoners, plays every angle, murders every exam, laughs at every teacher's joke, lives for extra credit, hangs out with professors before and after class, and along with a cabal of other gunners and ass kissers, scores invitations to their homes for brunches and barbecues and even gets hired to babysit their children. I give up on Shelly. She's not my type. My type defined as any woman showing a vague interest in me.

At our first class, Dr. Gaw hands out equipment, including latex gloves, goggles, and what I really want, nose plugs, which I stuff into my nostrils, hoping to at least partially deflect the stench. The nose plugs don't help, so except for gloves, I go commando. I figure I might as well get used to the smell. I'll have to, if I ever do become a real doctor. Most of the other first-years wear as much protective covering as possible. One guy, a gunner, shows up on the second day of anatomy wearing a hazmat suit. The whole ball and tackle. Goggles and ventilation mask. Dr. Gaw says nothing, but I think I see her scowl flutter, and I imagine her dropping Hazmat's grade.

Tim and I scramble to find seats together. Tim, I've learned by now, has exactly zero mechanical aptitude. A week into medical school, we've eliminated the possibility that he will ever become a surgeon. He struggles to pull on his *gloves*. This first day, I face him and yank them on for him. Once they're secure, I turn back and find Dr. Gaw standing over me. She reeks of formaldehyde. She holds a moist body part in one bony gloved hand.

"Dr. Youn."

How the hell does she know my name?

"Yes, Dr. Gaw?"

"Which valve of the heart am I holding?"

Am I glad she said *heart*. I thought she was holding a liver. I take a shot. "Mitral valve?"

"Congratulations." Do I detect a trace of a Nazi accent? "This is the *aortic* valve." She spits the words at me. "You have the deductive ability of a monkey. I pity your future patients, Dr. Youn."

She limps away.

Tim whispers, "If it makes you feel any better, I thought it was the small intestine."

Dr. Gaw suddenly materializes in front of Tim. Where did she come from? It's as if she stepped out of a fog.

"Do you have something to add to the class, Dr. O'Laughlin?"

"Me? No. Not at all. Not at the moment."

"I assumed as much. If you have any reasonable hope of passing this class, I would suggest that you and Dr. Youn refrain from talking and joking and making fools of yourselves. Oh, and a helpful suggestion. As doctors, you will find it useful if you can distinguish the heart from the small intestine."

I'm shaken. I've never found myself in such unfamiliar territory. Academically—from elementary school through college—I have always excelled. I'm the school scholar, the student hotshot, the freaking *valedictorian*. Within seconds, Dr. Gaw has trashed all that. To her, I'm the class idiot.

I'm left with two choices. I can shrink away. Or I can bounce back.

It takes me two seconds to decide.

I am going to *dominate* anatomy.

Starting tomorrow.

Today I'd like to disappear.

MOMENTS LATER, WITH Dr. Gaw in the lead, we tour the anatomy lab, gunners and ass kissers fanning around her like a rock star's entourage. The rest of us hang back. I stay as far away from her as I can. We stop first at the gurneys.

"As you may have heard, most medical schools assign a specific cadaver to a small group of students, and they spend their entire first year dissecting and learning its anatomy. Often they form a peculiar attachment to their cadavers, even giving it a name. Bob. Heidi. Adolph."

She pauses suddenly. Her bottom lip quivers. Perhaps she's lost her train of thought. Or perhaps, hopefully, she's having a stroke.

"We don't do that. The bodies here have been prosected. Which means, Dr. Youn, that they have been dissected in advance by faculty and students in the elective dissection course."

She seems fine. Damn it.

"These bodies are intact so that we can study the head, neck, muscles, nerves, blood vessels, and so forth *together.*"

She whips the tarp off one body, leaving the head covered. The abdomen is exposed, and all the nerves and blood vessels have been tagged by blue index cards with names and arrows pointing to internal structures.

"That is such a clever method," Shelly says.

"I agree," Dr. Gaw says. "Especially since I devised it."

I'm positive Shelly didn't pull that out of her ass. She must have researched Dr. Gaw in order to have this information locked and loaded.

"Of course, it was some years ago. But there has never been any reason to change."

"If it's not broken, why fix it?"

"Indeed, Dr. Burkhart."

She beams at Shelly. Shelly flashes back a *We are so connected, after this let's go for manis and pedis* smile. She's good. I can't stand her.

"Our gross-anatomy course will cover the entire human body, one system at a time. We will study the head and neck in one of the last sections, so for most of the course, the bodies will be displayed with their faces covered. For the next three weeks, we will study the abdomen and all its vital organs. Questions?"

Why does she look at me? I brace myself. Here it comes. Another sarcastic crack establishing once again that I am the class dunce.

"Good."

I'm spared.

"Each body part that I point out to you today will be on your lab practical exam in three weeks."

An undercurrent sweeps through the room. Gunners whip out notebooks. Scribbling commences. The word *exam* gets my attention, too. I decide to change position. I step forward to get a closer look. I move casually, furtively, outside Dr. Gaw's line of vision. In fact, I walk behind her.

"Dr. Youn, you've decided to join us. Astonishing."

Eyes in the back of her head. It's official. She's a ghoul.

Dr. Gaw, her back to us, gunners practically Velcroed to her, approaches the plastic bins at the far end of the lab. She taps the first container with a bony finger. "Inside these containers, you will find individual body parts for you to examine. This one"—she passes her palm over the top—"contains hearts. The one next to it contains livers. The next one, kidneys. And so on. Each container has a label stating which parts belong in it. If you take a body part out, please be sure to put it back and into the correct bin."

She whirls on us, a bony finger extended like a witch's wand. "Do not even *consider* taking a body part home with you. That will be grounds for expulsion."

I expect Dr. Gaw to warn me by name here. Hell, I expect her to frisk me to see if I've sneaked a kidney under my shirt. Instead she settles for a hairy-eyeball stare. It's enough to make me perspire.

"Take a few moments now and familiarize yourself with the various bins. And then we will begin our study of the abdomen."

She lays the word out—ab-do-*men*—as if it's part of a satanic feminist curse.

I start for the bin farthest from the gunners, stop, retrieve Tim. He waves me away. He looks a little under the weather.

"Let's check out the lungs, maybe toss around a liver." I grab Tim's elbow, attempt to steer him toward a bin in the back. "Body parts. Organs. This stuff fascinates me."

"You go. Enjoy." He leans over, steadies himself against a desk. His complexion darkens, turns green, the color of a fairway.

"You all right?"

"Never better. Have I mentioned that I'm a tad squeamish?"

"You're a klutz, you're squeamish, and Dr. Gaw hates me. We have this class *wired*."

"Score."

"You want some water?"

"No, I'll just puke and pass out and I'll be fine."

He lowers himself, head aimed down, lands with a thud at a desk. He rummages through his backpack, pulls out a towel, and presses it against his head. He smiles sickly. "You might want to move back in case I go projectile."

I give him a thumbs-up and peel out toward the plastic bins at the back of the lab. I find myself walking in the gunners' wake.

"I heard that last year someone stole a spleen, took it home to study," an ass kisser whispers to Shelly. "Smuggled it out in her backpack. Never got caught. Aced the exam."

"That rocks," Shelly says, wheels turning.

That *rocks*? These people are insane.

I veer off on my own, start with the bin marked *liver*. I move on to *heart* and *lungs*. I cruise from bin to bin, taking mental inventory of the contents. *That bin, number three. Packed with hearts swimming in formaldehyde. The next one, lungs. Filled to the top. The one after that, overflowing with livers—*

Then it hits me.

These are human organs. They belonged to actual people. People who cared enough about helping others to donate their organs so I—all of us—could learn to be a doctor.

I stop at the last bin against the wall.

It's open.

I look down and see a pile of severed hands.

Dozens of hands.

Floating in a pool of preservative.

I look at these hands, the hands of strangers, hands that appear to be reaching out to each other.

I stare at these hands. I feel suddenly as if I'm somehow invading these people's lives. I feel like an intruder. I did not expect this. I suspected that I would have a strong reaction when we study faces. I'm afraid that I will become too attached, too emotional. Doctors need to be detached, right? Impersonal. What is more personal than our face?

Our hands.

We use our hands for everything—to touch, to write, to build, to play, to cook, to clean, to feed, to feel, to guide, to caress, to love. Our hands serve us as extensions of our minds and our hearts.

I look at these floating hands, at the fingers, the fingernails, the bones, the knuckles, and I picture them as the hands of fathers, mothers, sisters, brothers, children, best friends, loved ones, the hands of people who once had thoughts, opinions, hopes, and dreams. These are anyone's hands. These are everyone's hands. They could be my hands.

I feel myself drifting off. I'm no longer here. I'm no longer in this classroom and anatomy lab. I've entered a different state of mind. I feel small and mortal and humbled and grateful. Deeply grateful.

And I feel that I have been given a gift and that I have a mission and a responsibility. I feel obligated to the people who gave us their hands.

I lift my head from the bin of hands. Across the room, Dr. Gaw's piercing purple eyes puncture my gaze. For the first time I don't care about her. I don't care what she thinks or what she says. I don't care if she doesn't like me and never will. I don't care about her at all.

Then something happens that I never could have predicted or imagined.

The old witch smiles.

7

Nerd Room

We live in the Nerd Room.

The Nerd Room looks nondescript, even benign. Long and rectangular. Filled with thirty study cubicles. Creamy walls. Beige wall-to-wall carpet. Overhead fluorescent lighting that hums soothingly and rarely flickers. No windows to distract. No music pumped in. No-talking policy, which we ignore. Great location. Adjacent to the medical-school student lounge that's loaded with good stuff—cracked and broken-in leather couch, basic cable, snack machine with the good candy, soda machine, Ping-Pong table, and a communal desktop computer that runs fitfully and often freezes due to the countless viruses that have infected it because of the amount of porn certain students keep downloading. I won't mention names (Tim, Ricky).

Tim, Ricky, James, Daisy, and I descend on the Nerd Room every Friday night. Except for bathroom breaks, meal and snack interludes (none lasting over fifteen minutes), an occasional furious full-contact game of Ping-Pong to blow off steam, the periodic make-out session—I don't participate; nobody does except for James and Daisy, who recently broke off her engagement to refrigerator repairman Clark—we never leave the Nerd Room. Crashing on the carpet in our soul-sucking cubicles, we sleep haphazardly and infrequently. We emerge from the Nerd Room Monday morning, blinking, sweating, smelly, irritable but prepared, primed to do battle against Dr. Gaw's brain-shrinking, minutiae-laden gross-anatomy exams, or the weekly brain-crushing biochemistry tests that have already made Shelly pull out sections of her own hair, or the brain-teasing pathology open-book tests that Professor X seduces you into thinking will be a piece of cake but in fact have been designed to terminate you.

Overall, medical school means study. And then study some more. And when you finish all that studying, you will definitely feel the need to *study*.

I first studied in my dorm room. The stench of simmering khrua gling and boiling larb accompanied by the constant flushing of my neighbor drove me away. I tried then to study in the library, but I found myself distracted by the high volume of cute coeds roaming the stacks. I moved to the local coffeehouse, but I found myself distracted by even more cute coeds, some of whom worked there. Not only couldn't I study, but I spent a fortune on espresso drinks just so I could get a closer look at them, not to mention the time I wasted thinking up clever pickup lines, none of which I found the courage to try.

Once I commit to the Nerd Room, I feel both at home and in a low-level state of constant panic. I'm home because this is where my new family resides. By now the four of us guys have become inseparable and growing closer with each passing study hour. I imagine our closeness compares in some ways to that of a platoon in a foxhole. There are similarities to war—the stress, the fatigue, the physical exhaustion, the mental exertion, and the fear of getting blown away, in our case not by an enemy (unless you count Dr. Gaw) but by the constant barrage of exams.

I also find that I have to learn a new way to study. Throughout high school and college, I applied a simple shotgun approach. I memorized every bit of information in the assigned chapters in our textbook as well as every note I took, going over and over it as many times as I needed until I had everything down cold. I can't do that in medical school. There is too much material to comprehend and absorb. I have to adjust my technique. I have to learn to isolate what's most important. As the hours in the Nerd Room whip by and I realize I have too much material to cram into my head in the time left before the Monday-morning exam, I panic. Well, first I freeze, then I panic. And then I despair.

"How are we supposed to learn all this stuff?" I moan to Tim as we scarf candy bars and wash them down with warm Mountain Dew. "There's not enough time."

"I know. It sucks."

"Plus, all this junk food. I've put on about thirty pounds."

"I can see. You've really ballooned up."

I halt my Snickers bar halfway to my mouth. "Now I don't feel like eating this."

"I'll eat it."

I slap the remains of my candy bar into Tim's waiting open palm. He two-hands it into his mouth. He smacks his lips, chews.

"We're all in the same boat, you know," he says.

I wait for him to finish what I realize was my lunch.

"We're all crazy, dude. We're all obsessive-compulsives. They know it. That's why they make every course pass-fail. To take the pressure off."

"So why do I feel so *much* pressure?"

"How should I know? You gonna finish your soda?"

Before I can say yes, he snatches my Mountain Dew and chugs what's left. He burps and slaps me on the back.

"Good talk," he says.

Sleep-deprived, adrenaline pumping, sugar-charged, head down, locked *in*, I blast through the eight o'clock Monday-morning anatomy exam. I attack those one hundred multiple-choice and two essay questions like a warrior. A wounded punch-drunk warrior; still, a warrior.

I destroy that test. I bolt out of the exam room, high, confident, proud. Within minutes, I second-guess every answer. I'm sure I messed up at least twenty and I'm positive I forgot a third essay on the back. Over-hearing Shelly and her gunners shrieking, "So *easy!*" doesn't help. I stagger back to Owen Hall, tumble into my room, crash completely clothed onto my unmade bed, pass out, wake up after dinner, shower, open a bottle of AXE or whatever the latest cologne I bought promising that women will swarm all over me and lock their legs around me until I cry for mercy, put on a gallon of the stuff with a roller, change into my best "playa" outfit, hop on my Huffy, and meet Tim.

In med school, Monday night is party night, and so we will, either at the USA Café or at James's off-campus apartment. When it comes to women, James is miles ahead of Tim and me. Well, miles ahead of me. A month in, and he already has a girlfriend. A girlfriend who dumped her fiancé for him. Plus, James has gone out with other women. More than two. Doubling my output. My hope is that he's convinced Daisy to invite a pack of her friends, attractive, smart, funny, *willing* friends, ones whose lives will not feel complete unless they hook up with me.

Tim and I arrive on our Huffys, each of us balancing a six-pack of Molson on our handlebars. Not as easy as it sounds. On the way, we swerve constantly and miraculously avoid crashing into each other. Inside, the party has begun without us. We pass around the brews. Scope out the talent. Nothing yet. In the living room, seven early arrivals dance the shopping cart. Bunch of posers. I'll show them *how* later.

Tim peels off, honing in on a less than gorgeous coed who's thumbing through James's CD collection. He winks at me before he leaves. You have to admire the guy. I wish I had half his guts. I'd kill for a quarter of his confidence.

I shuffle over to the snack table, inhale a handful of nachos. Ricky, in Hawaiian shirt, Bermuda shorts, and flip-flops, lands at my side. He frowns, a stricken look on his face. "What is that *smell*?"

Takes me a minute. "Oh, it's my new cologne."

"It smells like ox urine."

"Really? Maybe I should wash it off."

"I didn't say it was a bad thing."

"And you are familiar with the smell of ox urine how?"

"Oh, Anthony, the places I've seen."

A party of three enters, two hot unfamiliar women, undergrads, flanking a preppie jock type.

"Excuse me," Ricky says, ogling the jock. "My date's here."

He moonwalks toward the trio. The preppie guy laughs. I make eye contact with one of the hot undergrads.

"Mine, too," I say to myself.

I PITCH A shutout. Both of the hot new arrivals drool when I announce that I'm a med student. I lose one when I go into a little too much detail about my jaw surgery. The other bails when I rave about my mother's cooking. I get them back momentarily when we go hip to hip in the "Achy Breaky" dance. I wow them with my moves. They laugh, they swoon, then the dance ends and they leave. I pound one beer, then another. I'm halfway through beer three when Tim and the not so gorgeous coed come out of a back bedroom. His hair's flying all over, and she's wearing his baseball cap sideways. I drop onto the floor, slide my back into the wall. I hold up my beer and toast Tim and this evening's winner.

"I want you to meet somebody." Tim to the coed, who wriggles into her coat. "This is Tony, my best friend and the coolest guy I know."

"Hey," I say, reaching out my hand. I look at Tim and see a blank stare. Clearly, he doesn't know her name.

"Ingrid," she says, squeezing two of my fingers.

"Ingrid," I repeat. "Exotic."

"Danke. Are you a med student, too?"

"Yes, I am."

"Are you going to be a heart surgeon, too?"

The look of astonishment that slams onto my face, followed by my uncontrollable howl of laughter, causes Tim to practically shove Ingrid out the door. He sticks his head back inside. "Hey, Youner, you mind wheeling my bike home?"

"Yes, I mind. It's a giant pain in the ass. Wheel your own damn bike home, dude."

I don't say this. Another beer or two and I might.

"No problem. You two have a good night."

That's actually what I say.

"Thanks, man. I owe you. Later."

He whispers something to Ingrid that cracks her up. And then they're gone.

How does he do it?

James, I get. James has movie-star looks. Young Redford. A Jonas brother. Handsome and vulnerable. We once went on a road trip to Toronto. We heard they had some crazy little women there, and I wanted to get me one. Particularly in this one bar, the Easy Rider or something. We walk in, order drinks, lean back against the bar to check out the scene, and a blond, blue-eyed Kate Hudson wannabe walks straight up to James and starts making out with him. No hello, no buy me a drink, no nothing. Just bang. Mouth to mouth. Tongue to tongue. Tonsil to tonsil. Stunning. Can it be just looks? Can looking like a movie star be all you need? I kind of look like a tall Mr. Miyagi in *The Karate Kid*. So far that hasn't been a big plus.

Tim has it going on, too, but in a different way. He has a gift. He doesn't discriminate. He goes after women he knows he can get. And if he's horny, he goes all out. He once drove from Philly to Saratoga to hook up with an easy girl he knew from high school. Nine hours for seven minutes of pleasure. You have to admire that. I guess. And Tim refuses to take no for an answer. He's got the tenacity of a used-car salesman. I mean this as a compliment.

I need help. I want to be Tim's wingman. I think about my turning point.

A week ago.

Friend of mine tells me about a party off campus. Frat party. Invitation-only. Bouncers at the door. My friend happens to be the president of the fraternity, so we have an in. He doesn't invite us officially, but I convince Tim that we're solid enough to crash.

We park our Huffys a block away. We've learned by now that riding up on our bikes juggling six-packs on our handlebars reduces our cool factor by at least half. I can't afford to lose that much.

We hear the party before we see it. Loud, out of control, a future visit from the cops a guarantee. We turn up the street and see people spilling out of the house, filling up the porch, packing the sidewalk. We slide and squeeze our way to the front door. Two linemen blockade the door, shaved heads glinting in the moonlight. "We're full. We're not letting anyone else in."

"Seriously? But I'm friends with Kal."

Bouncer one pats a stomach the size of a barrel. "So am I. Like I said, the party's full."

"But we're medical students." Tim. Insistent, whiny, annoying.

"Medical students?" A female voice. Slurry. Sexy.

"Absolutely."

"Over here."

We follow the voice to the right of the porch. A girl, sorority type, way out of my league, Tim's, too, hangs out of a first-floor window. She waves. Her long wild hair swishes. "Come on. We'll let you in."

Another girl fills the window. They extend their arms. Tim and I clasp their hands like we're rock climbers and pull ourselves inside. We tumble onto the living room floor. A shriek, giggles, beers slapped into our hands. Cigarette smoke fills the room. The two girls who let us in laugh, sip fresh beer from glasses, grin. Dimples everywhere. Expensive white teeth. Hair for miles. *Smoldering.*

"Med students, huh?"

"Yeah," Tim says.

"Cool," Knockout One says.

"I always wanted to marry a doctor." Knockout Two, licking and slurping the foam off her beer.

"We're not doctors yet," I say, my glasses steamed up, blinding me. "Hahaha."

Tim elbows me a shot in the ribs. I double over. My beer sloshes.

"You guys get high?"

Knockout Two produces a pipe, starts packing it.

"Uh, nah, thanks," I say.

Tim hits me with a look that says, *I will kill you if you screw this up.*

"You don't indulge?" Knockout One. She pouts, allows a whole bunch of hair to fall over one eye. I follow her hair down and get a glimpse of her body. We're talking *Penthouse* hot. She shakes her head at Knockout Two, who makes Knockout One look like a troll. Tim *is* going to kill me. I expect him to torture me first.

"Your loss." Knockout Two.

Knockout One wraps her hair around three fingers. "We heard med students like to party, but I guess we found the only two who don't."

Knockout Two does a little hop, points off. "Look, Jerry and Dwayne got in! Jerr-eeee!" Giggling, waving the pipe, they bolt.

"And there they go," Tim says.

"I'm sorry, man."

Tim snaps his head back. "For what?"

"Wait. I thought when they brought out the pipe and I turned it down, you were pissed."

"Not at all. Forget it. We can do better."

"In this lifetime?"

"Maybe not. Hey, at least there's food."

We cruise the snack table, pile paper plates high with chips, dip, popcorn, cookies, doughnuts, and I think, *Tim is right. At least there's food. And Tim. And James. And Ricky.*

And at least I have them.

. . . .

BACK AT CHEZ James. Monday night a memory. We're looking at Tuesday morning, two A.M. It all starts again in nine hours with biochem. Tim's gone, and I remember I promised to wheel his Huffy home. A pang of depression gnaws me. Once again, I'm alone. My beer buzz gone, I feel wasted, a sexless blob. I melt into the warped hardwood floor that smells of cedar and spilled beer.

"Look at you."

Ricky. Hawaiian shirt, Bermuda shorts, barefoot.

"Hi, Ricky."

"Oh, Tony, baby. You're upset, aren't you? Sad. Horny. Frustrated. You didn't get any action tonight, did you?"

"Ah, no, nope. I did not."

"Well, here you go."

He drops onto my crotch.

"Get the hell off me!" I sit up and toss him off my lap. He roars and races out of the room. He howls all the way down the hallway.

Yes, I'm over my gay "thing." I love Ricky. He's one of my closest friends.

But no offense, Ricky, I need a woman.

I ALSO NEED lessons.

I tend to obsess. Tim, I'm happy to discover, obsesses as much as I do. By our calculation, we spend one out of every two minutes of our lives in the Nerd Room plotting, planning, and cramming for exams.

We spend every other minute obsessing over women.

I admit to Tim that I need help. I tell him how crushed I feel when a girl turns me down. My already fragile ego feels ready to crumble into powder. "Why can't I get a woman? What am I doing wrong?"

"It's all in the preparation. The pregame," Tim says. "You need to prepare with the same intensity and dedication as you do for an exam."

101

We sit in the student lounge eating a pizza we had delivered to the back door. We scarf the slices almost whole, fearing that Shelly and her squad of gunners might discover us here, mug us, steal our pizza, and leave us for dead.

"I don't know how to break the ice," I say. "I say something ridiculous. Then it goes downhill from there."

"I'm taking you under my wing," Tim says.

"I'm game."

"First, I want you to know that this is an outrage. You're good-looking, you're funny, you're smart, you're a great guy. No way you should be spending your nights alone, listening to the Chinese guy flush."

"I'm with you."

He rests a hand on my shoulder. "That's about to change."

"What do I have to do?"

"Three things. First, subscribe to *Cosmo*."

I pause, wait for him to laugh. "You're serious," I say.

"Dead serious. *Cosmo* gives you an edge. I read it cover to cover every month. Just finished a very informative article. 'Thirty Feisty Foreplay Tips.' Must reading."

"Thirty? I can only think of two. I guess my foreplay's a little rusty. So's my afterplay. My during-play could use a tune-up, too."

"You can start with my old issues. But I want them back. Now, number two. You ready? This one's gonna hurt."

"Hit me."

"Do not talk about your mother. Ever. I know you love her. I love my mother, too. But your mother must never come up in conversation in a bar. Especially when you are hitting on a woman."

"I get nervous. I can't help it."

"I don't care. I don't want to hear you telling some chick how much you love your mother's soup. Swear to me."

"Fine. I swear. What's number three?"

Tim scans my face. He frowns, considers. He apparently wants to be sure I'm ready for number three. He kicks aside the pizza box.

Wipes his hands on his shirt. "All right, Grasshopper. Number three. The secret to the whole deal." Tim reaches into his pocket and pulls out a cigarette lighter. He flicks it once. A thin blue flame shoots up.

"A cigarette lighter?"

I'm dubious.

"Surefire," Tim says.

"I don't smoke," I say.

"I don't, either. Who gives a shit? Get yourself a lighter. Carry it with you at all times. You see a cute girl about to light up, you whip out your lighter, cup her hands in yours, look into her eyes, and you're in. Two moves. Lighter out, flick, deep soul-searching look. Bam. Phone number."

I snicker. Reach for the last slice. "That is total bullshit. No way I'm buying a cigarette lighter."

I BUY A lighter.

Nothing fancy. A Bic flick. A dollar fifty-nine at CVS. I lock myself in my room and practice. I walk around the room, try it out in different pockets in various pants and shirts. Front pocket, back pocket, shirt pocket. I settle on pants, left side pocket. Then I practice lighting it until I can whip that thing out and flick the flame up fast as an assassin.

Monday night. Party night. Tim and I hit a bar. I've read two issues of *Cosmo*, and I'm so good with my lighter I can twirl it and flick it in one motion. I'm ready.

We survey the room. Cute coeds abound. Tim spots his prey, a husky softball-player type sitting alone. Tim winks, sidles up to her, carrying two beers. He hands one to her. She blushes, laughs, touches his arm. Home run.

Leaving me, as usual, alone. Playing with my lighter. Doubting Tim's training. I drain a beer, order another, down that one. Two beers. That's all it takes for me to fall down a hole and crash-land into the town we call Pityville. I stare into the dregs of my beer and wallow. Hell, Ricky does better with women than I do. And he's gay.

I need to get rid of these beers. I locate the line to the bathroom, which snakes ten people long down the side of the bar, around a corner, past the pay phone. What a night. I have to wait an hour to pee. And there's Tim and the lady shortstop across the room, laughing, touching, gathering up their things, getting ready to head back to his place to play long ball. Any second now he'll ask me to wheel his Huffy home. I have to face it. I'm hopeless.

"Is this the line for the *bathroom*?"

I tilt my head down slightly and see the face of an angel.

She's ethereal. Beaming a smile up at me that could melt metal. Short hair. One dimple. Olive skin. Eyebrows that wave hello. A hint of Asian about her. Maybe Polynesian. I don't care. I love Asians.

"Huh?" I say. So debonair.

Her smile fades. She leans her back into the pay phone. She looks away.

Tim's words dance through my head. *Do not talk about your mother. Do not bring up her succulent octopus soup.*

Focus, Tony.

Do not mention thirty feisty foreplay tips.

Or is it thirty feisty foreskin tips?

I'm losing it.

And then a miracle happens.

The angel pulls out a cigarette.

Time stops.

She holds the cigarette between a long lovely index finger and a long lovely middle finger. She lifts her knee and fishes around in her purse. "Damn," she says. Still rummaging in her purse, "Do you have a light?"

Do I ever.

I slip my hand into my jeans pocket and, with mercurial speed, whip out my lighter, twirl it, flick it, *whoosh*. An inviting pale blue flame shoots up, tickles the air.

Two angel hands cup mine. The angel dips her head and lights her cigarette. She tosses off a cloud of smoke from the crinkled-up corner of her kissable mouth. "I'm Carly," she says.

"Good name. Strong. Yet feminine. I'm Tony."

Three minutes later, she gives me her phone number.

Two hours later, I call her.

We talk until dawn.

I never mention my mother.

We go out the following Monday night.

We date for four months.

We get through twenty-three of the thirty feisty foreplay tips before she dumps me.

Home run!

FIRST YEAR. SECOND semester. Six weeks to go. If I squint, I can make out a dim flickering light at the end of the long dark tunnel.

Most days and every weekend we hole up in the Nerd Room. Tim and I continue to schedule breaks to discuss women and plan our dating strategy. But with under a month to go, two seismic changes occur that throw us off our game.

First, Tim meets Jane. Jane is different from all the other girls I've seen him date or take home for the night. She's pretty. She's smart. She seems not at all desperate. She shakes Tim up. He's no longer obsessed with women. He is now only obsessed with Jane.

"I'm going to marry her," he tells me.

"Have you told her this?"

"No. It's too soon. Things are still fluid. I'm not sure she even likes me all that much. Which makes me even more obsessed with her."

"She may be too good for you," I point out.

"I know. I thought of that. Just motivates me more. Makes me work harder."

"So no more driving nine hours to Saratoga for a quickie?"

"Those days are over, my friend. I have a long uphill battle ahead of me. But she's worth it. She's the one, dude."

"You going out with her Monday night?"

"Haven't asked her yet."

"You're playing it cool. Masterful."

"Actually, she hasn't given me her number yet."

I whistle low. "Think I'll hold off renting my tuxedo."

"Only a matter of time," Tim says.

SECOND SEISMIC CHANGE.

I fall in love with anatomy.

It happens over time but begins as a result of my competitive nature.

Months ago. The day after Dr. Gaw humiliates me in class, I decide to fight back. I refuse to give her control of my life and of my medical-school education. My plan involves mental judo. I vow to make her not only change her opinion of me but to fall in love with me. This becomes *my* obsession.

I begin by asking myself a key question. Who *is* Dr. Gaw? Not sure I want to go there. I do know this. Dr. Gaw seems to despise the living. She's clearly gaga over her cadavers, enthralled with her bins of body parts, orgasmic over her prosected organs. Therefore, I will pretend to love what she loves.

Day two, I motor from the back of the lab, where Tim, equipped with smelling salts, hides, and push my way to the front, where I rub shoulders with the gunners and ass kissers. I take notes like a court reporter, laugh along with the ass kissers at Dr. Gaw's lame attempts at humor, and listen raptly as she gushes over her livers, spleens, and kidneys. I can play fascinated with the best of them. I share meaningful glances with the gunners. I ooh and ahh with the ass kissers. I smile with respect at Dr. Gaw. It's all fake, a front. I don't give a shit. I just want an A in this freaking class.

Then one day I do give a shit. It starts again with hands. For the second time, I walk by the open bin of hands, and I'm drawn in. Again, I see the humanity in those hands. I *feel* their humanity. My perspective shifts. I alter my entire view of this class and medical school in general. I don't care about Dr. Gaw, or the gunners, or getting an A. I think about all the body parts in the lab, and I imagine them belonging to people I know or people I've seen. Then I wonder who these people really were. I wonder how they lived their lives, where they worked, what they did for fun, what made them afraid. I wonder who they loved, and I wonder who grieved over them.

I drift over to the bodies that we will study, some under tarps, some lying naked, their innards exposed, and certain details that I'd never noticed jump out—tattoos, dental fillings, scars—and I feel light-headed. I am in awe of these people. Most of all, instead of feeling de-tached from them, as I assume most doctors do, I feel attached to them. Committed to them.

I can't say that I feel this way constantly, every second of anatomy class, every moment of medical school. I will often lose this feeling of reverence toward these bodies, especially when I'm grinding through my notes, preparing for an exam. But I'm able to bring myself back, to locate the humanity easily.

Especially when I look into the bin of hands.

FIRST YEAR. THE last week.

I don't want to scream it yet, but—

I HAVE SURVIVED MY FIRST YEAR OF MEDICAL SCHOOL!

I should make that into a bumper sticker and slap it on my Huffy.

Second year promises to be better. James and Ricky have invited Tim and me to share a house with them. According to Ricky, they've found a *fabulous* two-story colonial on Flower Street. So much potential. He's already painting and decorating. "It's going to be a showcase," he says.

"It has to be a step up from Owen Hall," Tim says.

"Hopefully," I say.

"You two wound me," Ricky says.

"I apologize," I say. "Work your magic. You're a male Martha Stewart."

"If only."

. . . .

First year ends with a jolt.

Bianca.

Two days left. I pop into the admissions office to drop off a form. I hand the form to a secretary and head out the back door. I screech to a stop.

Leaning over a desk, arms slicing the air, speaking with deep-throated passion in a Spanish accent, her legs lined with runner's calves bent and brushing the desk, her back arched, her ass tight in a short skirt swaying, stands the hottest woman I've seen this side of Gloria. A woman in a pin-striped suit sits at the desk, nodding like a mourner, as "Gloria" raises one hand to the sky. I blink twice to clear my head.

I shuffle forward to hear her voice. I see now that the vision is taller than Gloria, her cheekbones higher and cut like glass, her complexion off-white, her eyes aqua pools. What ruins me is her laugh. She roars, uninhibited, husky, gleefully, carrying away both the woman in the pin-striped suit and me.

Instinctively, I whip out my lighter.

"Sir, there's no smoking in here."

Pinstripe. She speaks like a principal over a loudspeaker.

"Sorry."

The vision laughs. What teeth. They *gleam*. Dr. Schwarzman would hand her a trophy. I snap the lighter shut, return it with a flourish to the side pocket of my jeans. "Would you have a drink with me tonight?"

I can't believe I say this.

She laughs. "Yes," she says.

"Awesome!"

Pinstripe shakes her head. Can't tell if she's happy for me or thinks the vision is out of her mind.

"Well, sorry to intrude." I start to leave. I'm about to hit the glass doors.

"Where?" Her voice so husky I can feel her breath from ten feet away.

"Ha." What an idiot. Then cool takes over. "USA Café."

"I'll find it. Nine o'clock?"

"Great," I say. "By the way, I'm Tony."

"Bianca," she says.

THAT NIGHT WITH Bianca, I'm in a zone. Every line clicks. Every joke kills. Every move devastates. And when I lead Bianca in the shopping-cart dance? Forget about it.

At our table, eyes trained on each other, hearts thumping from drink, the heat of the bar, and the closeness of our bodies, I say, "Tell me everything about you."

We sip our drinks, beer for me, sangria for her.

"I'm pretty boring," she says, which is such a lie. "I was born in Mexico, raised in San Antonio. I always wanted to be a doctor. I applied to about twenty medical schools to cover my bases. I had my interview today. I'm dying to get in here."

"Is this your first choice?"

"Yes. But it's so *hard*. Very competitive."

"You'll get in. I'm sure you will. It'll be so great. The two of us. We'll hang out all the time."

"I know, right?"

"When will you find out?"

A shrug. A slug of sangria. Bianca slurps down to the orange slice at the bottom. She runs the back of her hand across her mouth like a slap. Leaves a heart-shaped red lipstick blotch.

"They mail me the result in six weeks. I have to go back to Texas. Unless I can move in with you."

"Not a problem. My parents will love you. You can pass for Korean, right?"

"*Sí.*" Then she levels me. "I'm leaving tomorrow."

"What?"

"I know."

"That *sucks*." I must scream those words, because the bar goes quiet. "Now what?" I say after a while.

Bianca presses her hand to my cheek. "I had so much fun tonight, Tony."

"That's it? We may never see each other again."

"But if I get in *here*—"

Now I shrug.

"Well, it's late," Bianca says. "I have to pack—"

She stands, mouths "goodbye" to James, Ricky, and Tim, who grunt as a group, watching me carefully, concerned that I'm about to stroke out. I stand, nearly knock over my chair. "I'll walk you home," I say.

"It's okay. I want to be alone."

She kisses my cheeks European-style, one side and then the other, then lightly brushes my mouth with the tip of her finger. I watch her disappear out the front doors of the diner.

"I've never seen you operate like that, man." James noogies my arm. "You reminded me of me."

I crash onto my chair. "I'm never gonna see her again." I barely croak out the words.

Three pairs of hands clamp down, massaging my back, mussing my hair, kneading my shoulders. Ricky kisses my cheek.

"Hey." Tim lifts his hand off my shoulder and pushes over a plate of crispy, overcooked french fries drowning in ketchup. The way I like them. "At least we have food," he says.

These guys.

Where would I be without these guys?

III Second Year

8
—

Flower Street

Summer.

Two whole months off.

As I pull away from campus and head home, I review my first-year highlights.

I aced the hideous Dr. Gaw's *gross*-anatomy class and pulled honors in pathology and neuroscience, which pissed off Shelly and her gaggle of gunners. I made three great friends. Dated one cute girl for four months. Spent an immaculate two hours with the hottest girl on earth. I'll never see her again, but oh well.

Mainly, I lived through first year. And now I outline my plans for the summer. Starting with—

Sleep.

That's it. I just want to sleep.

I may also mess around on the guitar, read trashy novels, run, lift weights, and attempt to reach the highest level on the latest video game.

But mostly, sleep.

My parents greet me in the driveway. My mother clings to me as if I've just returned from a war. My father claps me on the back. He wrinkles his face into what I'm pretty sure is a smile.

"I did it, Dad. Made it through first year."

"Ah, first year, nothing. Second year *worse*."

"You're kidding."

"Second year kill you."

"Great. Thanks. Thank you."

"You want lunch? Mommy make soup."

The summer zips by. I do lose weight, muscle up, learn a bunch of new chords, reach the highest level, read some good junk, and sleep. I call James and Ricky several times, speak to Tim almost every day. We apply for and become accepted as orientation leaders. Now we're golden. We get the first shot at the hot new first-years. The moment we get our orientation schedule and group assignments, I bury Bianca. I don't even think about her. I'm moving on. I live by a new creed. *Next.*

Second year. First semester.

The first person I see on campus is Bianca.

She comes out of the bookstore hugging a canvas book bag stuffed with textbooks. I'm twenty feet away, driving the Ford Tempo, on my way to meet Tim at our new house. I do a double take. I hit the brakes and nearly take out a trash bin.

"Bianca!"

She turns at the sound of her name. Her face lights up when she sees me. I think. I'm pretty sure. I've flipped the dashboard visor down to shield my eyes from a brutal August sun. I leave the Tempo running and bolt out of the car. Horns scream behind me.

"Tony!"

I throw my arms around her and receive her cheek and a handful of canvas book bag. "How are you?" I ask.

"Great. I'm great."

"You got in."

"Amazing, huh?"

"I'm so happy for you. And for *me*."

"I know, right?"

An asshole leans on his horn. Another asshole calls me an asshole.

"I'm sort of holding up traffic."

"I see that. Uh-oh. Not good. A guy's getting out of his car. You might want to—"

"I'm going. Hey. Good to see you."

"Good to see *you*."

We lean in to each other, peck each other's cheeks European-style. I run back to my car, duck inside. I poke my head out the window. "Do you want to hang out? Get dinner or something?"

"Definitely. Absolutely. Call me."

I pull away to pissed-off bleating horns and a crapload of cursing.

In the middle of a lush tree-lined street, Tim and I stand on the sidewalk facing our new house.

The place looks as if it has leaped off the cover of *Better Homes* magazine. Two-story colonial. Manicured hedge lining both sides of the walk. A front porch with white railings and a swing. The smell of lilacs, rows of which rim a front yard as manicured as a fairway. A basketball hoop attached to a garage at the end of a driveway wide enough for two-on-two.

A screen door snaps open, and James, cut-off tee, hands on hips, steps onto the porch. "Hello, girls. Welcome home."

"Oh, *yeah*," Tim says.

"Wow," I say.

"Sick, huh? We totally lucked out. Let me give you the tour." He swings the door open, smirking like a real estate agent. We follow him in, so excited we're practically slobbering.

The inside tops the outside.

Living room with overstuffed couch, cushy chairs, TV, fireplace. Family room, another couch, bar, wine rack. Cozy kitchen fully loaded with glimmering new appliances. Half-bath in the hall for guests. Freshly polished hardwood floors throughout.

"You like?"

Tim and I nod and squeal like monkeys.

"And now our wing."

We follow him upstairs to two master bedrooms, each with an attached full bathroom. We identify James's room by the basketball rolled into a corner below a blown-up yearbook photo of Daisy. We identify Ricky's room by the bathroom with the tub lined in scented candles and a collection of duckies.

"Wow," I say. "So, where's our rooms?"

"This way."

Like a running back, James sprints down the staircase, taking two steps at a time. I jump a flight down to the landing to keep up.

"Small thing. Since I found the house and Ricky decorated, we thought we should get dibs on rooms."

"That's fair," Tim says.

"Totally," I say.

We skid across the family room floor, a tight twosome at James's back. He pulls up at a door beyond the kitchen that I hadn't noticed before. He taps the door with his knuckles. "Got your own private entrance."

He flings the door open and yanks on a string dangling from a socket holding a naked yellow lightbulb. He descends. I see only his back.

"Careful. Couple of these stairs are a little uneven."

I ease down a flight of rickety wooden stairs that buckle and squeak under every step.

"Oh, and watch your—"

Thunk.

My forehead slams into a low ceiling. Pain streaks across my head. My neck tingles. "Shit!"

"—head."

I steady myself, dip my head, and squat my way down the rest of the stairs. I hear a crunch. Wood splinters.

"That was my *foot*," Tim says. "Ripping through a stair."

"I'll get that replaced, no worries," James says. "But it's the bottom stair. You don't really need it."

I arrive at the shattered last step and hop over it. I land on a concrete floor. I smell mold. And I hope I'm imagining things, but I hear animals scurrying. James pulls on another string. A long fluorescent tube buzzes and more pale yellow light flickers over my throbbing head. Barely. I'm six-one. The light is six-two.

"This is the cellar," Tim says.

"Basement, yeah," James says.

"It's about fifty degrees hotter down here," I say. "It's like Guam."

"What are those?" Tim. He speaks in a deeply disturbed and hoarse monotone.

Two rooms, each the size of a hall closet, loom before us, separated by a flimsy wall that shimmers and sways. The wall can't be moving. Can it? It's a *wall*. The conk on my head must be causing me to imagine things.

"Don't tell me," Tim mutters.

"I'll take a shot," I say, massaging the golf ball–sized welt that's forming on my forehead. "Those two phone booths are our bedrooms."

"You have so much more privacy down here," James says. "Think about that. With all the partying going on upstairs, we won't be able to study. No way."

I'm pissed and my head hurts. "Do we have a bathroom? Or do we have to drive to the gas station by the exit ramp?"

"That's funny, Tony. You have a bathroom. A shower, too. Right through there." He waves at a doorway that opens to a laundry room.

I see only a dented and dusty washer and dryer. "Where?"

"Right there. In the back."

I storm into the laundry room and walk right into a cobweb that covers me like a net. I open my mouth to scream and swallow a mouthful of stringy, sticky goo. "Blah!" I claw at my face, punch at the web that's folded over my lips and nose.

"Nobody's been down here in a while," James says.

"What the *hell*." I spit out another mouthful of web, then bang farther into the laundry room. In the corner stands a portable shower. The kind of plastic shower you usually find at a trailer park—outside.

"This is our shower?"

"Uh-huh," James says. "Look at the time. I need to call Daisy—"

"Don't *move*." The evenness of my voice freezes him. Fastening my eyes on his, I reach behind me into the shower and turn on the water.

Something crawls onto my hand. Something with a lot of legs. Something that stings.

"Yaaaaa!" I jerk my neck back and bang my head on the shower door. "You have to be kidding me!" A matching lump rises, this one on the back of my head.

I close my eyes and thrust my hand back inside the shower and turn the knob to max. The shower groans, shakes, then screeches. Ice water shaped like a tear trickles out of the gooseneck shower spout and splats onto the back of my hand. The water drips for another three seconds and dies.

"Not to worry. I'll call the landlord and have him adjust that pressure," James says.

"I think *you* need a shower, James," I say.

"Yeah," Tim says. "He smells like shit."

"Guys, come on. We're friends."

I lower my head and walk toward him with menace. Tim falls in step next to me. He slams a fist into his palm. "We're about to go all *Dawn of the Dead* on your ass, Jimmy boy."

James starts backing up toward the basement steps. "How's this? We'll knock ten bucks a month off your rent. We square?"

Tim and I keep coming. James turns and flies up the stairs. I charge after him. He's a dead man.

Except I hit my head on the ceiling again. "OW! SHIT!"

I fall back into Tim. He yelps as his midsection sags, and the two of us tumble over each other and somersault down the stairs. We land in a tangled heap, sprawled on the cold concrete floor. Above us, the cellar door opens and slams, and James's footsteps clatter on the hardwood floor. The front door opens, and we follow the sound of James hitting the porch and running out of the house.

Alone in the basement, breathing furiously, Tim and I lie in silence, unable to move. My nostrils sting from what I'm sure is the stench of deadly advancing black mold.

"Well, you have to admit," Tim says after a while, "it is much nicer than Owen Hall."

IN ADDITION TO becoming an orientation leader, I sign up to be a second-year "older sib," a mentor to an incoming first-year student. For the next year I will serve as a kind of big brother and guide. I'm looking forward to showing some unsuspecting rookie the ropes, starting with this subtle piece of advice: *avoid Dr. Gaw.* While two beefy guys with names stitched over their pockets lay cheap outdoor carpeting—no pad—over our concrete floor, nail another plywood sheet to reinforce the wall between our bedrooms, and throw together a couple of makeshift closets out of a kit, I call Amy, my sib, and arrange to meet her for coffee.

As I wait for Amy to arrive, I think about Bianca. I haven't called her yet. Something about her attitude the day I saw her coming out of the bookstore.

"What's the matter with you?" Tim said over beers at the USA Café the night before. "You'll never get a chance with anyone hotter. Call her. Can't score if you don't shoot."

"I know. I just . . . I don't know."

"You're scared. Understandable. Bianca's the type who goes more for guys like James and me."

I waited for his laugh. There was none. He's serious.

"I just got my confidence back," I said. "I don't want it crushed again. That would set me back years. I don't have years."

"I hear you. That's why we have the two-date rule."

"I'm drawing a blank. That's a new one."

"That's because until recently, you never had two dates. The rule is simple. If you don't get any action by the end of the second date, do not go for a third date. Hear me? You go oh-for-two, the party's over. Drop her. It's not happening."

"I don't know if that's my style. I move a little slower than you."

"Not a question of style. This is a hard and fast rule. Two dates, no action, say goodbye. Trust me. Have I ever steered you wrong?"

"Constantly."

Waiting for Amy now, I doodle on a napkin. "Two-date rule," I say aloud. "Worth a try."

"What's the two-date rule?"

I look up. I gulp. The napkin flutters to the floor. Amy, dark hair, killer smile, hypnotic eyes, *stunning*, takes the chair across from me. Not sure what I expected. I did not expect her to look like this. I don't speak for a solid ten seconds. Inside my head, a voice chatters nonstop like a machine gun: *Hummina hummina hummina.*

"Tony, right?" Amy says finally to break the ice.

"Yes. Hi. Sit down."

"I am sitting. I'm Amy."

"Yes, I know. I mean, I figured. Do you want some coffee?"

"Don't drink coffee. Thank you."

And the meeting starts.

Because that's what it feels like. A business meeting. Amy folds her hands in front of her like a job applicant or a boss and launches into a series of tough, smart, well-prepared questions. I answer as best as I can, go early to my saver—*avoid Dr. Gaw.*

"I've heard that. Interesting, because she's won so many teaching awards. Apparently, she's intimidating. Word is, if she likes you, you'll do well."

"She didn't like me. I know. Hard to believe." I laugh.

She doesn't.

I think her lip starts to curl up in the first leg of a smile, but if so, she slams it right back into place, as if she's shutting a window.

"Anyway, I wore her down. I ended up doing okay. I'm sure you'll do great."

Amy fidgets, moves on to her next set of questions.

The meeting lasts for twenty minutes, and then she abruptly stands, shoves her hand in the direction of my chest, we shake, and she promises to contact me if she has any more questions.

"Actually, that's my job. I'll be checking in with you."

"Oh. Fine. Either way."

A bored eyebrow raise.

Good start to second year.

I'm living in a cellar and my sib hates me.

We're off and running.

ORIENTATION WEEK. I see Amy in the hall. I nod, I wave, she looks the other way. She can't be ignoring me. She probably doesn't see me. The next day we nearly collide as she walks out of the main lecture hall. I say hi. Loudly. Enthusiastically. She walks right by me as if I'm invisible.

What the *hell*?

For a moment I thought there might be potential with Amy. I found out through a friend that her last boyfriend was Korean! What are the chances? I've met only one other woman in my life who's into Korean guys, and she's married to my father.

Have I pissed her off? Offended her? What can it be? I go right to the most logical possibility. Body odor. Our shower does suck. You have to run around in there to get wet. But I still shower every day and pride myself on my hygiene and grooming. I dismiss the BO notion. What, then? I can't figure it out. I ask the expert. The Love Guru.

"What is her problem?"

Tim and I sit at lunch in the school cafeteria, picking at plates piled high with something brown.

"Classic case," he says. "Seen it a million times."

"Yeah? What is it?"

"ILS."

"What the hell is that?"

"Ivy League Syndrome. I went to an Ivy League school, so I know all about it. Very common. She's Ivy League and you're not. Translation? She thinks she's hot shit. She's used to having all these Ivy League suckups falling all over her. She's not interested in you. You're below her station."

"I thought maybe she was just shy."

"No, my naive friend. ILS. Easy call."

"You really think she would be more interested in *you* just because you went to an Ivy League school?"

"Definitely. But we're not gonna find out. I'm obsessed with Jane."

"How's that going?"

"Terrific. I'm this close to getting her number."

Should I really be listening to him?

9

No, But I Play One on TV

Three minutes.

Every second is do-or-die.

I squeeze into my starched white coat. The coat fits snug around the chest. Too snug. Feels like a straitjacket. The sleeves barely reach my wrists. I shrug to loosen up the shoulders.

Ready, Dr. Youn?

I manage a brief head tilt meant to be a nod.

I didn't hear you.

"Yes. I'm ready."

A bell rings. I scramble to the door, hold up my fist to knock, withdraw, remind myself, *You're the doctor,* and enter the office.

A young man in a hospital gown, thirties, fidgety, sits on an examination table (actually, a snack table with a sheet over it), dangling his legs over the side. He wears his hair—shoe-polish brown, wavy, and possibly dyed—long and in an Elvis Presley flip. A clip-on microphone lies next to him on the table.

Two minutes, forty-five seconds.

I pick up the microphone, fumble it, drop it, bend down, kick it, retrieve it, lose it, cup it, stand, dodge the patient's swinging feet, clip the microphone onto my coat, step forward, watch the microphone sail off and land on the examination table.

"Crap."

I hear distant laughter.

I snap the frigging microphone in place, lock it in to make sure it's not going anywhere, scowl at the patient. Not a good start. I adjust. I throw on a toothy, insincere smile. I'm grinning like Jack Nicholson in *The Shining*.

"I'm Dr. Youn."

"Monty."

Two minutes, thirty seconds.

"So, Monty, what would you like to talk about today?"

Good. Points there. Always ask open-ended questions. It's a better way to gather information. Patients will talk more if you are less specific. That's the key here—get the patient talking.

I prod him again gently. "So why are you here today?"

"I dunno."

Not good. May have lost a point there. Let me try this again. "How are you doing today?"

"Fine."

"Fine?"

"Yuh."

"There's nothing wrong with you?"

"Nope. I mean, other than, you know, a little bloody diarrhea."

Two minutes, fifteen seconds.

"What do you mean by a little? How often?"

"Four, five times an hour."

"And how long have you had these tarry bowel movements?"

"The what now?"

"Diarrhea. The bloody diarrhea."

"Oh."

"How long have you had bloody diarrhea?"

"I dunno."

This guy's killing me. He must see the sweat stains that have begun to form under my arms. Hard to miss. They look like the Great Lakes.

"Approximately how long? Take a guess. Doesn't have to be exact. This isn't a test or anything."

Big laugh. Monty looks like he's about to crack. He pulls himself together. "A guess-ti-mate," he says.

"Exactly."

Two minutes.

"I'm gonna guess-ti-mate . . . couple of years."

"Couple of *years*?"

"Yuh. Give or take."

"That's a long time."

"Expensive, too. I'm always running out of underwear. Have to buy new u-trow every other day. I get the twelve-pack at Kmart. Sets me back six bucks a pack."

"Wow. Fifty cents a pair. Quality stuff."

"Oh, yuh. The bloody shitting is not the only thing, either." He sniffles. Swipes a tear. Pauses long enough to park a truck.

One minute, forty-five seconds.

I shift my weight. I'm nervous as hell about the time. "What did you want to tell me?" I say. "What else is going on?"

"Well, Dr. Youn, see, it's like this. I was molested as a child."

This is his story? Bloody diarrhea and child molestation? It's a trick. I'm a doctor, not a social worker. He's trying to distract me. I have to get him back on track. Determine the condition. That's my job. That's the test.

One minute, thirty seconds.

"My stepfather. He was brutal. A animal. He come home drunk. First he beat up my mom. Then—"

"I'm sorry, Monty. Very sorry. We'll talk about your childhood in a minute. I want to get back to the bloody diarrhea."

"So gross."

"I'm sure. If you're buying a pack of underwear every other day—"

"I'm talking about my stepfather."

One minute.

Will I be marked down if I go for the guy's throat? Does throttling the patient count against you?

I want to run out of here. I want to rip off my white coat and bolt. Run the hell *away*. This is a nightmare. The hell with my grade. Screw it. I don't care anymore.

Okay, I'm lying. I care. I am not a gunner. But I care. How do I get through this?

Forty-five seconds.

I can't speak. I've gone mute. I can only stare. I stare at Monty with ferocity. Maybe I can divine the answer to his bloody-diarrhea symptom psychically. Stare into his mind and pull it out. Mind to mind. I stare harder. I must have wriggled my way inside his head because Monty blinks, looks away, pecks at some invisible lint on the exam table. I've gotten to him.

What's your condition, Monty? What do you have? Tell me. Just tell me.

Thirty seconds.

Deep breaths. Relax. Why does this course scare the hell out of me? Is it because I know I'm being filmed and that I will be dissected in front of the whole class later like a frog? Is it because I know Monty is an actor and is deliberately trying to throw me off? Is it because I know if I don't determine his disease within three minutes, I will be marked down?

Yes. To all of it.

You can do this, Tony. This isn't the hard part. This isn't brain surgery. This is a game. You're good at games. You're just taking a bloody medical history. Any moron can do this. Get a grip—

Wait a minute.

Bloody medical history.

"How's your mom?"

My voice is trembling.

"Huh?"

"Your mom. Your mother. How is she?"

Fifteen seconds.

Beep.

The warning shot.

If I don't get the answer right now—

"My mom?"

"Yes! Your mom. How is your *mom*?"

"Not that great."

"What'sthematterwithher?"

"She got the cancer."

"Rectal cancer. She has rectal cancer. Doesn't she?"

Ten seconds.

"I think that's the one."

"Have you had your prostate checked?"

"Yuh. Checks out. I'm clean."

"THEN YOU HAVE RECTAL CANCER!"

"I think I do."

"GREAT! THAT'S SO GREAT! NOW LET'S GO TALK TO THE DOCTOR! YESSSS!!!"

I point a finger to the sky, raise both hands above my head, lift the roof, pound my chest, slap five with Monty.

I win! I've done it! I've diagnosed his disease!

With two seconds to spare.

And no points deducted from my grade.

Eat my dust, gunners.

CLINICAL SKILLS. FIRST we talk to actors while being videotaped. Then we examine actors. Yes. We *examine* actors. We give them rectal exams, pelvic exams, groin checks. We use gloves and speculums. The exams weird me out, push me way beyond uncomfortable. Up until now I've seen three people naked in my entire life. And only one of those I wanted to see naked. Now I have strangers dropping trou in front of me on an hourly basis. One dude, guy in a Hells Angels T-shirt, Mohawk haircut, wearing no underwear, drops his pants, and his penis immediately—like instantly—rises and becomes erect. I look around the room to determine the object of his affection and, for the life of me, don't see what might cause such an extreme . . . reaction.

"Look out," Mohawk says. "Mr. Happy got a life of its own."

He snickers like a porn star as the entire class looks away. Two or three girls duck.

It's stunning what people will do for twenty dollars. No skill required, a major selling point. Just drop your pants and allow a bunch of medical students to stick their fingers up your ass and poke around with a speculum.

How was work today, hon?

Hard.

I ASK BIANCA out. I decide to go for it. Why not? We totally connected that one night at the USA Café. Not to mention she's drop-dead gorgeous. I hear she's not dating anyone, and since I have no prospects—I admit that I'm attracted to Amy, but she's got that nasty case of ILS, so no sense wasting my time—I call Bianca late one night from the Nerd Room. I suggest dinner and a movie. She's in.

I *prep* for this date. I swipe away a spiderweb the size of a tablecloth blocking the laundry room, put my head down, and take an extra-long ice shower, keeping my screaming down to the bare minimum. I floss, gargle, sculpt my hair. I douse my body with a quart of irresistible aftershave I steal from James and head out for my date with Bianca, dressed to kill in pressed khakis and starched white shirt purchased for the occasion at Macy's. I pick her up in the Ford Tempo, freshly run through a carwash, the inside cleared of all old *Cosmos*, empty paper cups, and balled-up fast-food wrappers, spotless enough to preen as a contender in a used-car lot. We drive to a restaurant I've meticulously researched, a place that takes reservations as opposed to giving out numbers.

Bianca seems a little distant at dinner. Tense. I'm not surprised. We're having our first real date. You have to expect an awkward moment here and there. Things improve by the main course. We've loosened up, the conversation flows easier. By coffee, we're laughing freely, even touching a little here and there. I'm starting to feel the old sparks fly.

"So, what movie do you want to see?" I've paid the check. I've almost recovered from the small heart attack that gripped my chest like a vise when the bill came. I had no idea that a plate of spaghetti and a dinner salad could set you back over twenty bucks. All told, with tip, the meal costs fifty dollars.

Bianca fiddles with her spoon. "Actually, I have to call it a night."

"Really? No movie?"

"I need to go home and call my mom. I call her every Friday night. If I don't, she worries."

"I didn't know you and your mom were so close."

"Oh, *very* close. So, yeah, another time, okay?"

"Sure. No worries."

"You're so sweet." She squeezes my hand.

I squeeze back. She pulls her hands away as if they've landed on a hot stove.

I drive her home. I park in front of her apartment. She smiles, tells me what a wonderful evening she's had, and gives my hand another affectionate squeeze. I lean over to kiss her. I come up with air. She's already gone, dashing up her sidewalk.

"That's one," Tim says.

An hour later, we're spread out on our mattresses in our Gitmo-like quarters, dissecting the date.

"I know," I say. "The two-date rule."

"She ices you again, game over."

"You know, it is possible that she's my dream girl and I'm her dream guy. She just can't handle it."

"It's too much for her," Tim says, considering.

"Overwhelming. At such a young age."

"Could be. Doubtful." He fluffs his pillow, casually reaches for the phone. "Would you mind taking a walk?"

"Jane," I say. "You got her number."

"The poor girl." A wicked smile. "It's all over now."

IF TIM CAN wear down Jane, I can get through to Bianca. All I need to survive the two-date rule is some minor action. A lingering good-night kiss. I'll even dispense with lingering. As long as we lock lips for at least the count of three. Then we can trash the stupid rule.

For date two, we reprise date one—dinner and a movie. No sense in reinventing the wheel. Bianca chooses the same restaurant; the meal again tastes delicious and again ravages my wallet. The conversation flows even easier this time. We're sillier, flirting more, laughing louder. I'm feeling good, even though I'm out over a hundred bucks total, and all I have to show for it is a series of hand squeezes you could get out of your cousin. No worries. I'll make my move later. I've been planning it according to a recent magazine article I read in *Cosmo*—"Making Your Move in the Movies."

Alone, the two of us, only the receipt and one wilting rose between us, Bianca reaches across the table and grabs both my hands. She squeezes lovingly and looks into my eyes. "I have to pass on the movie."

"You do? Why?"

"I have to call my mom."

"But it's Saturday night. I thought you called her Friday nights."

"I do. I forgot to call her last night. I have to get home."

"You can't call her later or tomorrow morning?"

"Oh, no. She'll worry. She'll probably call the police to see what happened to me. I'm sorry. I'm having such a lovely evening."

Lovely evening. Code for *dinner with a schmuck.*

"Me, too," I say, frustration cutting through me like a saw. Then she tilts her head and hits me with a bedroom smile. Slight flutter of her lashes. Lips parting. Crimson fingernail notched suggestively into her teeth. I'm dying here. How can you not be crazy for someone who's this hot and this close to her mother? I'm tempted to ask Tim for a reprieve, to establish a three-date rule just this once.

"If you want to go to the movie yourself, I'll take the campus bus home," she says.

Yeah. Like I'm going to put her on a bus. "No, no, I'll take you home. You should call your mom. I don't want her to worry. And I don't care about the movie. Next time—"

I catch myself.

There will be no next time.

Not according to Tim's rule. And not according to the silence that fills the car. I drive Bianca home and this time receive not even a squeeze good night. It's over. Two and out.

10

Second-Year Crush

Second year *worse*.

Way worse.

I'm ambushed by the sheer volume of information we have to memorize. At least I know what's on each exam—everything.

Second year, we move from traditional lecture classes in which professors spoon-feed us material that we regurgitate at exam time (I regurgitate with the best of them) to problem-based learning, or as we nimbly refer to this style, PBL. We split into groups of ten and, guided by professors who aren't doctors and seem to have no clue about teaching us medicine, we realize we have to learn this stuff ourselves.

Every couple of weeks, PBL courses focus on a different body system, called problem domains, which include: infectious disease and immunology (bugs); disorders of development and behavior (birth defects and crazy people); major mental disorders (even crazier people); hematology/neoplasia (cancer); urinary tract; pulmonary; cardiovascular; neurology/musculoskeletal; digestive; and metabolic/endocrine/reproductive (sex—yeah, I wish). At the start of each domain, we receive a list of required reading and an outline of learning objectives. These couldn't be more vague or diabolical. A favorite that Tim and I quote for weeks in a game-show announcer's voice: "Know the physiology of digestion."

The nebulousness of the PBL domains shakes us up. Gunners start to crack. Ass kissers don't know which asses to kiss. Some students lighten the intensity of second year by extending classes into a third year. Not a bad idea if you have the money or don't mind owing $150,000 after medical school instead of the more common knee-buckling amount, a mere $100,000. I don't have the stomach for that kind of debt.

Six weeks into second year, I have my schedule down. A typical day:

6:30 A.M. Wake up. Consider showering. Stare at laundry room and tiny portable shower. Envision myself running naked through massive cobwebs, swarms of venomous, undocumented insects, gritting my teeth as I furiously soap up and shampoo while intermittent darts of ice stab my skin. Screw showering.

7:30 A.M. Attend PBL small group. Eat breakfast on the way—coffee and Mars bar.

10:30 A.M. Study in Nerd Room.

12:00 P.M. Lunch, throw down three PB&J sandwiches made at home, complain.

12:15 P.M. Study in Nerd Room.

4:00 P.M. Work out (I'm lifting weights and getting *ripped*, abs of steel).

4:05 P.M. End workout. Kidding. Not really.

5:00 P.M. Dinner. More complaining. Some seething.

5:30 P.M. Study at home. Unless there's an exam. Then study in Nerd Room.

12:00 A.M. Wind down. Take two ibuprofens. Drink a beer. Stare at TV. Feel guilty for (A) not returning phone calls from parents and (B) not studying enough.

12:15 A.M. Sleep. Well, try to sleep. Usually stare at ceiling and fight off more venomous, undocumented insects and giant spider.

3:00 A.M. Cry.

. . . .

THE WEEKS BLUR. Among my housemates—Tim, Ricky, and James—I struggle the most with adjusting to the PBL style. These guys seem to be able to isolate what's crucial in each domain. Unlike me, they sift out the unimportant stuff.

I'm not used to crystallizing and compartmentalizing. I much prefer the shotgun approach: blast away at everything. I just don't have enough time. This causes me to freak out before every test. Even though I study more than any of my housemates, I sleep the least. I *try* to sleep. I drink tea, listen to soothing music, attempt yoga, meditation tapes, sleeping pills. I even try a phone session with a shrink. Nothing helps. My stress level increases. I sit down at each test, stare at the bubble sheet, and watch the multiple-choice questions swim across the page. Words float. Letters scramble. I feel as if I'm looking at an eye chart. I lurch through each test, barely scoring enough points to pass. Even Tim outpoints me. After one especially frustrating exam, I stagger home and look at myself in the mirror. I'm pale, wild-eyed, hair sailing off in ten different directions as if I've shoved my fingers into a light socket. I've turned flabby, having abandoned weight training. Replaced it with a regimen of candy bars. I wear a pathetic, blotchy Fu Manchu mustache to cover a field of newly sprouted acne. My shabby clothes fall off my body. I'm wiry as a coat hanger.

Ricky walks by, stops, stares. "I'd say you look like a homeless person, but that would be an insult to homeless people."

Second year. Taking its toll.

"The problem is all you do is study and worry." Tim, lying in bed, fiddling with the phone cord. He's just hung up from a revoltingly gushy phone conversation with Jane. The phone is still steaming.

"What else is there?"

"A social life, dude. You need to find yourself a wo-man. Take your mind off things."

I have to admit that since things with Jane have amped up, Tim has seemed more relaxed. He certainly doesn't stress over PBL tests the way I do. Well, nobody does.

"And where would I find such a wo-man?"

"Let me think about it. What about— Oh, wait a minute, I forgot to tell Jane something."

But even as Tim redials her number, I know.

ONE DAY THE ice thaws. *Crack.* Just like that. With the shock of a ninety-degree day in January.

A week ago. A chance encounter in the hall outside the gross-anatomy lab.

I see the ghoulish shadow of Dr. Gaw as she places a liver on every desk—I'm amazed she even *has* a shadow—and hurry by only to find myself face-to-face with *her* as she heads into the classroom.

"Hi, Tony."

Bright, warm, ice-melting smile.

"Amy. Hi."

"I've been meaning to call you. I have a couple of questions."

"Oh?"

She's the last person on earth I expect to call me.

"Or, you know what, if you want to meet later—"

I'm facing hours of studying for my upcoming urinary-tract exam, but what the hell. I need a wo-man, right? But *Amy*? I thought she hated me.

"How's five o'clock?" She's positively *glowing*. "After the ghoul sets us free."

"It's a date."

Is it?

It is. Sort of. We sit across from each other in the medical-student lounge, sprawled in ratty armchairs, sipping bitter lukewarm cocoa we've gotten out of a vending machine. Amy sips, frowns, puts her

Styrofoam cup on the floor, and leans forward, her hands folded as if in prayer. "I owe you an apology."

"For what?"

"I've been a little . . . cold. You know, when I see you in the halls, on campus, the library. I've been kind of cold."

"You're not cold. You run the other way."

She blushes, laughs, dips her head.

"I wouldn't call that cold," I say. "That I would call repulsed. Revolted. Disgusted."

"Okay, *okay*. I'm sorry."

We sip our cocoa. This stuff tastes like motor oil.

"I'm not repulsed," she says.

I laugh. I like this girl.

"Do you have questions?" I say.

"No," she says. "I just wanted to get together."

I like her even more.

"Um." I smack my lips. "This hot chocolate is *delicious*."

We both nod officiously as if we're at a cocoa tasting.

"That taste," she says.

"Bittersweet, I believe. Perhaps a hint of milk chocolate."

"I was going to say mulch."

Maybe it's my state of mind, my lack of sleep, my need to connect, or my sudden comfort with her, but I lose it. What's even better is that Amy loses it, too. We laugh until tears come.

"Wow." Composed. Tears dried on napkins. "I haven't laughed that hard in years. There was nudity involved."

"Yours?"

Okay. I love this girl.

"So, I want to know. Why did you hate me?"

"I told you. I didn't hate you." She pauses, rubs the arm of her overstuffed chair. I find that kind of sexy. "You want the truth?"

"No. Lie. Yes, I want the truth."

"It's sensitive. You have to be discreet."

"I am. Everyone confides in me. I know a ton of secrets. I have a horrible memory, so you can tell me anything."

"It was Tanja."

"Your roommate?"

She nods. I scarcely know Tanja. I've seen her maybe twice. Tanja is large, shy, Navajo, and unpleasant. I'm not a big fan.

"She has a crush on you."

"What?"

"Had. She claimed you first before I could protest. She had such a huge crush that I felt I should back off. I didn't want anything to come between Tanja and me. I have to live with her."

"And that's why you hated me?"

"That's why I was cold."

"I get it. I think. You women. So confounding."

"We are challenging. By the way, Tony?" She speaks into her Styrofoam cup, the sides of which she has begun to crumble between her fingers. "I'm having the best time."

She mumbles this.

"What?"

"You heard me."

"I didn't."

Amy stands abruptly, stretches. "Well, big sib. I have a ton of stuff to do."

"You think you have a lot to do now. Wait."

"Walk me home."

We gather our stuff. I want to put an arm around her, hold her hand. I want to *kiss* her. But I don't do anything. I shove my hands in my pockets and keep my eyes glued to the ground. I don't want to spoil what has been maybe the best hour of the last decade.

We reach her dorm, stop at her front door. Our only moment of awkwardness sets in. We don't speak. We don't move.

"I will call you," she says. "With questions."

"I want you to."

"You can call me, too."

"I will. With answers. Maybe. Doubtful. But you never know. Even a blind squirrel finds his nuts sometimes. That didn't come out right."

She shines that ice-melting smile on me like a high beam. "We don't even have to talk about med school."

"Good. Great. I like that."

"So, again, I'm sorry. Friends?" She holds her hand out. We shake. We don't let go for a long time.

"Well, see you," I say. I can't tell which of us breaks away first. I turn to go, turn back. "What happened?"

Amy tips her head slightly, frowns. Really cute.

"With Tanja?" I say. "What happened to her crush on me?"

"She went lesbian."

I nod. "Good choice for her."

She grins, pivots, heads toward her dorm. I watch her go, my eyes fixated on her back. When she hits the door, she raises her hand and waves. Never looking back at me.

Wow. Is it possible? Do I got me a wo-man?

WEEKS OF PBL domains blow by. I bust for each exam, study more than anyone I know. With all this work and angst, I still barely eke by on every test. But now most nights, when I wind down, I add another activity between flossing and channel surfing—a phone call to Amy. We joke, we complain, we laugh, we gossip, we flirt. On occasion, during study breaks, we meet at the med-school lounge for bad cocoa. We're friends now, confidants, and I know we're both interested in more. I can feel it. I think. I'm fairly certain. But with Tim's two-date rule hanging over my head like an ax, I'm afraid to take our friendship further.

"You should ask her out, Youner. Officially. Move this thing along," Tim says.

"But what if nothing happens by the second date?"

"You bail. *Next.* You know the rule."

"That's what worries me. I don't want to mess this up. I like her too much. I don't know what to do."

"Man up. Show some spine, dude. Oh, no. What time is it? I have to call Jane. She gets pissed when I'm late."

With first semester a painful memory and second semester relentlessly pulverizing us, Ricky takes over and moves things along for me. He sees that we're all walking like zombies and that we need to blow off steam. He decides that we will host what he calls the med-school bash of all time, a party that will become legend. He invites a hundred of his closest friends. We chip in for food and kegs. Ricky decorates, chooses the perfect theme for Michigan in February—Wacky Waikiki. In the Nerd Room, I invite Amy. Officially.

"I'm confused." She's mangled her cup into a ruin of Styrofoam debris. "Are you inviting me to this party as your date or your sib?"

"Yes."

"Which one?"

"My date."

"Your date."

"Yes."

"Are you sure?"

"No."

She reaches out with her foot and bashes my boot with hers. "I accept."

"Cool," I say. "I'm nervous. I don't want to do anything to screw this up."

She punishes the last of the cup. "Then don't."

Two nights before the party. I reach for the phone to dial Amy, and the phone rings, stuns me. I laugh, pick it up. "Hey. I was just going to call you. We're like two bodies with one brain."

A husky coo. "That's what I think, too."

Bianca.

"Whoa." The phone slips, falls out of my hand, bangs on the concrete floor. I reel it back up by the phone cord. "Bianca. Hi."

"It's been a while. Why haven't you called me?"

"Why? Well. Second year. It's totally brutal. Like boot camp. You have no idea. I've been studying round-the-clock. Nonstop. Twenty-four/seven. I barely have time to *breathe*."

I'm rambling like the Rain Man.

"Hey, I hear you're having this awesome party."

"Yes. Yes, we are. Ricky's idea. It'll be a total scene. I only got invited because I live here."

"Is it okay if I come? Ricky said it would be."

Where is Ricky? I need to strangle him.

"I'm so excited about this party," Bianca says.

"Sweet," I say.

"I'm really excited to see you, too," Bianca says.

Gulp.

"Yeah. Me, too," I say. "Sweet."

We hang up.

My forehead feels hot to the touch.

FOR THE NEXT two days straight, Bianca hijacks my thoughts. I cannot kick her out of my head. Her exotic looks. Mocha skin. Wild black hair. That accent. Those lips. Those hips. The body that drives sane men insane. *Really excited* to see me. That's what she said. She called me out of the blue. Out of nowhere. She'd been a little cool when we went out. Not cool now. Not cool on the phone. Hot. Hot for *me*. She's had a change of heart. It happens. Take a look at what else is out there, and you find yourself falling in love with what you had before. Almost had. Could've had.

Calm down, Tony. Take it easy. Chill.

Really excited to see me. *Really* excited. I heard those words. Tim's stupid two-date rule. She's Latina. She has different rules. Latina rules. It might take more than two dates. Could take three or four or seven dates. So what? This is a smoking-hot woman. How many dates should you take with a woman this hot? What's *that* rule, Tim? Because Bianca—sizzling-hot Bianca—burns up my dreams. One question. Probably not important now. But keeps popping up.

What about Amy?

My own words boomerang into my brain and knock Bianca into a corner.

I don't want to do anything to mess this up.

"Then don't."

SATURDAY NIGHT. SEVEN o'clock. Party starts in one hour. I lie in my bed, comatose. I haven't called Amy in two days. I've gone deep undercover. Incommunicado. First time in months we've gone over a day without speaking. I'm frozen. I close my eyes and see Bianca wearing a sheer white dress. She circles around me, wiggles her finger to come to her. I move toward her. I stop. I blink and see . . . Amy.

Bianca.

Amy.

Bianca.

"If you don't get your ass out of bed, you're gonna lose both of them." James. Standing in the doorway. Easy for him to say. As soon as the party starts, he'll have a dozen women draping themselves all over him, even though he's still with Daisy.

"I'm sick," I say. "I have some kind of flu."

Ricky now. At the foot of my bed. He pulls the covers off me. I'm wearing only my boxers.

"If you don't get out of bed by the time I count to three, I'm getting in there with you. One."

I'm on my feet. Wobbling toward the laundry room shower.

"No, no, no," Ricky says. "Tonight you use the big-boy bathroom."

I take an hour in Ricky's bathroom. Finally, clean, coiffed, clutching a plastic cup half filled with brew that I hold against my chest, I hide in a corner as the party unrolls. Bianca arrives first. She removes her coat slow as a stripper and shakes out her hair. She's wearing a short, tight skirt and see-through blouse. Wait. Is she not wearing a *bra*? Holy shit. She's not wearing a bra! I'm not 100 percent sure, because my glasses have fogged up.

"Tony!" Bianca lassos my neck with both arms. Then she kisses me on the mouth. American-style. "You look great, Tony."

That is such a lie. I look like crap. I haven't slept in six months.

"You. Too. Look great." I'm talking like a caveman.

"I've been doing a lot of thinking." Bianca traces the rim of my cup with her finger. "About us. We need to spend more time together. Starting tonight."

"Well, ha. That would be certainly, you know, a change."

I guzzle my beer. The living room has filled up. Wall-to-wall med students. Music throbs. People start to dance. I'm feeling feverish again. I need to lie down. Ricky squeezes by, a dozen leis ringed on his shoulder. He lifts one off and slips it over Bianca's head. Kisses both of her cheeks. He winks at me. Then dances by. He looks back at me, slaps his cheek like a shocked diva.

"Are you all right?" Bianca asks me.

"Who? Me? Sure. Yes. Fine."

"You seem jumpy."

"Yeah, yeah, no. Second year, you know? Takes its toll. You'll see. I don't wish it on you, but. Oh, love this song." And then, idiotically, I sing along, faking most of the words.

Bianca eyes me as if I'm a mental patient. "You sure you're all right?"

"Fine. Honest. Um-hm."

"Then get me a drink."

"Okay. Good. Be right back." I mime pouring a drink and putting it into my imaginary cart, grin, and push away from the wall.

And that's when I see Amy.

She stands alone, scanning the room, looking for me, her coat draped over her arm. She wears jeans and a sweater. She has her hair pulled back, cut and shaped for the party. I have never seen anyone look hotter. She sees me and waves. I feel as if the floor is about to open up and suck me down. Or maybe that's what I wish for.

"You're acting so strange. I'll go with you." Bianca grabs my hand. Amy sees us and packs up her smile. Her face flushes purple. She nods, sick, then slips her coat back on and heads for the door.

"Amy!" I drop Bianca's hand. I break into a run, nearly take out a gunner, slide by, then back up and face Bianca. "Bianca, listen. The two of us. It's not gonna happen. I'm interested in someone else. I'm really sorry. I have to go."

I turn and sprint, weave between James and Daisy, sidestep Tim and Jane, spin around Ricky and a guy on the swim team. I cut in front of Amy and block the door as her hand is about to circle the doorknob. "Hi."

"Excuse me. I'm leaving."

"You're not. You can't."

"Get out of my way."

"You're not going. If you go, I'm going with you."

"I have another party to go to. I have a *date*. Go back to your mysterious exotic friend."

"She's not my friend."

Cute-as-*hell* head tilt. I want to kiss her right now.

"No?"

"No. She's my Latin-American cousin. I think she was adopted."

"Nice boobs. You can see them from the bookstore."

"I hadn't noticed." I reach over and stroke Amy's hair. She closes her eyes for a split second, then swipes my hand away. I grab her fingers, fold mine through hers. She squeezes my fingers white.

"I dated her twice, like months ago, before you. Nothing happened. I haven't spoken to her since. Ricky invited her tonight. She shows up and she's all over me. I think she's psycho."

"She would have to be."

We cling to each other's hands.

"Would you like a drink?" I ask.

"No, thanks."

"May I take your coat?"

Amy stares at me. I can almost hear her mind whirring, calculating, deciding—*Should I make a run for it, or . . . ?*

"Please," I say.

"If you ever go radio silence on me again, I'll kick your butt."

"Fair enough."

I help her off with her coat.

"How about that drink?" she says.

We hold hands all the way to the keg.

MAY. SECOND SEMESTER ends.

Unless you're a second-year medical student.

School's out for summer, but we still have a month to go. A month of hell. We end our grueling second year and jump right into studying for the United States Medical Licensing Exam Step I Board Exam (USMLE), or the Boards. By reputation, the Boards rival the MCAT as the most important test an aspiring doctor will take. To this day, my doctor friends and I debate whether the Boards deserve that reputation. There is no debate about this: I never study harder for a test in my life.

My studying begins the day after second semester ends. Along with almost every second-year med student I know, I enroll in a USMLE review course. The course goes for three weeks, Monday through Saturday, eight hours a day. Once we complete the course, we have one week left to cram for the all-day exam. Tim and I give up the house to James and Ricky and lock ourselves in the Nerd Room for fifteen hours a day. I leave my cubicle only to stretch, to eat peanut-butter-and-jelly sandwiches, to bitch to Tim, and to call Amy. We know the importance of sleep, so we're home at Flower Street by eleven each night. Even though I'm getting some sleep, the grind is wearing me down. I give up everything except studying. I no longer look like a homeless person. I look like a strung-out homeless heroin addict.

I drive myself based on the fear of failure. If I don't pass this treacherous eight-hour exam/brain tease this time, I will have to take it *again*. I need no other motivation. Besides, I can't imagine how I could possibly study harder. If I fail this test, I don't know what I will do. More than once during this killer month of brutal studying, I feel that I will have to quit.

By the day of the test, I'm a jittery mess. I haven't shaved, I've showered days ago—how many days ago, I don't remember—and I don't recall when I last changed my clothes. Even more worrisome, my brain feels vacant, as if I've retained nothing. Glancing around the exam room, I see that everyone else looks worse. I get no consolation there. Okay, some.

Part one of the Boards, a four-hour morning session, begins. I look at the test and can't make out a single word. I can't focus. The page shimmies. The letters swim around and plunk back down on the page, out of order and written in a language I don't know. I start to panic. I shut my eyes. My life flashes forward.

I have flunked out of medical school. My father orders me to sit down at the dining room table. He slams a stack of books in front of me. He tells me that I am not allowed to leave this room, ever, that I will have to study these books for the rest of my life.

I jerk back to reality. The letters miraculously unscramble, form into words, connect into sentences. Not only do I recognize the first question, I know the answer. I insert earplugs to reduce the noise in the examination room, pick up my pencil, and *attack*. We break for a fifteen-minute lunch. I inhale two peanut-butter-and-jelly sandwiches, my staple. Why mess with success? We return for part two, four more hours.

A month later, Tim and I are lounging on the living room couch when the mail carrier delivers the results. We tear open the envelopes like nervous Academy Award presenters. I don't believe it. I've passed! Even better, I beat Tim by five points.

And that concludes medical school, year two.

Now I can finally play doctor.

For real.

IV Third Year

11

First Do No Harm . . . Oops

Confession.

I hate hospitals.

Question.

Is this going to be a problem?

What do I hate specifically?

I keep a list.

First, the smell. You step off the elevator and it hits you, acidic and icy and metallic with a hint of disinfectant, designed to distract you, make you think you've wandered into a rather large janitorial closet instead of a planet of sick people. Same idea as that pine-scented strip the guy at the carwash hangs on your rearview mirror. You get into your car, and *ahhh*, you're transported into a fresh pine forest in the middle of some glen. Your nose buys the deception for exactly two seconds before you're down to earth, back behind the wheel of your Ford Tempo, the air laced with something vaguely mint-green, artificial, and chemical. Hospitals can go as heavy as they want on the ammonia and mask it with Old Spice for all I care. We're not fooled. We know where we are.

Second, the air. Illness, disease, and, especially, death rise up from the afflicted and bounce off the shiny linoleum in a mist, hovering above us in a pale haze. The hanging cloud comes with an odor, the smell of brown, a musty odor I previously associated with a dank, forgotten corner of our cellar, piles of clothes unworn and packed away in the back of a dark closet, and my grandparents.

Third, the sound. An off-key stew of humming, whirring, beeping, metal chair legs scraping, wheelchair wheels creaking, human groaning, moaning, and howling, rumbling sporadic voice-overs pouring through overhead speakers, green-paper footsteps, coarse breathy inappropriate laughter, urgent, sad, whispered plans, the occasional scream, the scratching of forks and spoons along unbreakable plates, the swish of blood pressure cuffs, the crackle of blinding and sporadic fluorescent lighting, muffled shrieks, and mumbled prayer. I do have potential, because to me, this mash-up sounds like music.

Fourth, the fear. Wide-eyed and breathless. Swirling down the corridors, oozing through walls.

Theirs. And mine.

DAY ONE, THIRD year. My first of five two-month clinical rotations in the hospital.

Internal medicine.

Elevator at my back, I turn down the corridor, walk like a gunslinger. Well, in my mind. In reality, I inch forward in my short white coat that barely conceals my quivering chest. I feel like a nervous waiter. In slow motion, I bang into the nurses' station and hold up my hand.

Tony Youn here. Reporting for duty.

I don't say this. I can't speak. I'm struck momentarily mute. A robotic nurse, eyes down, mumbles the particulars. Where to park (Lot C, Level 3, Aisle 2; I will never find my car). Where to eat (gag-a-teria, second floor, or the sketchy Burger King across the street, or the best bet, vending machine belly-up to the bathroom). Where to sleep (on-call room, next to the elevators, featuring a bowed metal bunk bed with cement mattress, choose up or fight for the bottom with the intern I'm assigned).

"Is this him?"

Voice like a bartender. I search for where it came. Look left, right, finally down. Find someone in a long white coat. Female, but that's a guess. Wearer of a permanent pirate's scowl. A dark bush of a unibrow that stretches ear to ear and shades two purple eyes like an awning. I'm still going with female. Or Danny DeVito in drag. Okay, I'm right. Female. Beneath her long white robe, I recognize a definite female configuration, breasts and such. Her hair is the clincher, pulled back in a tight black ponytail that she swings like a machete. She speaks again and confirms.

"I'm Nancy. And you are?"

"Tony. Anthony. Tony."

"Wild guess. Are you *Tony*?"

A roll of her purple pin eyes. Then a sigh that could blow out a birthday cake. "Here's the deal."

She sizes me up, which makes me uncomfortable, because the top of her head barely reaches my chest.

"I am your *mother*."

She may not mean it, but she shouts this, causing a work stoppage in the entire area code. I nod, or try to. Midnod, my head jiggles out of control. For a moment I'm a bobblehead. Nancy's gin-soaked alto hones in.

"I *own* you. You do *exactly* what I say. You have questions? Keep them to yourself. I'm not interested. I don't have time. Just follow my orders and stay out of my way. Understood?"

"Got it. Yes."

"Good. A smart one." A violent jerk of her head, and she suckerslaps me across the face with her ponytail. "And that was your orientation. Let's go, Tony-Tony. We got sick people backed up like a pileup on the I-96."

She's on the move, ponytail slicing the air. I match her stride for stride, too scared to lag behind, adrenaline pumping, keeping us neck and neck. She motors down the corridor, puffing like a tractor. We stop at door number one. She grinds her palm into the molding, sneaks a shot back at the nurses' station. "Here's the deal."

I lean in. Nancy checks me into the door frame. "I don't know you, but I don't like you."

"That was fast," I say.

"Nothing personal. I don't like anybody. I'm married, and I seriously don't like him. He's a *lawyer*."

She spits the word out like a mouthful of shell. She pulls back an inch, gives me space to breathe. Not much space. The width of a tie.

"Not gonna lie," Nancy growls. "I hate this. All of it. The job, this place, these people. This job? Want to know what they pay me? Shit. They pay me *shit*. Actually, that's not true. They pay me less than shit. I'd kill to get paid shit. You getting this? Am I getting through?"

"Oh, yes. Definitely."

"Good. I thought you took a dive on me there."

"I'm totally with you."

"We'll see. Because that would be a major change from the usual line of third-year numbnuts they give me. Okay, *Tony*. Here's the drill. Take the pulse, draw the blood—"

"Wait. I thought the phlebotomist drew blood."

"Every day but *today*. We're not waiting around for her lazy ass. So you lucked out. Do the draw, mark the chart, and move on. Don't waste time making small talk with the gomers. Got it?"

"Gomers?"

"The chronically ill who end up here and waste our time. They never leave and they never die. That's a GOMER. Stands for GET OUT OF MY EMERGENCY ROOM. Read *House of God*, lame-o."

She puts her shoulder to the door.

"Uh, Nancy, thing is, I've never actually drawn—"

I'm too late. She's barged into the room and is charging toward the first patient on the shift. Old guy sitting in a chair, gown pulled up to his waist. Lovely way to start the day.

She wraps her thick fingers around his wrist, her eyes beamed off into space, imagining, I presume, a different career choice. She drops his wrist as if it's a slimy dog bone, scribbles something on a chart. "Do the draw," she says to me.

"As I mentioned a moment ago—"

"Do the *draw*! We don't have all day."

Hands shaking, mouth dry and tasting of paste, I fumble with the needle kit she hands me.

Word of advice.

When you've got a razor-sharp implement in your hand and your job is to puncture someone's flesh, take your time. Not great to search for a vein when you're on the clock.

Put another way, there's no such thing as a speed blood draw.

"Ow! Goddammit! Fuck you doing?" Gomer with the gown yanked up. Screaming as I stab his biceps. "OWW!"

"Sorry, sir, I just—"

Pay dirt.

"Yessss!" Needle in one hand, I fist-pump with the other.

"How about you dial it down a notch, Tony?" Nancy, under her breath.

"What's with him?" Gomer. Using his free hand to take a side trip inside his gown. Wow. This I don't need.

"It's his first day," Nancy says. Follows with a mumble to the universe, "Fucking third-year pain in my balls."

"Pardon my enthusiasm," I say to the vial of gomer blood rising. "I love my job."

AN HOUR LATER, we've run through eleven patients, most of them gomers. We double up on some. Nancy listens to heart and lungs while I draw blood. Without a word, we've become an efficient tag team. Leaving door eleven, speeding down the corridor, dodging her kung fu ponytail, I wheeze, "You are fast."

"I should get paid on commission. By the head. Speaking of which."

She's gone, ramming into the restroom.

I'm stranded and confused. Do I chance a pee break? Earlier this morning I dropped my pager into the urinal. Which, given Nancy's charming personality, remains the highlight of my day. No. Best to hang here and loiter by the restrooms like a drunk. I bend my forehead to the cool bathroom wall and peer down at my formerly crisp short white coat, no longer remotely crisp or white. I'm now wearing a rumpled multicolored heavily weighted *sack*, crumpled from leaning against a morning's worth of gomers, multicolored from intermittent fountains of bodily fluids, blood, pus, urine, and swill, otherwise known as breakfast, contributed mostly by patients with a splotch of my own flop sweat, and weighted down from accumulated stuff I've jammed in my pockets—new pager, hammer for banging on knees, stethoscope, pens, prescription pads, three-by-five notepad, yellow highlighters, hand sanitizer, and one medical how-to book, which I have yet to crack open and doubt I ever will.

Nancy bursts out of the ladies' room as if sprung from a slingshot. She chicken-wings her arms. I fall in step next to her.

"Hour two," she says, whipping me twice with her ponytail. "The fun never sets."

She hauls ass around the corner and skids to a stop at door number twelve. I think. I have lost count. I know this: the patients' faces have started to flip around into a psychedelic circle. I'm briefly light-headed and momentarily lost. Chalk it up to two years of eating nothing but crap, doing little exercise, the shock of facing an hour straight of nonstop sick people, and trying to keep up with Intern Nancy. I vow to start running and lifting again. Why do I decide this *now*? Is it because I'm gasping for breath before each blood draw?

I feel the death stare on me.

I crash-land back to earth. "Yes?"

I don't know what Nancy's thinking, but I don't like the look on her face. She offers up a smug smile as if she's just figured out the punch line to a private joke. She jabs her ponytail at me, which I manage to duck. I smugly smile back, but she doesn't notice. She consults her clipboard, tinkles her fingers over a name. "Zingerman," Nancy says.

"Gomer?"

"Probably. New admit." Flicks at the name as if it's a speck of lint. Furrows her furry unibrow.

"What?" I say.

"Stop that. I told you, no questions."

"Sorry."

She swats the air as if striking a mosquito. "Here's the deal."

I lean forward precariously. I'm an inch away from tipping over.

"You do the medical history. I'll hit the gomer next door and the one across the hall. Couple of drive-bys. Meet up with me two doors down."

"Wait, wait, wait. You want me to go in there *alone*?"

"Duh-uh."

"This is my first day. I've been doing rounds for exactly one hour. I'm a little green."

Nancy's not buying. Or caring. "Don't go near her with anything sharp. Take her history and get the hell out. Bang-boom. Tell me you can't handle that, and I'll bust you down to another tern, someone who, unlike me, will be a bitch."

I must be gaping because Nancy says, "Close your mouth."

"I didn't expect to be thrown into the fire the first day—"

"Don't be a wuss."

Eyes staring up, locking to mine. I feel myself flush. I spin away, face the door. Hesitate.

"Give her hell."

Nancy growls and slaps my ass.

I OPEN THE door to Mrs. Adele Zingerman, seventy-eight, my first live patient ever. She sits across the room in a chair, legs folded at purple ankles.

"MRS. ZINGERMAN!" I shout. "HELLO!"

Okay, a little less volume. Let's start with that.

I cross the room in two steps. I arrive and hover over Mrs. Zinger-man. I sing softly, "Good morning, good *morning.*"

What the hell am I doing, *Singing in the Rain?*

I ease onto the edge of the bed, fumble in my pocket for a pen and a three-by-five. I grin at Mrs. Zingerman. I try to remember my class in clinical skills. Step one. Put her at ease. Ask an open-ended question.

"Hello, Mrs. Zingerman."

She coughs, grimaces, grins back.

"So what brings you here today?"

Textbook. Doctor Talk 101. How I've been trained. All that time I put in with dead bodies and live actors is kicking in.

I flash a broad smile. Click the pen. Poised to write. Mrs. Zinger-man again grins, grimaces, says nothing.

I speak again, slower and louder. "WHAT BRINGS YOU HERE TODAY, MRS. ZINGERMAN?"

Nothing.

I scratch my head with the pen. Mrs. Zingerman laughs. What the hell? Might as well keep scratching. She got a kick out of it. Scratch, scratch, scratch. I make a silly yet kind face. She stares through me, creases her mouth into a frown. Maybe she doesn't speak English.

"What kind of problem are you having today? Can you tell me?"

Mrs. Zingerman opens her mouth. A sound trickles out. Half a grunt, half a croak. Not a sound I've heard before. She pushes herself to her feet, stands unsteadily. I stand, too, extend my arms, ready to guide her. She takes a step. Weaves.

"Do you—are you—where are you going—?"

She lurches forward, takes two more shaky steps.

"Do you need to use the bathroom?"

She freezes. Her eyes bulge. She gasps, gurgles, takes another step, and falls to the floor. She lies there, motionless, soundless.

"Mrs. Zingerman?"

She doesn't move. She doesn't grin, gurgle, or gasp.

"Are you okay?"

Wait a minute. Is she—? No. She can't be.

"Mrs. Zingerman? Hello?"

Are you SHITTING me?

I drop down, feel for a pulse.

No pulse. No heartbeat. No breath. No sign of life.

I'm new at this doctor stuff—I'm still a medical student—but I'm pretty sure this means that Mrs. Zingerman is dead.

I have killed my first patient.

This can't be good.

It may be some sort of record, but I know it can't be good.

Will I get marked down for this?

I crouch over Mrs. Zingerman, thinking, *What do I do?*, and then Nancy's tanklike frame fills the doorway and I hear "Youn, what the fuck is taking you so long . . . *SHIT!*"

Time stops. Fractured words dance across the room, *saddle pulmonary embolus*, screams of *"Code! Code!"*, then whirring of machinery, crashing of footsteps, a tide of white-coated bodies surging in, and one man, Dr. Ed Moncrief, exuding a steady cool, pushes through the crowd to take over. He wears a long white coat, but he may as well have on a leather jacket. He is that cool. I stand to the side and watch in some state of awe, still stunned but no longer afraid. Unlike Nancy, who's a terrorist, and me, who's a rookie, Dr. Moncrief is a *doctor*, and everyone in the room knows it, defers to him, and gets the hell out of his way. He is the star in the room, and the light shines only on him as he works over poor dead Mrs. Zingerman, checking for her nonexistent breath and pulse, jolting her nonbeating heart with paddles, pounding her lifeless chest. We stand in the shadows, helpless observers, his audience in the dark. Finally, after five minutes of literally trying to revive the dead, Dr. Moncrief calls it a day. "No cure here." Sung in a glee-club baritone.

Moncrief stands, making sure we all notice that he towers over everyone in the room. He pronounces Mrs. Zingerman officially deceased and announces her official time of death like a news anchor. Pin eyes blinking contempt, aimed at me, Nancy scribbles a frazzled something onto her clipboard. Moncrief spins out of the room, halts at the doorway to again check the time. "Lunch," he says, and pivots toward the gag-a-teria.

Nancy, I know, will have to answer for this. Not that she could have stopped Mrs. Zingerman from dying, but she should not have left a third-year medical student alone with a patient—even a gomer—on his first day. Hell, in his second *hour*. She will have some explaining to do.

She starts after Moncrief. I step toward her. She whirls and bumps me with her hefty shoulder, then eyeballs me with a laser look designed to reduce me to a pile of ash. "Good job," she says, forming a blockade with her body. "I don't know what you said, but you killed her."

"You actually think it was something I said?"

Hand up. A stop sign. "No—fucking—*questions*."

Some emotion Nancy vaguely recognizes—fear, horror, sadness, helplessness—passes across my face, because her eyes widen and glisten. "Oh, fuck. Okay, look. It was a blessing in disguise."

I nod, understand. "She had a fatal illness and it was just a matter of time."

Roll of her eyes for the five hundredth time of the morning. "No, dipshit. It's a blessing that you got your first one out of the way. Patients die. Get used to it. This is a *hospital*."

This begs for a response, but I have temporarily turned to stone. Meanwhile, Nancy's moment of humanity passes.

"Meet me back here after lunch for round two. Thirty minutes. Let's see what kind of damage you can do this afternoon."

"I can't do any worse."

She's gone, rumbling down the corridor toward a burrito.

I DO NO further damage in the afternoon. At least I don't kill any more patients. Except for poor dead Mrs. Zingerman, I call the day a success. Nancy hasn't canned me, and the dozen or so lacerations on my face caused by her flying ponytail have started to scab and heal.

"Yippee. You made it through day one, hotshot." Nancy, an elastic in her mouth, tortures her hair into a bun.

"I couldn't have done it without you."

"No shit."

"Well, okay, then. Guess I'll see you in the morning."

"Yes, you will. You'll also see me tonight, you lucky stiff."

I blink furiously.

"We're both on call. What a coinkydink. Here, partner." She tosses me her pager.

My mouth flops open. Goes well with the uncontrollable blinking.

"You seem mentally challenged. Have you been tested? Listen up, superstar. Here's the deal. That's my *pager*. If someone pages me between now and six A.M., *you* answer it. If it looks like blood, guts, or death, wake me up. Otherwise, leave me the fuck alone. I need my beauty rest."

She guns her eyes into mine, dares me to flinch. I'm ready for her. "Sweet. I'm your screener."

"I was gonna say scut monkey, but we'll go with screener. I don't hand out this privilege to everyone, by the way. My *screener*. I like it. Oh. In case you're wondering, you'll sleep next year. Night-night."

Hair stacked on her head like a hut, fumbling at the top buttons of her long white coat, she disappears behind door number one.

I'll sleep next year.

Hell, Nance, don't spoil me. I bang into door number two.

The call room.

A closet with a saggy cot, a coat rack, a bulletin board cluttered with notices dated a month ago. Tighter, darker, and more depressing than my bedroom on Flower Street, which, before this moment, I thought impossible. I strip down to my boxers, slip on scrubs I find hanging on the backside of the coat rack, and collapse onto the cot. I slam the pillow over my head and stifle a scream.

. . . .

NOBODY PAGES YOU with good news.

You never pick up a page that reads, *Congratulations, Tony! You've hit the lottery! You win 84 million dollars!*

No. Every page brings you a variation of *bad*. When I answer Nancy's first page, I emerge from a snowflaked stupor to a bonking yellow message that announces a spiking fever and uncontainable discharge. Jarred awake, I feel like a firefighter aroused to save a flaming city block. Adrenaline *rush*. I'm on it!

Two minutes later, I chase Nancy, who lumbers down the slick, barren corridor. She moves fast for a troll. I jog to keep up. It may be too early—or too late—for small talk, but it's after midnight, and this is my first night on call and I'm wired.

"I have to admit. I'm excited."

"Here's the deal," Nancy says, whipping around, voice fuzzy, as if she's been chewing on a bar rag. "We're putting out fires."

"That's just how I feel. Like a firefighter."

"Shut up." She burns rubber around a corner, halts, leaves a skid mark in front of an open door. Moaning flies out, bounces off the walls. "Our job is to make sure all these patients survive until six A.M. Then we hand the baton off to the morning crew and get the hell out of Dodge. You got me?"

"I do."

"We're plate spinners. Keep 'em in the air, never let 'em fall."

She bulldozes into the room. I'm right behind her. Putting out the fire.

THE PAGES DON'T stop. They come every fifteen minutes. All seem to contain the word *blood*. I'm thrilled by the first one, charged up for number two, ready to rumble for number three. Number four frankly annoys me, number five pisses me off, number six sends me diving under my pillow. By number seven, I'm as surly as Nancy. The eighth call does me in. Pushing on a gomer's distended belly, Nancy grunts and carves the air with a cracked whisper. "Tony? Would you like some action?"

This perks me up. I so want to be a part of this. I'll do anything besides answer her pager and nip at her heels like a puppy. "You bet."

She hands me a pair of white latex gloves. I snap them on like the surgeon I hope someday to be.

Nancy smiles. I *think* she smiles. Put it this way: something happens with her mouth that doesn't scare me. "Relieve the pressure on this patient's colon."

"I'm sorry?"

"Get your hands up there and pull."

Now she really is smiling. Like a homicidal maniac. Her pager hums. I flip it off my belt and make out words like *immediately* and *panic* and *bloody discharge*.

Nancy's smile fades. Her face goes dark. "Dig in, Tony."

She whacks my shoulder. I hesitate. Feel my jaw vibrate.

"Now!"

Trying to block out the patient's moans, I hesitate, then tunnel in, panning for gold.

Rotation one. Day one. Internal medicine with the sadistic intern Nancy.

The shits.

DAY TWO. I'M late. Or so says Nancy, who fills the cafeteria doorway as I exit carrying a coffee and a glazed doughnut.

"What time is it, Tony?"

"Good morning." I twist my doughnut hand and peek at my watch. "Six-twenty-five. I still have five minutes."

"*I* get in at six-thirty. Which means *you* need to get in an hour before me to do prerounds on all the patients *before* I get here."

"I'm sorry. I didn't realize—"

"Get the doughnut out of your face and start with the patient in 507. Frank Fremont. Fifty-five years old. In for an MI."

"MI is of course—"

I hold. Wait for her to fill me in. She holds back, leaves me hanging until melting doughnut glaze drizzles onto my fingers.

"Myocardial infarction," she says finally. "Which you didn't know."

"He had a heart attack, huh?"

Slight quiver of the lower lip. I've grazed her. Not for long. She battles back, counters with a left-right combination.

"Yes, Tony. Cardiothoracic surgery wants to take him in for a four-vessel CABG, but Mr. Fremont won't consent to surgery. I've tried to talk him in to it, but he seems to find my manner somewhat . . . off-putting."

"No way."

"Perhaps you can convince him that having the surgery would be in his best interest."

"Me?"

"Don't spend longer than three minutes in there. It's a waste of time. He's a POS."

Another dumb look.

"Piece of shit. Move it. And get here an hour earlier starting tomorrow. Five-thirty sharp."

"I will. My mistake."

"You won't be needing these." She whisks the coffee and doughnut out of my hands and thunders by, bashing my shoulder like a third-grade bully.

12

Role Model

I stand outside room 507 and read through Frank Fremont's chart. *Admitted three days before. Sudden onset of chest pressure. Diagnosis—severe coronary artery disease and mild heart attack.* I scan further. *All four arteries clogged nearly 100%. Bypass of blood vessels recommended immediately and urgently.*

"Mr. Personality." A nurse's aide about the same age as my mother stops on her way to the nurses' station. She looks over my shoulder at the chart. "Good luck in there."

"Why?" The blinking again. "What I mean is . . . *why?*"

"Tough case. He doesn't speak. Well, that's not true. He says 'Leave me alone' and 'Let me die.' He also won't eat and refuses an IV."

"I can handle this guy. I've been on the job for almost two days."

"Did I mention that he's a junk dealer and he hasn't bathed for I'm guessing at least a week before the admit? *Stinks* in there."

"You're not scaring me. Okay, maybe a little."

She laughs. "Go get him, kid."

I flap the chart against my thigh and knock.

Nothing.

I knock again. Again, nothing. I ease the door open a crack. "Mr. Fremont?"

"Get the fuck outta here."

What do you mean, he doesn't speak? I got him to talk right away.

I push the door open all the way and step in.

The stench hits me, whoosh, like a wind. Blowing sour like the retching smell from a Dumpster behind a Chinese restaurant. I clamp two fingers over my nose and step farther in. The shades are drawn. In shadows, I make out a gaunt man in a hospital gown, slumped in a chair next to the hospital bed. I stop at the edge of the bed, allow my eyes to adjust to the dark.

"Hello, Mr. Fremont. I'm Tony Youn. I'm the medical student on the internal medicine service. Mind if I talk to you about your medical situation?"

Frank raises his head. He looks like a ghost. He lifts a scrawny hand and dismisses me. His bones protrude through his wrists. Pockmarks spot his face like divots. He licks his lips, then lowers his head.

"Could we talk about the surgery the doctors are recommending for you? The surgery might save your life."

He chuckles. Shifts in his chair. Kicks at the floor with a paper shoe. "Leave me alone."

I don't move. After a moment, I sit down on the edge of the bed and wait. I have no idea what to do or say, but I know I can't leave.

Suddenly, I hear myself speak. "Can I tell you about something that happened to me?"

He sniffs.

I lay his chart down on the bed next to me. Then, accustomed to the dim light, acclimated to the foul smell, I tell him a story.

I WANT TO tell you about my mother.

My mom is very traditional. She's basically just your typical mom. The family caretaker and cook. The one who raised us. My dad is the breadwinner, the family disciplinarian, the ruler of the house. But if you asked me whom I look up to most in my life, who would be my role model, I would say my mom.

A few months ago I got a call from my father. My mom had played tennis in the early evening, and that night, in the middle of the night, she began to feel short of breath. It kept getting worse. She finally woke up my father and said she needed to go to the emergency room.

By the time they got to the ER, she could barely breathe. She was gasping for air. It was as if her lungs had filled up with gallons of water and she couldn't manage even a tiny, shallow breath. My mother has never smoked in her life and rarely drinks. She exercises regularly. She's been the picture of health. And then this happens.

At the ER, they run some tests. They find out that she's in sudden heart failure. One of the valves of her heart has failed and her heart is no longer beating normally. This is causing her lungs to fill with fluid. She's literally drowning from the inside out. They rush her to the ICU, put her on a bunch of IV meds. She starts coming around. My dad spends the night with her in our small-town hospital, waiting for them to transfer her the next morning to a bigger, better-equipped hospital. Here. Where you are.

They move her here and my father calls me and my brother. We all meet at the ICU. The cardiologist schedules her for an echocardiogram. By the time I see her, the meds have kicked in, and she's breathing better. A nurse arrives, gives her another medication through the IV, a sedative for the procedure. It works quickly. My mother starts to drift off. My brother and I kiss her on the cheek and tell her we love her. My father says nothing. He awkwardly reaches over for her hand, holds it, then nods at her as they wheel her away for the procedure.

In my entire life, I've never seen my parents show any affection toward each other. They never kiss, hug, hold hands in front of me. I've never heard my dad tell my mom that he loves her. He's never told me he loves me, either. I know he does. He doesn't have to tell me. I'm sure it's a Korean thing.

After they wheel my mother into the OR, my father, brother, and I go downstairs to the waiting room. After a while, my brother gets up and looks for a paper. My dad and I sit across from each other. We don't say anything. Just sit there. In silence. Forever, it seems. I start to read. Then I hear this sound. Like a whimper. And then a gag. I look up. My father is sobbing. Tears are streaming down his face. I've never seen him cry. He can't control himself. He covers his face with his hands. I don't know what to do. I want to go over to him and put my arms around him. I want to rock him like he used to rock me when I was little. But I can't move. I think he'll be humiliated if I try to console him. So I don't. I just sit across from him and watch him cry. I've never felt so helpless.

Finally, he gets ahold of himself. He exhales deeply a few times. He blows his nose, becomes completely composed. My brother returns. The three of us sit quietly and wait, as if nothing's happened.

About an hour later, the cardiologist comes in. He explains that my mother needs open-heart surgery to repair the heart valve that has failed. He says if the surgery goes well, she'll be fine for a very long time.

She has the surgery. It's a complete success. The strangest part is that my mom never worried. She has this faith, this belief, that whatever happens is God's will. This faith gives her enormous strength. And enormous peace. I admire that so much. I wish I had that. I wish I had her strength. I want to be like her.

That surgery is the same surgery they want for you.

That surgery gave me back my mom.

MY PAGER GOES off. It flashes neon yellow. *What the hell are you doing in there??? Get your ass away from the POS and preround the rest of the patients!!!*

So Nancy. Such concern. Such compassion.

I switch off the pager.

"Now tell me your story, Mr. Fremont."

I don't expect he will. I expect that I have wasted my time. I expect that he will ask me to leave. I pick up the chart, stand, start to leave.

"My wife died ten years ago."

Frank speaks slowly in a smoker's rasp. I sit back down on the bed.

"Breast cancer. She had a lump in her breast for years, but her doctor said not to worry about it. She finally went for a second opinion. This doctor found out that the cancer had already spread to her lungs and brain. Nothing they could do. She died six months later. To me, she was . . . everything."

He coughs.

"After she went, my life ended. I have a daughter. She married this guy. We don't get along. Put it mildly. I got a granddaughter. She's five. I don't see her much. I own a junkyard. I sell scraps for a living. I don't bother nobody. Then one day this. My daughter doesn't know I'm here. I didn't tell her. She wouldn't care. She doesn't care if I live or die. End of story."

"You sure?"

Frank shuffles both of his paper shoes. He looks past me, into the shadows, then he faces me. "What do you mean?"

"Sometimes people have a hard time expressing what they really feel." I picture my father sobbing across from me in the waiting room. "Mr. Fremont, I'm young. I don't know that much about life. But I do know that if my dad was sick, I'd want to know. And I think, in some way, my mom—" A catch in my throat strangles the rest of my thought.

"What?"

I clear my throat. "I think my mom had her surgery for us. Like I said, whatever the outcome, she felt it was God's will. She was ready to go. But *I* wasn't ready to let her go. Neither was my brother. Neither was my father. And she knew it."

"So . . . you think I should have the surgery?"

"That has to be your call. You have to make that decision yourself. I know the doctors are good here. They saved my mom. And I'll bet your daughter's not ready to lose you yet. I bet no matter what you think, she wants you to play with your granddaughter for a long, long time."

Frank slowly begins rocking in his chair. "I'll think about it," he says.

I grab his chart and stand again. "Good luck," I say.

"Thank you," Frank says. "For talking to me."

He wheezes, then extends his hand. I grip it and we shake.

"I'll see you again," I say.

OUTSIDE FRANK'S ROOM, Nancy waits. Fists pumped tight on her hips, blood drained from her face, she washes me with a drizzle of spittle before she spews. "WHAT THE FUCK WERE YOU DOING IN THERE?"

"What you told me. Trying to convince him to have the surgery."

"I told you to take THREE MINUTES."

"Sorry. I lost track of time. He's such a talker."

"Get your ass rounding. We are so behind. If you make me miss lunch."

"I'm on it."

I start to trot away. Nancy clutches my biceps in a death grip and nearly lifts me off my feet. She jams me into a watercooler. She grinds her head into my chest, arrows her purple devil eyes into my forehead. "And if you ever turn off your pager again, I'll bust you so bad you'll spend the rest of this rotation washing out specimen jars. We clear?"

I nod.

She cups an ear.

"Yes. We're clear."

"Dork." She releases me. "I was just starting not to hate you."

ROTATION ONE. DAY three. I get to sleep in my own bed in the comfort of my own dungeon on Flower Street. Heaven. I can unwind on my own time and talk to Amy. We talk nightly when I'm not on call. I vent about Nancy, she rails about the PBL domains. We hang up gushy after an hour. I set my alarm for four-thirty and drift off to Tim cooing to Jane. Ah. Medical-school romance.

The next morning, while rounding the fifth-floor patients with Nancy, I take a chance. "I'm gonna check in on 507."

Nancy thumps her clipboard against a meaty thigh. "The POS."

"Yeah. I told him I would."

"Tony, if you take longer than two minutes."

"I won't. I promise."

I break into a sprint. I slow down by the nurses' station, wave at the same aide I saw yesterday.

"He's gone," she says.

I lean my elbows on the nurse's desk for balance. "He *died*?"

"No, idiot. He's in surgery." She rolls her eyes, then pats my hand, the way my mother would.

Of course, I want to shove this news into Nancy's face like a pie. I have to wait first. Make sure the surgery goes well and Frank's out of the woods. Then a strange thing happens. I lose my taste for revenge. I don't really care about Nancy. It's not about her. It's only about Frank.

That night in the call room, between a barrage of pages—Nancy has once again honored me with the privilege of being her screener—I think about my mother. I think of how much she must worry about her family. I know she prays for all of us. Then, even though I've sort of pushed religion aside since I started medical school, I decide to pray for Frank. I'm not in very good standing at the moment, so I'm not sure my prayer will be heard. But I figure praying can't hurt. So I pray. I ask God to help Frank through the surgery.

The next couple of days waste me. The nights I'm on call, I eke out a couple hours of sleep, but never consecutively. By the time I finish prerounding Nancy's patients at five-thirty, I can barely stand. I'm back on her good side, though. She sees how hard I work and notices that I actually help her more than get in her way. Plus, I greet her every morning with a Starbucks venti latte and a glazed doughnut, my treat.

Her cheeks puffed out like a chipmunk's, she slurps her latte and, with a foam mustache riding her upper lip, says, "Tony, if you think you can win me back with coffee and junk food, you're right."

Rotation one. Day four. I get a page. It's from the fifth-floor nurses' station. *Come to 507. Bring your tern. No emer.*

"We're wanted in 507," I tell Nancy.

Nancy does it again for the second time in four days. Her lips twitch and slide into that weird narrow uptick that may be a smile. "Let's book."

She barrels down the hall. I speed-walk to keep up. She's like a human boulder on wheels. In a flash we hit 507. Nancy, her breathing rolling out in huffs loud as drumbeats, blocks the doorway. I stretch and peek over the top of her head.

Frank, IV tubes stabbing him everywhere, lies in the hospital bed. He looks even thinner, paler, but astonishingly, his cheeks shine pink, as if someone has dabbed them with makeup. A woman in mom jeans and a heavy sweater sits at his bedside. He catches my eye. He speaks without moving his lips. "There he is."

The woman cranes her neck. "Please, come in."

I squeeze by Nancy, whose head has begun to rotate. She grunts as I move by her. The room smells of Lysol.

"You did it," I say.

"I feel like shit," Frank rasps.

"He did well," the woman says. "You're gonna be fine, Dad."

"This your daughter?"

"Dottie," Frank says.

"Nice to meet you."

Dottie presses my hand between both of hers. Her eyes fill up. "You saved his life," she says. "Thank you, Dr. Youn."

A groan from the hall. Nancy. No doubt gagging on her doughnut.

I touch Frank's shoulder, which feels as brittle as a bread stick. "Hang in there, Frank. You're on your way. Proud of you."

He sniffs, holds up a tubed hand. "You say hi to your mom," he says.

Later that night, lying in the call room, staring at Nancy's pager, mercifully silent for almost three minutes, I replay my first week as a medical student in the hospital. Two thoughts spin through my mind.

The first is a quote by Hippocrates: "It is more important to know what sort of person has a disease than to know what sort of disease a person has."

The second comes out of the mouth of Intern Nancy. As we walked away from Frank's room, she whispered loud enough for the entire hospital staff to hear, "*Dr.* Youn, my ass."

IN THE END, after our two months together, Nancy admits grudgingly that of all the medical students she's worked with, I have been, by far, the least pain in her balls. She rewards me with a high grade and glowing recommendation. I'm thankful for that and for clarifying what I already know for my future: I have no interest in dealing with disorders of the heart, liver, pancreas, kidney, and spleen—I don't find human physiology and how organs work all that fascinating—and I will not pursue a career in internal medicine.

As it turns out, neither will Nancy.

Nancy will change career paths and become an orthodontist.

I can see her now, plowing her fingers into strangers' mouths and sadistically bending and tightening small strips of metal around their disfigured and mangled teeth until they squeal.

I've no doubt that she's happy.

13

"Miracle of Birth Occurs for 83 Billionth Time!"

Clinical rotation two.

Obstetrics-gynecology.

I love babies. Who doesn't? But I will never be a baby doctor.

No offense, Dad. Nothing personal. It's the lifestyle. It's just not me. I always saw you as a great ob-gyn. A warrior. A hero. A champion. You kept our phone number listed and gave it out to all your patients, just in case. They took you up on that. They would call our home days, nights, weekends, and holidays. One Saturday night, I'm sixteen, hanging out in our basement playing *Super Mario Brothers* with my nerdy friends, and the phone rings.

"Hello?" I cradle the receiver into my neck so as not to jar my controller.

"Dr. *Youn!*" a frantic woman shrieks.

"No, this is Tony—"

"GET THIS FUCKING BABY OUT OF ME! IT HURTS LIKE HELL! *AHHHH!*"

"Dad, it's for you."

I place the receiver down with a clatter and return to the game. Screaming mothers in labor don't faze me. I'm used to these calls.

I'm also used to hearing my dad leave the house in the middle of the night, the wheels of his car crunching down our driveway, enduring his crankiness due to exhaustion and overwork, and accepting his absence at school events because he's been called away to perform an emergency C-section. And while I am awed by the miracle of birth, I tend to embrace the sentiment put forth in a headline found in the satirical newspaper *The Onion:* MIRACLE OF BIRTH OCCURS FOR 83 BILLIONTH TIME!

I won't be going into the family business.

DAY ONE.

The night before.

I practice suturing.

Every night for at least an hour, as I have for the last three months, I stitch.

I started with a rudimentary suture kit I picked up from my dad. Over time I advance. I head over to the hospital and collect packets of old sutures the lab guys are about to toss in the trash.

I work through a half-dozen knots, beginning with a surgeon's knot we saw demonstrated first year. I maneuver over and over and in and around the clamp called a needle driver. I manipulate all of the knots with ease and master all of the instruments until they feel like a part of my hand. Then I stitch some more.

I practice on a pig's foot.

I keep Porky's piggies in my freezer.

I stuff the foot in a Ziploc bag between a frozen pizza and a pint of Ben & Jerry's Cherry Garcia.

One night while we're snuggling on the living room couch, allegedly watching an old movie on TV, Amy announces that she has a craving for ice cream. She charges into the kitchen and rummages around inside the freezer. She returns dangling the Ziploc bag containing Porky's foot.

"Explain," she says.

"Oh, that. It's my lucky pig's foot."

"Am I supposed to rub it and make a wish?"

I snag her hand. "Worked for me."

I reel her back onto the couch and tell her that one of the gunners in my anatomy class told me that the skin of a pig comes closest to approximating the texture of human skin. When our local supermarket meat department sells out of pig's feet or misses a weekly shipment, I go for the next closest thing—a chicken breast.

So every night I practice suturing on my pig's foot or chicken breast.

I know in our rotations that doctors will not require us to remove a gallbladder. I'm doubtful we'll be called on to take out an appendix.

I do know they expect us to suture.

I'll be ready.

I believe in practice—putting in the time—and discipline. Always have. Whether I'm playing the same chord on my guitar until my fingers cramp up, or hitting a thousand backhands, or spending hours and hours suturing a pig's foot, when I'm called on to perform, I want to be prepared. No, that's not right. I *need* to be prepared. I refuse to be that medical student who excels in the classroom but screws up in the field.

I also pride myself on my manual dexterity.

That's why I'm shocked at how clumsy I am the first time I pick up a suture kit. I feel like I have ten thumbs. It takes me a full hour to get the hang of the surgeon's knot. Once I do, I practice it so many times that I can tie the knot blindfolded. I offer to demonstrate on Amy. She declines. Wuss.

THE OB-GYN ROTATION feels like a reality show.

Day one. Our intern hands us each a checklist of procedures we need to observe or perform in order to pass the rotation—perform cervical checks, rupture membranes, attend a cesarean section, and assist in a designated number of natural births, meaning catch a bunch of kids.

Ever the vigilant student, I study the huge dry-erase board at the labor and delivery nurses' station that displays the patients' names and the stage of labor they're in. On call nights, I locate the patient who's furthest along, dash into the delivery room, introduce myself to patient and doctor, get into a squat, receive the baby, then hose down my shoes—newborns arrive into this world with a splash of goo, guck, ooze, warm fluid, and the edible though not quite delicious placenta. Or so I'm told. I've never been tempted. Perhaps someday when I'm a father. As an appetizer with fava beans and a nice Chianti. After the requisite amount of oohing and ahhing, I leave mother, child, and sometimes father, retire to the call room, and add one more check to my list.

One day I get the call.

I drop onto a stool into receiving position as the delivering mom hits high notes only a dog can hear and pushes her baby out into my awaiting mitts.

"Yes!" I say, thrilled that I've caught the baby properly and successfully handed the newborn off to the doc. I scream also because, with this birth, I meet my quota for the required number of natural births I have to assist.

"Good job, Tony," says Dr. Singer, the attending physician.

"Thank you, Doctor. Well, congratulations. Beautiful baby." I start to leave.

"Hold on," Dr. Singer says. "You still need to stitch up her episiotomy."

Not sure why he's picked me to suture up the small incision he's made in this particular woman's vagina, but I'm not going to complain.

"You ready for this, Tony?"

I picture my pig's foot. "Totally."

I'm ready but nervous. I realize this is the first time I've sutured anything but frozen meat. I take a deep breath, close my eyes, and visualize myself suturing.

You've done this a thousand times, Tony. Ten thousand times. This is a small tear. Nothing to it. Piece of cake.

I open my eyes. I'm not even consciously aware of starting. Within seconds, I'm *into* it. With Dr. Singer guiding me, I begin by tying a surgeon's knot. Then, slowly, I start suturing. Smoothly. Effortlessly. Flawlessly.

"He's good," the mom says, nuzzling her two-minute-old baby.

"He is," Dr. Singer says. "You've got surgeon's hands, Tony. And great dexterity."

"Thank you. I practice a lot. I bought my own pig's foot. Got it in the meat department at Kroger."

"Nice. A lot of students aren't aware of the similarities of the fleshy membranes in a woman's vagina and a pig's foot."

"The texture's surprisingly similar."

"Although once you get into the actual *folds*—"

"Guys," the mom says, "I'm right here."

I stitch on in silence.

FUNNY WHAT FREAKS you out.

Of course, you never see it coming. That's partly what freaks you out. The element of surprise.

One of the last days of my ob-gyn rotation.

I've met all my requirements, finished checking off everything on my list. I join a pack of med students and follow them into a delivery room to observe a woman in active labor. I walk in as the mom— attractive, young, her face drenched in sweat, sitting up in stirrups— begins to push. She grunts, groans, screams, and heaves forward with her pelvis. The baby begins to crown. The air crackles with excitement. But I am grossed out.

Because she's got six toes on each foot.

Two pinkies on each foot. Doubles. Four pinkies in all.

She's pushing out her baby with every last ounce of her strength, she's yowling, swearing, huffing, and all I can think is *My God, she has six toes.*

I cannot take my eyes off her feet.

It's like I've wandered into a sideshow at the circus.

That's wrong. That's not fair. I'm sure she's a wonderful, lovely person. But—

Six toes?

What about the baby?

Will her baby have six toes? What about fingers? Will the baby have two pinkie fingers? Or two thumbs? Or two middle fingers? Maybe this kid will grow up to be a super freak and be able to flip off four people *at the same time.*

What is wrong with me? I have to stop staring at this woman's six toes and become a professional. Right now. I'm sure that everyone in here is staring at *me* staring at her. I sneak a glance around the room.

Everyone is staring at her toes. We're all so focused on the woman's feet that I hope one of us snaps out of it and remembers to catch the baby.

In the realm of the unusual, I doubt that a woman with six toes giving birth will rank as the most bizarre thing I will ever see in my life, especially if I spend longer than ten minutes on the Internet. I've already encountered the teratoma, a cancerous mass with its own teeth and wisp of Troll doll hair, and gazed at photos of the guinea worm, a parasite that burrows into the flesh and has to be wound out over a stick, but for some reason, seeing the six-toed mom creeps me out. Go figure.

Finally, the baby, a butterball, flies out of the womb as if kicked down a waterslide. We duck to avoid the splash—ob-gyn students should be issued ponchos instead of scrubs—cluster around her, and deliver a group gasp.

Five toes. Five fingers.

The attending nurse gently lays the baby on the mom's breast (only two of those) and pulls the thin white monogrammed hospital sheet over her feet.

I feel as if I've made this whole thing up, as if the mom's six toes existed only in my mind. One by one we straggle out of the delivery room. I'm the last to leave. Something stops me. The hairs on the back of my neck bristle. I turn back. At that moment, the mom shoves her foot out of the sheet. She wiggles—

Six freaking toes!

Like a hand shooting out of a grave.

No. I will never become a baby doctor.

14

If You Don't Cut, You Suck

Clinical rotation three.

General surgery.

Surgeons, I'm told, call their corner of the hospital world the home of the gods. They revel in their motto: "To cut is to cure."

Or as Shelly the gunner warns me after completing her surgery rotation, if you're planning on becoming a doctor other than a surgeon, you're not becoming a doctor at all. She, of course, plans to become a surgeon.

I walk the corridor with Intern Dan, lean, lithe, muscles rippling through his scrubs, aloof soap-star looks, a hundred-dollar haircut sculpted in place by *product* assuring that his flowing perm shall remain impervious to hurricane-force winds, a tiptoe walker and low talker, so low I have to strain to hear. Dan doesn't waste any time.

"You gonna be a surgeon?"

"Yes. I think so. I'm leaning that way."

"It was a yes-or-no question."

"I'm strongly considering it."

Dan slows up, plops a condescending hand on my shoulder. "It's the only way to go." He speaks so softly that I find myself trying to read his lips.

"I hear you. It's just that, you know—"

"What?"

"No, no, nothing. With these rotations, you get to sample—"

"Sample? Sheeeet."

Dan plucks a limp orange Stimudent from his pocket and starts picking his teeth like a rancher.

"If you don't cut," he murmurs, low, "you suck."

DAY ONE. EIGHT A.M.

Tim, Shelly the gunner, and I sit in the hospital cafeteria an hour before our daylong orientation, during which we will watch videos detailing the rules of surgery, including the proper way to put on our scrubs and where and how to stand during operations. Shelly and I scarf a breakfast of bagels hard as hockey pucks, cream cheese that spreads and tastes like spackle, and scrambled eggs that bounce. We wash it all down with murky lukewarm coffee. Tim, his complexion wan, his motions jerky, eats nothing. He sips orange juice, eyes front and vacant.

"The orthopedic surgeons make the real money—three, four hundred K a year," Shelly says, scraping eggs onto the fat half of her bagel with a knife. "They're studs. The jocks of medicine. Smart, too. Like that hottie Intern Dan. Right, Tim?"

"I guess," he says.

"They make that much?" I say.

"Oh, easy."

"But that shit, man, that's not even surgery," Shelly says, flagging her fork like a conductor's baton. "That's like carpentry."

Tim coughs.

"I was talking to Eddie Graham? You know him? Fourth-year? Former lacrosse player? Anyway, he did a monthlong orthopedic elective. *Insane.* You wear like an astronaut's suit. You take these spikes, jam them into the unconscious patient's knee, and pound away, bang, bang, bang. Every time you whack the thing, bone splinters, chunks fly everywhere, bone juice spurts and splatters over everything, and blood gushes, whoosh. It's hilarious."

Shelly takes a massive bite of bagel and egg, somehow shoving the whole half into her mouth at once. "You know the best part? The accessories. You have to wear these boots, like waders, because you literally slosh through a river of bone juice. Plus, you have to wear waterproof scrubs *over* your scrubs. And goggles thicker than regular goggles. They're like a splash shield. By the end of the day, they're completely caked with bone juice—"

"Can you *not*!" Tim glares at Shelly, his eyes glazed.

"You look green," I say.

"You should eat something," Shelly says to Tim, chewing with her mouth open.

"Jesus," Tim says. He presses his palm into his forehead, mops up a lake of sweat.

"He's squeamish," I say.

"A tad," Tim says.

"He's not that great with his hands, either," I say.

"I flunked shop class in high school. I have stone fingers." In misery, he pushes away his orange juice. "How am I gonna get through this?"

"Tell them you're gonna be a shrink," Shelly says.

"Oh, that's a good idea," Tim says. "Then Intern Dan, that hottie, will flunk me out of my surgery rotation, and I'll end up doing my residency at Cal State Magic Mountain."

"I could be a surgeon," I say.

"Oh, in a heartbeat," Shelly says. "It's so sexy."

"My father would be overjoyed. I'm not orthopedic material, though."

"True, dat," Shelly says. "You need more bulk, mister. They would not let you into their little jock fraternity. You're not their type."

"I know. I'm just a scrawny Asian nerd."

"You're not scrawny," Tim says. He shivers, moans, and lowers his head onto the table, his reflection weaving in the orange juice glass.

. . . .

ORIENTATION GOES ON for eight hours. Shelly claims a seat in the front row, takes copious notes, asks thoughtful questions, and ass-kisses everyone in sight. Tim hides out in the back, a mute for the day, rocking his head in his hands, fighting to remain upright in the darkened room. I sit behind Shelly, watch, learn, memorize six basic rules—

- We must change into scrubs before crossing a large red line on the floor separating the OR from the rest of the world. I fear that this line is electrified and will fry anyone who dares to cross in street clothes.
- We must wash our hands for at least five minutes before each surgery with a special antibacterial soap that not only kills every germ floating anywhere near your flesh but chafes your skin until it resembles reptile hide buffed with an electric sander.
- We must wear goggles. Wraparound welder's glasses similar to the ones we strapped on in shop class. This causes Tim a painful high school memory of attempting to make a wallet.
- We must familiarize ourselves with the surgery we will attend. If we walk in unprepared, the resident or attending surgeon will humiliate us, abuse us, and then boot us out of the OR.
- We must learn to keep our hands above our waist at all times. This restricted area above the belt is known in the OR as the sterile field. The moment you inadvertently or surreptitiously drop your hands out of the field, I expect lights to flash, alarms to blare, guards to appear. If you have a sudden uncontrollable urge to itch below the belt, don't. Bite your lip and suck it up.
- Finally, and most important, we must learn how to stand during surgery. Never lock your knees while standing in the operating room. This increases your chances of fainting, swooning, falling, and smashing your head on the floor, or worse, fainting and falling face-first into the patient's cut-open belly. It has happened.

. . . .

THE NIGHT AFTER orientation, my father calls. "General surgery good, no?"

"I don't know, Dad. It's early. The first day. I have to think about it."

"Think about *what*? What else you do? Huh?"

"No, it's great. But I also like the idea of family practice—"

I may as well have said that I like the idea of becoming a serial killer.

"*Family practice?* Work all day, all night, weekend, make no money. Go broke! Surgery only thing. Psychiatry? No. Too many crazy people. Pediatrics? No. Little kids, little dollah. Surgery! One proceejah, two thousand dollah!"

"You make a lot of sense. I'll definitely think about it."

"Fine. Think. Then do surgery. Trust Daddy."

I hang up, wondering how many other sons actually disappoint their fathers by becoming doctors.

FOR THE NEXT several weeks I accompany Intern Dan during a series of brief, uninteresting, even dull surgeries. He snips flesh for biopsies, removes appendices, repairs hernias, drains cysts. Nothing approaching sexy. One day, though, halfway through the rotation, he offers me the ultimate treat.

"Tomorrow morning," he whispers low. "The Whipple." He pauses reverentially.

I nod dumbly like I'm new to English. I've never heard of the Whipple.

"You don't have to attend." Dan snorts. "Totally optional."

"Oh, no, no, I definitely want to attend."

"Good answer." Dan chucks me under the chin and backs down the corridor, shooting me with a finger pistol.

That night I read about the Whipple procedure, known formally as a pancreaticoduodenectomy, daunting doctor-speak for the removal of the pancreas and duodenum in patients who have cancers of the gastrointestinal tract. Finally, a meaningful surgery. I'm psyched. What I don't find out until the following morning when I'm about to scrub up is that a typical Whipple surgery takes nine hours.

"Did you say nine hours?" I ask this casually of Keisha, a nurse who looks like Samuel L. Jackson in a dress.

"Did you not notice on the scheduling board that the OR has been booked out all day? Did you not pick that up?"

"I did," I say. "I just wanted to confirm."

"Uh-huh. Well, I run this show. So listen to me. You're looking at nine hours *minimum*. Usually more like *ten*. No recess, no lunch, no bladder breaks. And I hope you're wearing comfortable shoes." She claps her hands with a sudden ferocious crack. I jump two feet. "Let's go!"

She herds me toward the OR, pulling up at the red line as if it's a force field. "Drop your pager on my desk," she says. I hand it over like I've been caught holding a bottle of water by airport security. She places my pager at the edge of her blotter. "I hope you turned it off. Because if your pager beeps during these nine hours?" Keisha opens a desk drawer. She reaches in and pulls out a pair of scissors the size of gardening shears. They gleam like razors. "I will read your page *aloud*, and then I will cut the cord on your pants. You can finish the surgery in your skivvies or nekked. I don't care. Am I clear?"

I nod like a three-year-old.

Keisha faces me, telescopes me with her eyes. She sees something that troubles her. Guilt? Fear? Insurgency? Whatever she sees, she wants to trample it. She snaps the metal jaws of the scissors shut with a clang. "You *understand*, Mr. Youn?"

"Yes, sir. I mean, ma'am."

She eases the scissors onto the desk next to my pager, sits down first with a shimmy and then a thud, and begins to chart the surgery, eyeing me all the way.

She's right.

She saw something.

She saw a petrified medical student picturing himself standing for nine hours in unspeakably embarrassing underwear.

I pray that I've turned off my pager because there is an excellent chance that Amy will page me. We can't go nine hours without contacting each other. We're brimming over with immeasurable amounts of lovey-dovey nonsense that we must communicate. And since I can't get to my pager because of the Whipple, she *will* page me.

It's what she will say that unnerves me. Our pages vary from cute and funny to cute, funny, and pornographic. I can live with cute and funny.

In my mind, I hear my pager beeping. I see Keisha reading my page to herself, slowly shaking her head, then reading Amy's off-color message aloud. I see her lifting herself up from her chair, folding her fingers into the scissors, snapping the menacing metal mouth in the air, walking toward me, bearing down, and cutting the cord that holds up my pants, revealing my—

Joe Boxer underwear. A gift from Amy. Yellow cotton fabric, soft, cozy, covered entirely by Joe Boxer's big smiley cartoon face, little tongue poking up in the corner.

From the Joe Boxer collection called Mr. Licky.

I'm a dead man.

THE WHIPPLE SURGERY begins. The attending physician and chief resident take their places on opposite sides of the patient's abdomen. The junior resident and Intern Dan set up at the patient's thighs. I'm kicked down to the foot of the operating table, where I'm blocked by their six-feet-four-inch frames and am able to see absolutely nothing. I think about the next nine hours. What fun. I just have to keep my hands above my waist, try to squeeze my head in or around these human tree limbs so I can see *something*, and pretend to care. Most of all, pray that Amy forgets to page me.

Twenty minutes in, Intern Dan decides that this Whipple might in fact be *his* moment, his time to shine in front of the attending physician. He must take charge of me, young Mr. Medical Student, for whom he somehow wrangled an invitation to this private party, and use this operation as a teaching opportunity. Dan, serious, his low murmur filled with gravity, begins quizzing me about surgical anatomy to see if I've done my Whipple reading. I have. I answer each question. I see what he's doing. He's trying to look good and trip me up at the same time. Feels like I'm a pledge in a fraternity. We have a name for this line of questioning. We call it pimping. In med school, we have two types of pimping. Pimping meant to teach, we call benign. Pimping meant to humiliate, we call malignant. I'll call Dan's pimping stage five malignant.

Two hours in. Everyone's sweating except me. Thankfully, Dan's run out of questions, or I've frustrated him by knowing the answers. He's gone silent, stony. And with seven hours to go, I still haven't seen much action except for a couple of brief exciting moments of blood and guts. Feels like a waste of time. I begin to drift—

Ten days ago.

I'm on call. My trauma pager goes off. I race out of the call room and meet Dr. Z in the hallway. We blast through the double doors leading into the ER and rush to the trauma bay, where we meet the trauma bay doc, Dr. A.

"Twofer," Dr. A says. "Drunk driver broadsided a retired firefighter. Both in bad shape. I'll take the driver."

Dr. Z and I gown and glove up. I assist him as he works on saving the firefighter's life. Next to us, Dr. A attends the drunk driver, who pelts us with nonstop obscenities and vicious laughter. I concentrate on doing anything I can to help Dr. Z save the firefighter. After a couple of hours, Dr. Z knows there is nothing more he can do. The firefighter succumbs to a massive hemorrhage from a torn aorta. Shaken, Dr. Z calls the time of death and retreats to speak to the firefighter's family members, who have gathered in the waiting room. The drunk driver survives. He screams for higher doses of pain medication. When we refuse, he threatens to call an attorney. At one point he hollers at a nurse to bring him a beer.

I want to punch him in the face. I round on him the next morning. He continues to scream for meds and verbally abuse the nurses. As we prepare to discharge him, I find Dr. Z.

"I need to ask you something. What happens when we discharge him? Can we call the police to pick him up? He committed *murder*."

"We can't do anything," he says.

"It's ridiculous," I say. "It's unfair."

"Tony, we're not cops, and we're not judges. Our job is to provide medical care. Period. Doesn't matter if a patient is a scumbag."

"But doesn't it bother you?"

"A lot. But the more you do trauma, the more you see these things, and the less they affect you. I'm not proud of admitting that, it's just true."

Lying in the call room the next night, I know that the field of general surgery will burn me out. I'm too emotional to deal with the intensity of trauma and other life-and-death surgical procedures on a regular basis. My emotions would cloud my judgments. I would've gone after that drunk driver. I would've called the police. I would've—I don't know what I would've done, really—but I know I could never be as cool, objective, and detached as Dr. Z.

Sorry, Dad, I'm just not made for general surgery.

Now, who can I get to tell him?

"*Retractor!*" the chief resident growls through his mask. "Dan, hold the retractor!"

Back at the Whipple, someone slaps a steel tool resembling a pair of pliers into Dan's hands. He fastens the retractor in place onto the patient, holding back the edges of the surgeon's incisions so that the attending doctor can get a better look at the patient's insides.

"You hold it in place, Tony," Dan whispers. "Keep your hands steady."

Since nobody's moving to make room for me, I snake between Dan and the chief resident, crouch so that I've got a good angle, grab the retractor, and stay locked in that position for the next two hours. Despite being almost on top of the action, I see nothing.

Then it happens.

About an hour into my crucial retractor holding, my pager goes off.

The beep echoes through the operating room. Nobody speaks.

"What is that?"

The chief resident. His gruff voice roars through his mask.

"Tony?" Keisha taps my pager on her desk. She doesn't even try to disguise the wave of malicious joy that's seeped into her voice.

"Yes, see, ah." I've momentarily lost the ability to form actual English sentences. "That would be my pager. I forgot to turn it off. I'm very, very sorry."

"Who would be paging you in the OR?" The resident. This is the first time he's turned in my direction. The only time he's acknowledged my existence.

"I'm sure it's my, you know, girlfriend. It's not important."

Keisha snorts. "I told him if his pager goes off, I'm gonna cut off his pants."

She slides the scissors out of her drawer. She rubs her meaty palm over the blade.

Everyone laughs. The tension in the room leaves.

"Where did you get those?" the chief resident says, a nod toward the scissors. "Looks like a murder weapon."

"Oh, *yeah*." Keisha laughs.

"Read the page," the attending physician says. "Aloud."

My neck goes hot. "I really don't think—" I squeak.

"I'd love to," Keisha says. She clears her throat for effect. She holds my pager up to eye level and pauses as she first reads Amy's message to herself. "Aw. This is so sweet. Very touching. *Hey, Hot Buns, you bringing the hot dog tonight?*"

I nearly drop the retractor into the patient's stomach cavity. The other doctors, and Keisha, lose it.

"Oh, man," the chief resident says. "I'm crying."

"We'd better be quiet or we'll wake up the patient," the attending physician says.

"I think I should snip his pants so we can get a look at that hot dog," Keisha says. She snaps the scissors open.

"Guys," I beg. "Please." The last thing I need is for them to see my smiling Mr. Licky Joe Boxers.

"Feels like he's got something to hide," Keisha says.

"My hand's sweaty," I say. "I don't want to drop the retractor into her stomach."

A second of silence, then another outburst.

"Good one, Tony," the resident says. "Okay, people, back to work."

Instantly, we're back to business. Except for holding the retractor for another hour, I am forgotten.

That night, after standing through ten hours of Whipple surgery, I unwind with a beer at Amy's apartment.

"So, how was the Whipple?" she asks me. "Did it really take nine hours?"

"Ten," I say. "Ten unbelievably boring hours."

"Something exciting had to happen in all that time. Spill."

"Nope," I say, sipping my beer. "Absolutely nothing."

IT's AT THIS point in our relationship, seven months in or so, that I start to feel tiny, intermittent drips of uncertainty. In lonely moments in the call room, leafing through issues of *Cosmo* so old and worn that the covers crack, I bombard myself with questions: Are we moving too fast? Too slow? Are we too comfortable with each other? Are we too good to be true?

And the biggest question of all—

Does she love me?

I love her. I know that. She knows that. I think. I'm pretty sure. I've never actually *told* her I love her, and she's never said she loves me, but—

Yes, *but*. Therein lies that drip . . . drip . . . drip . . . of doubt. Does she feel the same about me? What if she likes me a lot but doesn't quite *love* me the way I love her. What then? Where are we then?

I take action. I decide we need an intimate overnight away from here. But where? I ask the maven of all things romantic.

"So you want to shack up for the night?" Tim says.

"Well, yeah, I was thinking somewhere discreet, quiet, romantic."

"I'm picturing candles, soft music, incense, hot tub in the room."

"Exactly. That's what I'm talking about. Do you know any place?"

"Hi Dee Ho Motel. Grayson and Fifth, downtown. Ask for a Jacuzzi suite. They have a student special every Monday night. Thirty-nine bucks, including tax, cash only. I'm told."

"Is it nice?"

"I hear it's quite nice. I've personally never been."

"Really. Kinda *sounds* like you've been."

"Never." He snaps off his reading lamp. "Mention my name, they'll comp you on the Magic Fingers."

The following Monday night, I whisk Amy away from the grind and intensity of our everyday lives and head off for our romantic getaway. We make a pact. For the next twenty-four hours, all topics are on the table—except school.

Things start with a bang. We get lost. I find downtown with no trouble, but Grayson and Fifth seem never to intersect. The longer we loop around, the sketchier the neighborhood becomes. Finally, by sheer luck, we turn up a blind alley and approach a ratty two-story building in need of immediate remodeling or razing. A precarious neon sign dangles over the front door announcing HI DEE HO. The letters hiss and blink. A green VACANCY sign sits in the window next to a rattrap.

"If you close your eyes," I say, "you'd swear you were in Niagara Falls."

"My eyes have been closed," Amy says. "I'm curious. How much did this set you back?"

"That's the amazing part. Forty bucks, including tax."

"Amazing, all right. I think you got ripped off."

"It can't be as bad inside. Let's try it."

"You go," Amy says. "I might bump into people I know."

I stare at her.

"I'm kidding."

"I knew that. I think. I'm going in." I peer around for potential murderers, see no one suspicious, ease out of the car, and run to the front door. "Cover me," I call back.

Five minutes later, room key in hand, the Ford Tempo stashed in a leaky carport a floor below our room, we push open the door to our Jacuzzi suite. We step a foot into the room and nearly ram into a filthy oversize bathtub slathered on all sides with a brown residue resembling chocolate pudding. A flickering floor lamp with a family of buzzing flies trapped inside the lamp shade teeters next to it. The stench of dirty gym clothes wafts from the bedsheets.

"Aren't you going to carry me over the threshold?" Amy says.

"You're so romantic."

"Actually, my feet are sticking to the floor. Not sure what the sticky stuff is, but I'm not walking in it."

I swoop her off her feet and cradle her in my arms. I take a step and pretend to drop her. She squeals, laughs.

"Amy," I say.

"Yes, Romeo?"

"I love you."

She yanks her head back and looks at me dead-on. For a moment I think she is going to leap out of my arms and sprint out of this room, out of my life.

"I know," she says. "And I love you."

In that moment everything changes, and settles, and soars, and shakes us up. But a weight lifts off my heart.

We kiss. Lips locked, eyes closed, we lurch in the direction of the bed. I know we're getting close because the sour smell that I usually associate with an open PE hamper hits us right between the eyes.

"Put it in reverse, big boy," Amy says, her eyes still closed. "Now slowly, back up to the door, put me down outside, and let's get the hell out of here."

15

Shrink Rap

Clinical rotation four.

Psychiatry.

I fear this rotation. The thought of sitting in an office from nine to five every day, listening to people drone on about their awful parents, inconsiderate children, intolerable husbands, bitchy wives, and boring jobs fills me with terror, the terror that as they reveal their innermost secrets and kinky fantasies, I will fall dead asleep.

"Happens all the time," Shelly the gunner warns me. "You gotta watch yourself. Some poor schmuck's whining about how much his life sucks and you nod off? You will be marked down."

"Tim says shrinks call those people the worried well."

"I call them cash cows. Whatever. Anyway, if you can stay awake, psychiatry is the cushiest rotation. Sign up early tomorrow, try to get Lindstrom, my guy. The best. We both fell asleep. So embarrassing. He snores."

I wake up the next morning with a record-breaking dose of diarrhea. I spend the entire day in a fetal position on the floor of our phone-booth-size bathroom on Flower Street. Note to self. Never eat another bean burrito from a vending machine.

The next day, recovered, I arrive in administration eager to receive my psychiatry rotation assignment and prepare for two months of rest, if not sleep. To my horror, I have been matched with Dr. Levine, the only shrink left, a psychiatrist in private practice with whom I'll be covering the maximum-security prison in Ionia.

This can't be right. What happened to listening to the worried well and their boring problems? What happened to *cushy*? I have to get out of this. I try to get people to switch with me. I find no takers. For some reason they seem put off by the words *maximum-security prison*. I'm stuck. I resign myself. I will be traveling with Dr. Levine to administer antidepressants and provide therapy to hard-core prisoners, the worst of the worst—murderers, rapists, child molesters, and money managers.

"Word of advice," Tim says. "Do *not* fall asleep."

He smiles smugly.

DAY ONE.

I drop my car off at Dr. Levine's condo, and we drive in his car to Ionia maximum-security prison, known as I-Max, thirty miles away. Dr. Levine is a runner, short, trim, and jittery, with a manicured orange Afro and a face flecked with freckles, a cross between Alfred E. Neuman and Carrot Top. But Dr. Levine is anything but a cartoon character or raving comedian. He wears thick horn-rims and speaks quietly and kindly and without a trace of humor.

On the drive up, he tries to put me at ease. "Basically, I listen, say very little, write medications. That's about it."

"Doesn't sound bad."

"It's not, really. I ask how the prisoners are feeling, if they're hearing any voices—"

"Wait. If they're hearing *voices*?"

"Yeah. Pretty common. Among murderers, especially."

"Uh-huh. I'm just going to be a fly on the wall."

"I would. Oh, and avoid looking the murderers in the eye."

We drive the rest of the way in silence. I look out the window and flash on a picture of Shelly and Dr. Lindstrom snoring away in their leather chairs while a member of the worried well whines about her difficult mother. And I have to worry about an ax murderer hearing voices?

How is this fair?

FROM A DISTANCE, you might mistake the cluster of nondescript buildings for a military barracks or boarding school. Closer in, you notice the fence that surrounds the buildings, and as you get closer still, you see not only the added mesh of barbed wire that sits on top of the fence but the mesh on top of *that*, consisting of rows and rows of ferocious, glittering razor blades. In my imagination, fueled by years and years of comic-book reading, I-Max looks like a lumbering, sleeping beast with a mane of gunmetal hair.

Once Dr. Levine announces our names into a call box, the first of what will be three gates clanks open. We drive to gate number two, manned by guards who inspect the car and wave us through to yet another gate, where more guards inspect the car again, even more thoroughly. One slides under the car, holding a taut vibrating wire attached to a small box. I hear him grunting and scraping at the belly of Dr. Levine's dusty Camry. Eventually, he slides out and, from his back, waggles a thumbs-up.

Admitted onto the prison grounds, we pass through several more checkpoints, this time on foot, where we empty our pockets and various guards, male and female, search us, pat us down, feel us up, and electric-baton us. Each checkpoint requires us to show two forms of ID and our medical credentials. At last, searched, scoured, and plucked clean, we walk into an open area somewhere in the center of I-Max, where I feel watched, as if I'm prey.

We head to the medical center, walking across a prison yard where ten inmates play basketball, others lift weights, some play chess, and one lone orange-suited inmate with scraggly blond hair strums a guitar. If I hadn't gone through eight checkpoints, been identified and searched, and seen the razor wire on the fence that surrounds us, I might think I had wandered into an urban park in any city in the United States. The idea that these basketball players, weight lifters, chess players, and guitarist have all committed heinous crimes beyond my imagination and yet are allowed this seemingly carefree time for relaxation, even fun, unnerves me. Their victims will never again play hoops, pump iron, play chess, or hear music. I have no answer and offer no moral judgment. It simply feels unsettling and out of whack.

We spend the bulk of the day in the medical center—a metal table and chair facing two more metal chairs, where Dr. Levine and I sit and talk to inmates. The day passes slowly. The inmates speak softly, sullenly. Most are heavily medicated, their conversations detached. Late in the afternoon, the nurse on duty leads in a slight, frail-looking guy, no more than five-six and 135 pounds. He wears leather restraints on his wrists and steps deliberately and lightly, almost on tiptoe. He twitches and smiles sadly, revealing a smattering of small yellow teeth and wide gaps in his mouth. His thinning hair lies like strings of hay across the top of his head. His forehead is long and goes on forever and is lined with what look like tread marks. He keeps his red face puckered tight, like a weasel's. He sits down at the desk across from me and Dr. Levine. Dr. Levine flips through his chart.

"So, Raymond, how you doing?"

Raymond shrugs, twitches. "Doing fine," he says. "Really well."

"Good," Dr. Levine says. "And the meds?"

"Fine." Raymond twitches again. He pulls his leather-shackled wrists up above the table so he can scratch his nose. "Yeah, working fine since you changed them. I'm not hearing any voices."

"That's good," Dr. Levine says.

"Yeah," Raymond says. "It is."

Twitch . . . twitch . . . twitch.

"Is there anything you want to talk about?" Dr. Levine says. "Anything on your mind?"

Raymond looks at me for the first time. His face goes dark, almost as if a cloud passes over him. His eyes flutter, then open wide. He keeps looking at me, unblinking.

"So, anything you want to discuss?" Dr. Levine asks.

A calm descends over Raymond like a window shade dropping. He pinches his eyes and looks at me, harder. He stares. I squirm. Look away. When I look back, he's still staring.

What do I do? Where do I look? Don't stare at him. Do I pretend to look up something in my notes? Do I flip through his chart and pretend I'm reading? Look *away*.

He keeps staring.

"Raymond?" Dr. Levine says.

He keeps staring.

"Raymond, what's going on?"

He keeps staring.

"How are you feeling? Talk to me."

He keeps staring.

"It's okay, Raymond, you can tell me. What's on your mind? What's going on? What are you feeling right now?"

A beat.

Raymond lunges at me, leaping over the table.

"I'M COMING HOME WITH YOU, PRETTY BOY!" he screams.

I shoot out of my chair. "GAAAAA!" I shout, slamming myself back against the wall.

"I'M COMING HOME WITH *YOU*!"

I see then that his legs are chained to the table and the leather restraints hold back his hands so he can't get close to me. The door flies open, two guards grab Raymond on either side, unchain his legs, lift him off his feet, and carry him out of the room. My entire body, flat against the wall, quivers. My throat is caked shut.

"How did you—?" I croak to Dr. Levine.

"Panic button. Under the table. You okay?"

After a moment I feel the blood return to my face, the quivering stops, and I nod. I stagger away from the wall and sit down.

"You want some water?"

"That would be great. Dr. Levine?"

"Yeah, Tony?"

"This is my first day in this rotation, and I'm just a medical student, but I'm not sure the new meds are working."

For the first time—and only time—in our two-month rotation, Dr. Levine smiles.

Then the door flies open and Raymond, eyes aflame, stands in the doorway. He punches his shackled hands at me.

"I'LL BE WAITING FOR YOU IN THE CAR, CHINA MAN!"

Twitch. Twitch. Twitch.

16

This Is Spinal Tap

Third year. Clinical rotation five.

My last one.

Pediatrics.

The rotation that changes my life.

My attending physician, Dr. Jay Pyle, wears his silver hair long, either flowing down to his shoulders or knotted into a ponytail. His face, lean and red from a lifetime of too much sun and red wine, is cut with kindness and laugh lines. His nose, sharp and strong, veers crookedly to the left, the result of blocking a punt in high school with his face. He played cornerback and ran back kickoffs and made All-City. When he smiles, which is often, he squints and his pale blue eyes twinkle. He was raised in Manhattan, and his accent comes at you hard, with a touch of a patrician lilt; he was a kid of both the Harlem playgrounds, where he played street ball, and the halls of Dalton and the brownstones of the Upper East Side.

We hit it off the first day.

"You're good with your hands," he says, a smile panning from cheek to cheek. "The word's out."

"Really?"

"Oh, yeah. I may have to take advantage of you. Isn't that what I'm supposed to do? Take advantage of my third-years?"

"Absolutely. I'm here to serve."

He grins again. "I'm liking this. All right. Let's begin a little rounding. Watch out for room 223. Baby with strep. FLK."

"FLK?"

"Take a shot. You won't offend."

I picture the letters. "Wild guess. Funny-looking kid?"

Dr. Jay Pyle steps back. "Tony Youn, you have a future in medicine." He slings an arm over my shoulder.

THREE WEEKS IN.

One morning I arrive a half hour before rounds. As I sign in, the charge nurse tells me that Dr. Pyle is already in with a patient on the ward.

"You should get down there," she says. "There's going to be a spinal tap. Something to see."

I enter the room and find Dr. Pyle sitting with a young, frightened couple. The dad holds the mom's hands. They are nodding numbly. Their faces have gone the color of chalk.

"We have to take a sample of the spinal fluid," Dr. Pyle says. "It's the only way to test for meningitis."

The parents look up as I step farther into the room. I half-smile, wave. The parents sit up straighter, wave back.

"There he is," Dr. Pyle says. "So I want to explain what he's going to do. I want you to know exactly what to expect. No surprises." More nodding. These poor people look as white as mimes. "He's going to stick a four-inch-long needle into your baby's back, right between the bones of the spine, and he's gonna draw out a small sample of spinal fluid. We send it right down to the lab, they do a culture, and we'll find out what's going on."

Wait a minute.

Did Dr. Pyle just say *he*?

He's going to stick a four-inch needle into your baby's spine?

He as in . . . *me*?

"How you feeling, Tony?"

"Good. Great. I feel great."

I think I'm going to be sick.

I feel warm and my head is spinning.

I'm actually doing this?

My first medical procedure ever is going to be a spinal tap on a four-month-old?

What doctor in the world would trust a third-year medical student to perform a spinal tap? Dr. Pyle has to be nuts. If I were a doctor—*when* I'm a doctor—would I ever let a medical student do this? Hell, no.

"Tony is unbelievable," Dr. Pyle says. "He's gifted. You're in great hands. I'd trust him with my own kid."

My emotions begin to swirl, switching back and forth. Simultaneously, I'm—

Nervous as hell. Immensely proud. Nervous as hell. Incredibly excited. Nervous as hell. Unspeakably thrilled. Nervous as hell. Amazingly pumped. And—

NERVOUS AS HELL.

"Let's scrub up and do this. It's all you, Tone."

Dr. Pyle puts a charge of confidence in me that I have not felt from anyone. It fills me up, seeps into me, pushes under my skin.

I'm still a wreck.

I have no time to picture the procedure in my head, to see myself inserting the needle, drawing out the fluid. I have no time to *prepare*.

Okay, what's the worst that can happen?

I can miss, puncture a blood vessel or hit a vertebra, causing permanent paralysis—

This is not helping.

I feel light-headed. Dizzy. Nauseated. Like I'm going to faint. Yep. I'm going to pass out. The medical student doing the spinal tap is going to fall, boink, right onto the floor. Perfect. Dr. Pyle is going to look like a total and complete jerk. And I will end up failing out and sharing a shrink practice with Tim.

Tony, get ahold of yourself. You can do this. This is your moment.

I look at Dr. Pyle.

He grins. I want to say to him, "Seriously? You trust me to do this?", but the look on his face tells me everything. He has no doubt. I think about Frank Fremont and how I convinced him to have the surgery that saved his life, and I think about suturing up the episiotomy and practicing for months before that with a pig's foot, and I know I'm ready. I know I can perform this spinal tap, that I can perform it well, and that I will perform many more procedures in my lifetime; this is merely the first. I no longer feel flush and unsteady, and nervous as hell leaves, replaced by a sort of adrenaline-pumping nervousness bordering right on the edge of something I might actually call . . . a rush.

Dr. Pyle holds the baby. He lays his tiny body down in perfect position, and I insert the needle into his back and pull it out, and the fluid we see is clear, and the baby is crying, but I'm grinning and Dr. Pyle shrugs proudly, as if he had no worries, none, ever, and all I feel is total and complete exhilaration. I want to shout in triumph, but I see the terrified looks on these young parents' faces, kids really, only slightly older than me, people who might someday *be* me, and maybe Amy, too, and all I hope for is that the culture comes back clean and shows no meningitis and that their baby will be all right.

And when the result does come back negative, I feel for one fleeting moment as if I'm on the team, as if I belong.

As soon as my shift is over, I call Amy and tell her about my surprise spinal tap and the rush I felt. She whoops into the phone, then after we talk for a while, she goes silent and I can tell she's crying. I want to celebrate with her, but I know she has a brutal PBL domain exam on Monday and an inhumane amount of material to digest before then. Been there.

With a day off, I decide to fire up the old Ford Tempo, hit the road to Greenville, and spend some quality time at home with the 'rents.

The truth is that while I'm flying high at this moment, overall, I feel lost. I'm in the middle of my fifth and final clinical rotation and I have no idea what kind of doctor I want to be. Our school designs the rotations to allow us to sample the possibilities, to set us on a path so that in fourth year, we can "choose our own adventure." But I'm more confused now than ever.

As I drive, I consider my options again, for the millionth time.

Pediatrics? My father's voice blasts through the car's speakers: *Tiny people, tiny dollah!* I love working with Dr. Pyle, but I'm not cut out to be a pediatrician.

Surgery? I hear my father's voice again, but this time he's pushing me: *One proceejah, big dollah!* But the road to specialized surgery is so long, grueling, and intense. I'm not made that way. And clearly, I'm not orthopedic-surgery material. General surgery? I refuse to end up like Dr. Z or Dr. A, fifty-five years old, sleeping in the hospital, stumbling out of the call room at three o'clock in the morning to deal with a trauma. I will burn out if I don't first flip out.

Obstetrics and gynecology? No.

Internal medicine? I can't see myself spending my life investigating the secretions of the pancreas. As fascinating as that may be.

Psychiatry?

I'M COMING HOME WITH YOU, PRETTY BOY!

Tim, have fun.

I don't see myself in any of these fields. I feel stuck.

I suppose I could go into family practice. It's so easy. Three-year residency, and the last year is a walk in the park. You're essentially done in two years, no pressure, and you're left with a ton of free time. I like to dabble. I can get more serious about my guitar, maybe join a band. Maybe I'll even get an MBA on top of my MD. True, you don't make a lot of money at first, but my other interests could lead to more money coming in. When I measure money versus lifestyle, money doesn't always win. Why not take it easy? I think I've found it. Family practice. Perfect for me.

Great. I have a plan.

I'm going into family practice.

I know that my father desperately wants me to become a surgeon. Sorry, Dad. I'm a grown man. I make my own decisions. This is *my* life.

Isn't it?

WE'RE AT HIS tennis club, batting balls back and forth. It's been a while since I picked up a racket, probably not since high school. I played so much back then that I could hit winners with my eyes closed. No more. Today I'm a hacker. Balls slice off the rim of the racket, squirt out of bounds. I whack my forehand with so much power that balls sail over the back line and bang off the back wall, or I turn my wrist too far over and balls whap into the net. My dad, quicker and stronger than you'd think, takes his tennis seriously. He lunges at balls you swear he'll never get to and returns them with nasty topspin. He's ferocious. With him, there's no such thing as a simple volley. You always have to be on top of your game. We don't keep score, we just hit. Words to live by.

I remember once when I was a kid, twelve or thirteen, my dad asked me to hit some balls with him one Saturday afternoon. I didn't refuse— I'd learned that lesson—but I volleyed with no enthusiasm. I jogged after balls he lobbed, I didn't run. I served lazily. I hit a few underhand. I didn't want to be there, so I didn't try.

After one rally in which I whiffed at a ball and then laughed, my dad stopped and stared at me across the net. He snorted. He picked up a handful of balls, turned his back to me, and began hitting balls to himself off the back wall. He hit the balls to himself again and again as if I weren't there. I stood alone on my side of the court and waited for him to return to volleying with me. He never did. He hit a bucket of balls to himself, then turned and walked to the car. I ran alongside him. He didn't speak to me until the next day. I learned two quick lessons. First, no matter what you do, do it well, with enthusiasm and heart. Second, respect your father.

Now, over ten years later, we hit to each other. I'm in every rally, or trying to be. I'm stinking, but I'm trying. He knows I am.

"You rusty," he says, not unkindly.

"I know," I say. "Frustrating."

"No time to practice. This good, though. Good workout."

"Yep." I grunt through a serve, which finally zips into the corner of the server's box and past him for an ace.

"Ah!" my father yelps, points the racket at me happily.

"Dad," I say. "I've been thinking about general surgery."

"Good field," my father says. "Transplant better. Or vascular surgery. Or neurosurgery. Or cardiothoracic surgery. Or colorectal surgery—"

"I know. And I like surgery. It's just that—" I can't finish.

"What?"

"I've been seriously thinking about family practice."

"Family practice? Instead?"

It feels as if the temperature has suddenly dropped thirty degrees.

"Also. In addition. In addition to general surgery. Keep my options open."

"Family practice, you make no money."

"I know. But the lifestyle is good. I think, you know, it's what I want."

The words hang out there, refusing to fade. My father tips his cap. The bill falls over his eyes. He scratches the back of his neck furiously. He pulls his cap back in place and walks to his position at the baseline.

"Your serve," he says.

THE REST OF the evening is chilly. We sit at dinner, the three of us, Dad, Mom, and I, passing one another bowls of food my mom has made, the only sounds the slurping of soup and the clicking of chopsticks. My mother tries to get the conversation rolling. She asks about my room-mates, my house, and casually wonders if I've been seeing anyone.

"No," I say, staring into my soup. "Nobody."

Yeah, that's all I need on top of the family-practice disaster. If I ever bring up Amy, mention that I have a girlfriend—a white girlfriend—I might as well start interviewing for another family.

"Plenty of time for girls after finish school." My father's mantra since fifth grade.

"You do have to concentrate on your studies," my mother says.

"Oh, I know Tony," Dad says, smirking, about to tell the punch line to an old family joke that nobody finds funny, least of all me. "He gonna marry a blondie." He roars at his own joke.

Of course, it is no joke. It's a thinly veiled threat.

So, how am I doing this weekend? Let's check my vitals.

I've rejected surgery.

I have a girlfriend.

Who is not Korean.

But hey, at least she's not a *blondie*.

I'm on life support.

I CAN'T SLEEP. I lie in my bedroom in my parents' house, the bedroom where I grew up. My mom has left everything in place here, like a room cordoned off in a museum—my books on the shelves, flanked by high school awards and trophies, my posters on the wall, clothes I will never wear still hanging in the closet. It's my room, but it feels as if it belongs to a stranger.

I bring my covers up to my chin, toss and turn in my twin bed, more uncomfortable even than my threadbare mattress on Flower Street. Maybe it was a mistake to come home. I felt homesick, yet whenever I come home, I regress. I'm a third-year medical student. I'm going to be a doctor, but within five minutes of being home, I become twelve. I want to please my parents, I want them to be proud of me. But at a certain point, you have to grow up. You have to make your own decisions. I'm sorry if my father is disappointed. I will have to accept that. And when I finally tell them about Amy, they'll have to accept that, too. If it means they kick me out of the family, so be it.

Two A.M. Still wide awake. My ankles hang over the bed. I'm tangled in my covers. I can't find a comfortable position. I feel claustrophobic in my own room. How did I sleep in this bed for so many years?

Three A.M. Finally starting to fade. Each one of my father's surgery suggestions dances in front of me, pounding like a drum—*transplant surgery, vascular surgery, neurosurgery, cardiothoracic surgery, colorectal surgery.*

I lose myself in my father's voice. My eyes slowly close. I start to float away—

I hear something at my door.

A scraping. A clawing. The door creaks open. My eyelids flutter. I'm coming out of the twilight state between dreaming and being awake.

Someone is coming into my room.

I half-open my eyes and catch a glimpse of the clock: 5:13 A.M.

"Move over."

My father. Standing over me. He's fully clothed. His breath, warm and smelling of green tea, brushes my face. "Move over," he says again. "Daddy needs to talk."

Obediently, I scoot to my right, sliding over as far into the wall as I can. My father lies down next to me, his weight making the twin bed sag. He folds his hands on his stomach. He says nothing. We both stare at the ceiling.

"Tony."

I swallow. "Yes?"

"Daddy has been . . . thinking."

I wait.

"If you want to go into family practice, it's okay. Daddy understands. You do what makes you happy."

"Okay," I whisper.

"Daddy just wants you to be happy."

"Thank you. That means a lot."

"You go broke. You probably have to move back home. But." He sighs, sniffs. "That's fine. If it's what you really want, it's okay."

"Thank you," I say again.

He reaches over and touches my hand. "Daddy," he says, his voice cracking, "is very proud of you."

17

Mommy Dearest

Nothing ever happens in pediatrics.

Until one night.

The night that changes my life.

2:23 A.M.

The time has been burned into my memory like a brand.

I'm half asleep in the call room. My pager goes off. I swing off my cot and hit the corridor. Dr. Pyle, an odd look on his face, waits outside the call room. "We've got to roll," he says.

"Where?"

"PICU."

"Pediatric ICU. Isn't that unusual?"

"Extremely."

He starts to jog, then in seconds, we're sprinting. We arrive at the elevator. He wails at the buttons. "Elevator's down in the parking garage. Let's take the stairs."

We bolt toward the end of the corridor, hit the stairwell, take the four flights to PICU two stairs at a time.

"What did the page say?" I gasp, falling half a flight behind Dr. Pyle.

He hesitates. "Infant," he says. "Attacked by an animal."

I stop for a split second at the landing.

"You coming?"

"Yes," I say, and push myself to run faster.

We reach the fourth floor, burst through the door from the stairs, and crash through the doors of the PICU. A nurse points to a corner room. For some reason, perhaps because of the number of people spilling out of the room, we ease our sprint to a speed walk, the soles of our running shoes slapping on the recently waxed floor. We squeeze by two women blocking the door, one dressed professionally in a pantsuit, incongruous at this hour, the other my age or younger, dirty-blond hair, tight jeans, tight top, face fiery and scraped, eyes glassy and distant. She's possibly high. Several people crowd around an infant's hospital bed, a pediatric surgeon, two nurses, a respiratory technician, a pediatric anesthesiologist.

"Hey, Joe." Dr. Pyle greets the pediatric surgeon. "What happened?"

The pediatric surgeon backs away from the crowd around the baby's bed. He speaks out of the side of his mouth as if he doesn't want to be heard. "I've never seen anything like it." He clears his throat. "Eight-month-old boy. Mom went out to a bar. Left the baby alone in their trailer with their pet raccoon."

I gasp.

Dr. Pyle lays his hand on my arm. "Don't tell me. No cage?"

"Shoe box." The pediatric surgeon pinches the bridge of his nose with two fingers. He speaks to the floor. "She comes back and finds the raccoon eating the baby's face."

I feel the floor sway. I reach out for the wall to keep my balance.

"My God," Dr. Pyle says. "How's the baby?"

"He's going to live. Both eyes are intact. But the nose, one cheek, upper and lower lips, gone. They're tubing him now. The plastic surgeon's on his way. We don't see any other injuries." He pauses. "He's lucky to be alive."

"Yeah," Dr. Pyle says. "What kind of life is that going to be?"

A rustle at the door, and the two women step in. The pediatric surgeon tilts his head toward them. "The mom and the social worker."

"I think I can pick out the mom," Dr. Pyle says. "Is there a dad?"

Joe shrugs. "I don't know. Cops are on their way."

Dr. Pyle whistles softly. "Who the hell leaves her kid alone with a raccoon?"

A commotion near the baby's bed. The anesthesiologist finishes inserting a breathing tube and steps away. Dr. Pyle moves over to talk to him, leaving an opening to the bed. I edge away from the wall and step closer to the baby. I want to see. I take one more step.

Dear God.

The baby's face has been torn off. There is a gaping hole where his nose used to be. He has no mouth, no lips. His gums appear through a gap in his flesh. His right ear has been ripped away, and half of his left ear hangs torn and jagged. His eyes, beautiful and blue, stare wide open. I stare into them and I say aloud, "Oh, God," and a lump rises into my throat. I feel nauseated, and I stumble out of the room and into the hall. I bend to my knees and bury my head in my hands.

In a moment Dr. Pyle squats next to me. "You all right?"

I blow out a slow breath. "I don't know. I honestly don't know." I turn my head toward him, exhale again.

His face has turned red. "In my twenty-five years of being a doctor, this is, hands down, the most horrifying thing I've ever seen."

I lower myself onto the floor. Dr. Pyle sits next to me. "There's nothing we can do. The baby's stable. The rest is up to the plastic surgeon. It's all him now. So. Here's what I'm going to do." He studies my eyes as if he's checking my vitals. "I'm going back over to the call room. I'm gonna try to get some rest. If I stay here, I'm afraid I'll say something to that kid's mom that I'll regret."

"I wish you'd stay here, then."

Dr. Pyle pops up to his feet. He offers me his hand. I take it, allow him to help me up. "Take the rest of the night off, Tony. I'm dismissing you. Go home. Get some sleep in your own bed. Come back around six. Something else insane happens, I'll page you."

I'm tempted, but only slightly. "I think I'm gonna stick around. I want to see what the plastic surgeon can do. Besides, the call-room bed is more comfortable than my bed at home."

His smile surprises me. "I thought you'd say that. I'll page you if I need you."

The baby's mom comes out of the room, fumbles in a large straw bag, pulls out a pack of cigarettes, jams one into her mouth, and heads toward an exit door.

"I have to get out of here," Dr. Pyle says.

I FIND A spare folding chair and camp out by the nurses' station. I catch a ten-minute power nap and awake at 3:01 A.M. to footsteps echoing in the corridor and a nurse's voice: "That's him. I've seen him on TV."

I look up to see a Ben Affleck clone with stubble, wearing starched scrubs and striding down the hall. He carries a small camera bag. He pulls up at the nurses' station. "I'm Dr. Kanner. Room 411?"

"I'll show you," I say. I offer my hand. "I'm Tony Youn. I'm the medical student on pediatrics tonight. Would you mind if I went in with you and observed?"

He grins. "Nothing happening over there, so your attending stuck you with me?"

"Actually, he sent me home."

Dr. Kanner raises an eyebrow.

"I wanted to see what you can do here," I say.

"A kindred spirit? Welcome to the club, Tony Youn."

We start toward the corner room. As we walk, the door to the stairwell opens at the far end of the hall and whistles shut behind the baby's mom. Even from here, fifty feet away, she lasers us with her eyes. She takes a step, teeters on what I see for the first time are precarious high heels. She arrives at the room ahead of us, folds her lower back into the doorway, and presses her foot into the floor as if she's crushing out a cigarette.

"Mommy dearest?" Dr. Kanner.

"Yes."

"Is she drunk or a complete idiot?"

"I don't know. I haven't had the pleasure."

"I'm an experienced physician. It's possible she's both." Dr. Kanner quickens his pace, pulls ahead of me. I don't know why I'm surprised, but he offers her his hand. "Mrs. Ellison?"

She hesitates, then extends three fingers with inch-long nails painted shocking pink. He tries to find a grip. She withdraws immediately as if she's afraid she'll catch something. "*Miss*," she says, and sniffs. She speaks in a high nasally voice, a trace of a southern accent.

"I'm Dr. Kanner, the plastic surgeon. I've been called in to look at your son."

"I figured. You been on TV, right?"

"Couple times."

"I seen you." She sniffs again, picks at something on her tongue. As she does, she sizes him up. She leans forward and reaches into the back pocket of her skintight jeans. She pulls out a photograph. "This here is Jerome two weeks ago. This is how I want him to look. Exactly like this. No scars. No nothing. Just the way he was."

"Well," Dr. Kanner says, running a hand through his hair.

"That's what you *do*, right? That's your *job*. I mean, you say you're a plastic surgeon. Are you a *good* plastic surgeon?" She looks at me. "Or some kid just starting out." Eyes roaming down Dr. Kanner's entire body. "You look awful young."

"I should examine your son, see what's going on," Dr. Kanner says.

He tries to step past her, but Miss Ellison reaches her arm across the doorway, blocking him at the neck. "You do this shit all the time, right? What do they call it? Face-lifts? You gonna fix my baby's face, right?"

He hands her back the photo. "I'm going to do the best I can. But I understand your baby has had some major deforming injuries."

She blinks, either not understanding or in deep denial.

"Your baby is severely deformed," Dr. Kanner says slowly. "I can only promise you that I will do my very best to make him look as good as I can. As good as humanly possible."

"Well, Dr. Kanner, that sounds like a load of shit. How old are you? How long you been doing this? This your first time? You are a *doctor*, right?"

She practically spits these words in Dr. Kanner's face. I smell the alcohol on her breath then. Dr. Kanner was wrong. She's drunk, an idiot, and an asshole.

"I'm a board-certified plastic surgeon," he says. "You can look me up. I've had all the necessary training and years of experience, and I'm here at three in the morning to take care of your baby. If you want me to go home, you'll have to take that up with the hospital administration. Right now I'm going to do my job, which is to figure out what I can do for your baby. Now, if you don't mind, *Miss* Ellison, get out of my way. Please."

A stare-down.

After ten full seconds, Miss Ellison drops her arm with a slap on her thigh and moves aside, allowing Dr. Kanner and me to pass.

I follow him to the foot of the bed. He scans the baby's body, moves up, and lowers his head over the baby's face. He studies every inch, as focused as a camera, then goes to the sink in the room. He scrubs his hands, pulls on sterilized gloves. He nods toward the supply cabinet. I pull open a drawer. He nods again, and I open some gauze packs and tubes of antibiotic ointment. He walks back to bed, peels open the baby's eyes, murmurs something that almost sounds like a prayer, then squirts an entire tube of ointment over the remains of the baby's face, laying gauze over the exposed areas.

"I'm going to take some pictures in a minute," he says. He drops his hand onto the baby's forehead and caresses his few thin blond hairs. "I'm gonna do my best, little man." He stands straight up, erect as a sergeant, yanks off his gloves, and shuffles into the far corner of the room. He reaches into his shirt pocket, pulls out a pen and small notebook.

"Let me give you an idea of what we're going to do." He looks up at me as if in afterthought. "You had any experience in plastic surgery?"

"No. I'm in my third year, last rotation. I've finished general, but we didn't spend any time on plastic surgery."

"Yeah, I know. I think you miss out. My humble opinion. But that's what fourth year is for."

"Choose my own adventure."

"Exactly. We'll talk. Okay, let's see what we can do." He begins sketching the baby's face on the pad. "You draw?"

"I do, actually."

For the second time since we've met, he lifts an eyebrow. "That will serve you well. There. Our first issue is that he's got a lot of growing to do. That makes the reconstruction even more complicated, as if it weren't complicated enough. For example, I could re-create his nose by flipping down the skin of his forehead."

Dr. Kanner draws an outline of a nose on the baby's face. "But the reconstructed nose probably will not grow with him in an anatomically proportional fashion."

"So, we're looking at further nose reconstruction as he gets older."

"That's almost a given. Our first priority here is to get coverage of his open wounds."

"I see. That way he won't have exposed cartilage and other organs of the face."

"Yep. We're going to need to bring in tissue from another part of his body to remake his lips and mouth. I won't be able to reconstruct his lips and mouth perfectly—"

He sketches in lips and mouth. As I watch Dr. Kanner draw, I realize I'm no longer tired. Despite the horror of the baby's mutilated face, I feel a kind of thrill, the thrill of possibility, the thrill of hope. For a brief single moment I imagine that I am Dr. Kanner. I am sketching the replacement face for the eight-month-old child, and I am the one accepting the responsibility for rebuilding his face. I wonder how that would feel.

Dr. Kanner snaps his notebook shut. "Time to talk to the mom again."

We step into the corridor, eerily vacant except for one nurse at the nurses' station. We head in that direction.

"Tony, if you want, call me and we'll have coffee," Dr. Kanner says. "This is not the time to talk about it, but plastic surgery covers a lot of territory. The obvious elective-cosmetic stuff to stuff that's, well, like this. Here's my card." He zips open his camera bag and hands me a business card.

"I will call you," I say.

At the nurses' station, Dr. Kanner scans the hallway, shrugs in confusion. "Where is she?"

"She went home," the nurse says.

It takes us both a while for this to sink in.

"She went *home?*" Dr. Kanner says.

"She said she was tired."

Dr. Kanner raises his index finger as if he's a student in class with the right answer. Then he forms a fist and knocks softly on the nurse's desk.

"Yeah," the nurse says. "I know."

"Well, I'm going to go back to the room," Dr. Kanner says.

"I'd better head back over to pediatrics. Thank you, Dr. Kanner." I offer my hand.

He grips it firmly. "Call me," he says.

FOUR A.M.

Back in general pediatrics. Slouching toward the call room. I walk in a kind of dream state. Images bombard me—the baby's face, Dr. Kanner's cool confidence, the unbelievable reaction of the baby's mother, the idea that I might want to look into becoming a plastic surgeon—

But I can't shake that baby's face.

How much can Dr. Kanner do? What will happen to that poor kid?

A baby's shriek jars me.

The shriek builds to a frantic cry.

After what I've just seen—

I stop at the nurses' station. A beleaguered nurse takes her time before she raises her head and sprays me with attitude. "Yes?"

"I don't mean to bother you, but that baby—"

"We're monitoring him. He's not in any distress."

"He *sounds* like he's in distress."

"He's not. Look, we got a lot of sick kids up here. We're not a baby-sitting service."

She turns away from me. I'm not even remotely pissed. Two weeks away from completing my last rotation, I get it.

When you constantly have to function on zero sleep, you sometimes get a little testy.

The baby's crying intensifies to a piercing wail.

I follow the sound.

I come to the door of his room, slide the chart out of the plastic holder on the wall outside, flip through it. Daniel Kwan. Thirteen months old. Half Asian, half Caucasian. Diagnosed with a respiratory syncytial virus infection.

In English—runny nose, wheezing, hard as hell to breathe.

I push the door open with my shoulder and walk in. Daniel, frail, small for his age, wearing a hospital gown and a diaper, his head reared back as he howls, a mop of brown hair sticking straight up, stands inside his crib, his tiny hands gripping the metal bars. He is alone in the room.

"Hey, buddy," I say. I reach my arms over the crib.

He stops crying, takes a step back, wheezes, sniffles, studies me with uncertain wide brown eyes.

"I'm Tony."

He gurgles, then holds his arms out and waddles over to me. I lift him out of the crib and press him against my shoulder.

"Rough night, huh? I hear you."

He whimpers, revs up, starts to wail.

"Hey, hey, it's okay. I got you."

I find a blanket lying on a rocking chair facing the window. I grab it with two fingers, drape it over Daniel, and sit down with him on the rocking chair.

His crying hits overdrive.

"It's okay," I say. "Shh."

I start to hum the first song that leaps into my head, the only song I can think of—"Every Rose Has Its Thorn" by Poison.

"You like metal?"

Daniel *wails*.

"Me, too. All *right*." I rock him slowly to the rhythm of the power ballad, humming the chorus.

"'Every rose has its thorn,'" I sing.

Daniel stops crying.

"'Every rose has its thorn, just like every night has its dawn—'"

Daniel coos. I fight to remember the rest of the lyrics, can't, so I repeat, "'Every rose has its thorn, just like every night has its dawn,'" over and over, softer and softer, until Daniel, precious baby, yawns, coos again, and fades into a sleep so deep that he snores.

"Oh, man. I saw some stuff tonight, Daniel. I saw some stuff."

I clutch him into my chest and rock him slowly.

V Fourth Year

18

Thanksgiving Story

Fourth year.

Choose Our Own Adventure.

After a solid year of endless days and sleepless nights of hospital rotations during which we felt mostly clueless and in the way, we ready ourselves for the year in which we find ourselves. The year we determine the kind of doctor we're going to be.

I alone on Flower Street feel uncertain. From day one, Tim has announced that he will be a psychiatrist. A wise decision. For the sake of humanity, he should be kept far away from medical equipment and sharp instruments. Ricky has opted for pediatrics and will work at a top children's hospital on the East Coast. James has fallen in love with internal medicine—somebody has to—and will spend much of his fourth year abroad.

I begin my summer of fourth year sitting in a medical building cafeteria having coffee with Dr. Kanner, seeking direction.

"I think of myself as an artist, I really do," Dr. Kanner says, pumping his coffee full of sugar. "You're always shaping, sculpting, creating, and re-creating, but your canvas is the human face and the human body. You get to make people over. It's amazing. Kind of powerful. Never boring. Have I hooked you yet?"

"I'm intrigued. A little overwhelmed, too."

"There is a lot. And you need to experience all of it, the whole breadth of plastic surgery, see what we do, cosmetic, reconstructive, the whole deal. You need to travel to Mecca."

And so, thanks to Dr. Kanner's patience and prodding, I start on a series of three one-month plastic-surgery rotations, beginning in the Mecca of the Midwest—Grand Rapids, Michigan.

SEPTEMBER.

Grand Rapids, Michigan, the Furniture City, population 197,000. Second-largest city in the state. Home of the minor-league West Michigan Whitecaps and the Gerald Ford museum.

In my month rotation, I have no time to take in a Whitecaps game, I skip the Gerald Ford museum, and I observe no furniture of note, other than the catalog-issue metal chairs, tables, and gurneys in the plastic surgery center's operating room. I'll live without experiencing these thrills. Because I take in something way cooler.

My first breast-reduction surgery.

For the squeamish—Tim, jump ahead—this is one bloody surgery.

Basically, the surgeon carves the breast completely apart, scoops out the insides, reshapes it, then puts it back together. And the blood? Rivers. Spurting. Gushing. Like a grenade going off in there. I watch, my mouth wide with wonder. How is this surgeon ever going to put that breast back together and mold it into something beautiful? Well, he does.

And what's more, I want to do it.

I'm so excited that after my first day, I call Amy to tell her that at the eleventh hour, when I was feeling lost, when Tim and Ricky and James had all found themselves and I felt like a kid left at the side of the road while the school bus pulled away, I figured it out.

I call my father and tell him that I won't be going into family practice. I will go into surgery after all, plastic surgery, hopefully, and if I don't get into a residency, I'll bite the bullet and go for general surgery.

"Oh, Tony," he says. "That's good, that's fine. But if you want family practice, it's okay. You go into debt, you won't be able to afford a house, or a car, or new clothes, or food, or shoes, and you cry yourself to sleep every night, but it's okay. Daddy's not mad."

"I'm not going into family practice, Dad."

"Thank God."

During my month in Grand Rapids, I assist on several breast reductions. Each surgery takes four hours. After my second one, the surgeon aims the spotlight right on me. He asks me to suture. My first reaction is *Wow, these people think I'm worthy.* I'm ready. And I know I can suture. I spent a year practicing on frozen pig's feet. Not the same as a live woman's breast, but still—

Then I realize that Grand Rapids *is* Mecca. I have to get accepted into a plastic-surgeon residency, and Grand Rapids is where I want to be. For a slew of reasons—close to home, close to Amy, everyone is welcoming and patient and kind, and it's the best plastic-surgery residency in the Midwest, if not the country.

I prepare to suture. I suddenly feel everyone's eyes on me. I start thinking, *They're watching me. They're checking out my hand-eye coordination. They're scoping my skills. This is a trial, a test. Like a final exam. If I mess up this suture, they'll never accept me into residency here.*

No, no, no. Now is not the time for my hands to shake. Great. I'm doing a suture solo, and here comes a nervous tremor. Beautiful. I'm a dead man.

I take a deep breath, visualize, see myself suturing this woman's breast, watch myself do it again, and then I begin and I'm smooth, and within seconds people stop watching me and move on to what they're doing. I relax, I take my time, I suture. I feel accepted. I feel as if I've arrived.

I want this.

NOVEMBER.

Next stop, the home of Abraham Lincoln, Springfield, Illinois, a boring six-hour drive away. Now that I've decided on plastic surgery, I want to check out the top residencies in the country. When it comes to hands, no place tops the clinic in Springfield, Illinois. And as I will discover, when it comes to small towns, nothing feels smaller than Springfield, Illinois.

I cram my Ford Tempo full of my clothes, books, and all the essentials I'll need for the month—tiny twelve-inch temperamental TV, a VCR I buy for two dollars at a tag sale, a mini-microwave Tim never uses because it occasionally smokes, one pot, one pan, two cups, two dishes, and a Korean sleeping cushion my mother forces on me. I say goodbye to my parents. My mom beams, my father crushes me in a hug. I stop at Amy's apartment after she's completed a grueling twenty-four-hour call with an intern who makes Nancy seem like Deepak Chopra. We hold each other, and then she whispers the sentence I've been dreading: "When you get back, I want to meet your parents."

"Great idea. I was thinking the same thing. When I get back from Springfield, we'll all have dinner. I'll check their availability. They're pretty busy—"

"Tony, I mean it."

"Look at the time. I better get going. Got a big drive ahead of me. Six hours. I'll call you when I get there. Love you."

I know she's really exhausted because she doesn't press it. We cling to each other silently. One last kiss and I'm gone.

SIX HOURS LATER, driving into dusk, I pass all things Lincoln—Lincoln's home, the Abraham Lincoln museum, Lincoln's Tomb, and the thirty-foot-tall Abraham Lincoln totem pole. And that, as far I can determine, covers all there is to see and do in Springfield, Illinois. Doesn't matter. I'll be wrapped up 24/7 at the hospital or hand clinic, both an easy walk from my apartment complex, a 1950s former motel with water-stained cement stairs on the outside leading to my second-floor walk-up. Road-weary, head pounding, needing a shower—I've driven the six hours straight through—I trudge up the flight of uneven stairs to my apartment and unlock the door. The smell of smoke nearly blows me back outside. I gag, hold my nose, and walk in.

I exhale, gag again. The place smells like an ashtray. In addition, the bare floor is so covered with dog hair that it looks like a shag carpet. I peek into the empty room and instantly retreat, my eyes burning from residual cigarette smoke. I shut the door and fight a sudden desire to gather my meager belongings, bolt down the cement stairs, reload the Ford Tempo, and drive the hell away from Honest Abeville.

Seeing an image of myself suturing in Grand Rapids, feeling newly welcomed into the plastic-surgery community—hoping that, anyway—I suck it up and decide to stay. I'll make the best of it. I'll barely be in this apartment. I'll only sleep here.

But . . . sleep where?

That's when I whisper a prayer of thanks to my mom. I unroll her Korean sleeping cushion, spread it out on the living room floor, and pile everything else onto the kitchen counter, including my clothes.

My apartment may be a rat hole, but at least I'll bond with a group of great people in the world of hand surgery.

THEY HATE ME.

At least that's how it feels. They're certainly not warm, fuzzy, and welcoming, like the Grand Rapids guys. It could be me. I've been out of sorts. You have to cut me some slack. Waking up every morning smelling like a casino, mouth tasting as if I've swallowed a schnauzer, can make a man irritable.

Day one. I get a glimpse of the chief of surgery in action during a team meeting in a conference room as he reams out the residents, who cower as he pummels them. He's unhappy with how they've treated a few of the plastic-surgery patients, and he's letting them know. He's apoplectic. He's taller than everyone in the room, a chubby-faced guy with a bush of black hair and large calloused hands the size of baseball mitts. I have to follow his ream-out act by introducing myself and making nice. Nothing better than gushing like a fool, saying, "Hi, I'm Tony Youn, the new medical student. Awesome speech." I, of course, say nothing. I smile, offer my hand. He crushes my fingers in a powerhouse handshake. He looks right past me as the surgeons slink out of the room.

No surprise that the clinic specializes in hand surgeries. Springfield lies in the center of farm country, which means farmers regularly slicing off fingertips, cutting off fingers, lobbing off entire hands. I watch with fascination as surgeons deftly reattach fingers and hands, reconnecting arteries, veins, and nerves, all done under a microscope. These plastic surgeons are masters of minuscule needles and tiny suturing, mavens of microsurgery.

The first time they invite me to suture, the chief resident hovers like a hawk, eyes fixated on my hands, scouring my fingers for the slightest evidence of tremor. They've started me off with a foot. If I manage to suture without trembling, they'll move me to a hand. I keep my hands still as stone, but as I begin, I start to shake.

Tony, you're good, I tell myself. *You can do this in your sleep. Slow down. Breathe. Now stitch.*

I calm down, move my fingers a fraction of a millimeter at a time. But it's too late. I know the chief has seen the tremor. He lurches away, mutters something. He's seen enough.

I have weeks left. I haven't really connected with anybody. I find none of the camaraderie of Grand Rapids. The surgeons in Springfield are all business—intense, impatient, distant—and not interested in engaging me. I no longer attribute this attitude to my dog breath.

I hit the clinic each morning at five. I round every patient on my own, fill out boring and basic paperwork, write progress reports— *Patient doing well. Wound looks good*—then I write down whatever the surgeon has suggested for the next step. An hour later, the residents arrive, round the patients themselves, read my reports, and sign their name. Two hours later, the attending surgeons come in, visit the patients with me, and sign their name on the report I wrote hours ago.

My job, as I see it, is to do everything I can to make their job easier, to save them time. I change dressings, write notes, look up lab-test results, input them on the charts. And when I can, I kiss ass. I'm not proud of it. But this is year four, the year we land a residency. I hear every day how tough the competition is for plastic surgery. I wouldn't love spending six years in Springfield, but if it's the only place that takes me—

Yes, I want to become a plastic surgeon that badly.

The week of Thanksgiving, I start to feel extremely homesick. I miss my family terribly and ache to see Amy. I dread the idea of spending Thanksgiving alone. I've been coming in at five A.M. every day, never missing a day, and I'm sure the residents will give me a couple of days off to drive home and spend Thanksgiving with my family.

During rounds one morning, I ask about it. "Thanksgiving's coming up next week. You think you'll be needing any help? Should I stick around? Or should I make plans to go home?"

"Yeah, stick around," the chief resident says, rumbling toward the door. "We can use your help. One of the residents will invite you over for Thanksgiving dinner."

I have to stick around? You have to be kidding. You don't need me. I don't do anything. I write stupid notes on a stupid chart. Nobody knows I exist. You can use my help? Seriously?

"Oh, okay, sure, that's terrific. Thanks."

I doubt he's heard a word I've said.

THURSDAY. THANKSGIVING DAY, 4:45 A.M.

I pull myself up off my sleeping cushion, take a quick shower to wake up, walk over to the medical center. I round the patients, make my notes, wait for one of the residents to show up. Two hours later, he strolls in. We speed-round the patients. It's Thanksgiving, after all. A wave of homesickness washes over me. I won't be going home, but at least I'll have a home-cooked turkey dinner with someone else's family. We finish rounding the patients.

"Well, I'm off for two days," the resident says.

"Right," I say. "The long weekend."

"I love Thanksgiving. It's my favorite holiday."

"I know, so great. Turkey, stuffing, mashed potatoes, gravy, buttered yams, cranberry sauce—"

"Cut it out. You're making me hungry."

I laugh. "Sorry. Got carried away. So, um, what time—"

"All *right*, buddy. I'll see you in a couple days. Hold down the fort, willya?"

He slingshots out of there. I guess he's not the resident assigned to invite me home for dinner.

WHEN I LEAVE an hour later, it's raining, the kind of pile-driving Midwest deluge that rakes your face and hits the pavement with the consistency of mud. I run to my apartment, climb the treacherous, slippery concrete stairs, and pull off my clothes. I take my second shower of the day, a really quick one, in case the phone rings with my official Thanksgiving-dinner invitation. I dry off, change into the best clothes I have, and sit on my Korean sleeping cushion, the only spot in the apartment where I feel clean, waiting for the phone to ring.

It takes me only about twenty minutes to realize that no one is going to call.

I turn on my tiny television and flip from snowy channel to snowy channel. I stare numbly at the Lions receiving their traditional Thanksgiving Day beat-down. During commercials, I find an old black-and-white movie with Jimmy Stewart, so sappy it chokes me up. I nap, and then at around six, famished, I brave the storm, and with the rain battering my windshield like gunshots, I tool slowly toward the center of town, looking for a place to eat. "I am gonna have my turkey dinner, damn it," I say as the wipers flap and crunch across the windshield.

In front of me, a large lad holding a tray full of food beckons. The sign reads BIG BOY. I pull in to the parking lot, find a space, throw my collar up, and dash inside. I shake myself dry in the small entryway.

"How many?" the perky hostess sings.

"One," I say.

She frowns painfully into the clipboard she holds. She raises up, hits me with a blinding smile she's clearly practiced in a mirror. "Right this way, sir."

Sir? I'm probably younger than she is, but whatever.

"Here ya go." She gestures toward a booth as if she's Vanna White. "Plenty of room for ya to stretch out."

I slide in, and she spanks a laminated menu into my hand.

"Happy Thanks*giving*," she says.

The booth smells of lemon Pledge. I tap my fingers on the edge of the table, then fan my face with the menu, even though it's about thirty degrees in here. I look around the restaurant. A party of four to my right. Three women to my left. A family of six across from me, taking up two tables. As far as I can see, I'm the only single in the place.

"This is officially pathetic," I say.

I lay the menu down on the table, edge out of the booth, and head out of the restaurant, passing the perky hostess standing like a sentry by her podium at the entrance. Her practiced smile twitches in confusion. "Did you want a different booth?"

"Kind of want a different life," I say.

I slosh back into the rain.

IN THE END, I celebrate Thanksgiving alone in my apartment with two root beers and a turkey sub I find mashed in the front case at a convenience store. This may not be what the Pilgrims had in mind, but it's all I got. I fall asleep to the sunny weatherman predicting more rain—why is everyone around here so damn perky?—and wake up, as usual, at 4:45 A.M. I drive to work, round the patients, write my notes, and walk out the door. I fill the Ford Tempo with gas, grab a bunch of PowerBars and a Big Gulp, and drive six hours straight to Greenville. One of the residents mentioned something a while ago about giving me a day off after Thanksgiving, so I'm taking it. I arrive a day late for Thanksgiving dinner, but it doesn't matter. I just need to be with people I care about and who care about me. Sunday morning I drive the six hours back to Springfield, this time stoked on turkey sandwiches from home, geared up for my last week in the world's most elite hand-surgery medical center.

The day before I'm set to leave, the chief surgeon calls me into his office, a dark narrow cavern on the third floor. He sits behind a desk the size of a conference table, his huge hands linked in front of him. "Sit down, Tony."

I reach behind me and find a chair.

"As you know, we interview for residencies in December or January."

I squirm in my seat.

"I figure you don't want to drive all the way back here, do you?"

"I don't mind. It's part of the process. Gives me time to prepare, too."

"You don't need to prepare. Let's do the interview now."

"Now?"

"Is that a problem?"

"Oh, no, no, now's good. Perfect. You're right. Saves me a trip."

I don't remember what he asks me. The questions lumber out of his mouth in slow motion. I do my best, but I know I muff the answers. I feel ambushed. The interview lasts under five minutes. He kicks back from his chair, stands. "You have any questions for me?" A throwaway. This interview is *over*. He's pushing items on his desk into his briefcase.

"Yes."

"Shoot."

"Do I have any shot of getting in here?"

His hand freezes on his address book midway from desk to briefcase.

A question he never expected.

He takes a moment. "Tony, you seem like a nice guy. Hard worker. Eager. Helpful. Prepared. But we have a lot of people who want to come here. Lot of qualified people."

I'm slow, but I don't think I aced the interview.

I leave the next day. On my way out of town, I stop at Lincoln's home and take the tour. Then I go to Lincoln's Tomb and check that out. I skip the Abraham Lincoln museum, but I park outside the thirty-foot-tall Lincoln totem pole and take a picture.

I don't want to leave Springfield, Illinois, without taking in the town's highlights, because I have a feeling I won't be back.

19

Beverly Hills Bloodsuckers

One bracingly cold November night in Springfield, alone in my apartment, exhausted from a string of crushing twelve-hour days beginning at five in the morning, feeling vulnerable, lonely, and sorry for myself, I call my mother and tell her about Amy.

I don't plan to. It just spills out. My mother, too, is alone this night, my father at the hospital delivering twins.

"I want to tell you something, Mom."

I hear her gasp. The urgency in my voice has prepared her for the worst—I've been arrested, I deal drugs, I've killed a man in Joliet, I've dropped out of medical school.

"I have a girlfriend."

There it is.

In our family, no one my age or younger has ever had a girlfriend or boyfriend. Or at least admitted it. None of the relatives, none of my cousins, none of us. It's not supposed to happen. We're Koreans. We work harder, study harder, achieve more, and we don't date. I've broken new ground. Amy is the first. I'm a dubious pioneer.

"A girlfriend," my mother says.

"Yes. Her name is Amy."

"Amy," my mother says.

I'm way ahead of her. I know her next question. I answer it before she asks.

"She's not Korean. She's white."

"Oh," my mother says.

"She's Christian," I add quickly. "White Christian Amy."

"How long?"

I've anticipated this, too. I swiftly do the math. Amy and I have been together for nearly two years.

"Three months," I say.

"Long time," my mother says.

"I've told her all about you and Dad," I say. "She's dying to meet you."

"I'm dying to meet her, too," my mother says.

I hang up, wondering what the hell I've done.

AFTER SPRINGFIELD, I have five days at home before I leave for my third and final one-month rotation. Thanks to an introduction from Dr. Kanner, I will be spending a month where the dreams of plastic surgery are made, Beverly Hills, California. I will apprentice under Dr. Romeo Bouley, one of the most famous and respected plastic surgeons in Southern California.

"You're in," Dr. Kanner tells me over coffee. "Bouley is a little different, but he's the best. Be prepared. Beverly Hills has a faster pace than Springfield."

"Death has a faster pace than Springfield."

"You have to see what this guy does. He's a wizard. He's also obsessed with women. He's outrageous. Watch yourself."

"I have a girlfriend," I say, and then I blurt out, "We're having dinner with my parents tonight. According to them, I'm too young to have a girlfriend. Makes sense. I'm only twenty-five. Did I mention she's not Korean? Should be a fun night."

"If you like that sort of thing. But hey, if it doesn't go well, Romeo will set you up."

WE'RE LATE. TOTALLY my fault. I picked up Amy twenty minutes late, stopped for gas, and I'm driving about forty miles an hour below the speed limit.

"Want me to drive?" Amy says gently.

I glance at her. I've never seen her look so beautiful. Kid cleans up nice. Plus, for the past year, I've seen her only in scrubs. Even in a conservative skirt and top, she's a knockout.

"Tony, seriously, you're driving like two miles an hour."

"It's a Korean thing." The stink eye. "Okay, I'm a little nervous."

"A *little*?"

"In my family, *nobody* dates a non-Korean. It's never happened. I'm talking throughout my entire extended family, like a bazillion cousins. It's unheard of."

"It'll be fine."

"I'm sweating like a pig."

"What's the worst that can happen?"

"My father will be charming, polite, cordial, and then we'll get home and he'll kick me out of the family. Not out of the house. Out of the *family*. I'll be excommunicated. A wandering Youn. My only hope is that in ten years, when we have kids, he'll soften up and let me back into the fold. My mom won't agree with my dad, she'll be torn up, but she'll go along with him because she has to, it's what Korean wives do."

We pull into the restaurant parking lot, and I fumble with my key as I turn off the ignition. Amy scoots over and kisses me forever. She finally pulls away, reapplies her lipstick in the visor mirror.

"Slight change of plans," I say.

Amy puckers. "Yeah?"

"I already know my parents. You go in without me, have dinner, bond, then call me later and tell me how it went."

"Genius." She drops her lipstick in her purse, snaps it shut, and gets out of the car. A moment later, she flings open my door and drags me out of the driver's seat. "Cowboy up," she says.

Excluding one clumsy move when I reach for a bread stick and knock over my water, requiring a new tablecloth, the dinner goes smoothly. My mother sits next to Amy, my father across in prime interrogation position. I expect him to grill her like a murder suspect, but he doesn't. He *is* charming and polite and even, in his own way, welcoming. I'm sure he's acting, putting up a false front. He'll wait until we're home before he goes ballistic. But right after we order, my mother drops a bomb.

"So, Amy, Tony tells me you're Christian."

Nice, Mom. I was counting on you to go easy on her.

"I am, yes."

"Do you go to church?"

Amy catches my eye.

"Actually, Mom—" I say.

"Mommy is talking to *Amy*," my father says.

"I go every single Sunday," Amy says. "I never miss."

"Every Sunday?" my mom says.

"Yes. It's a thing with me. I'm very religious."

My father violently snaps a bread stick in half, scaring the crap out of me. "Tony go?"

"Sure," I say.

"Sometimes," Amy says.

I look at her. She smiles at me, I catch it, smile back. "She's right. Sometimes. I should go more."

My father chews slowly, thoughtfully. Across from him, my mother reaches over, lifts Amy's hand, and places it between both of hers. Without saying a word, the two of them stand. Are all women's bladders in the world always in sync?

"Excuse us," my mother says. They walk hand in hand toward the bathroom.

My father mauls another bread stick. I can't read his expression, but I have a pretty good idea what he's feeling. I can certainly eliminate several options, overjoyed and delighted among them. Since they'll be locked away in the ladies' room for the next half hour, I expect that my father will take this opportunity to level me. I'm not going to argue with him. I'm not going to defend myself, and I'm not going to defend Amy. I'm a man. I have my own life, which includes, now and forever, Amy. At some point after we both graduate, we plan to marry and have kids, and if the color of her skin or her ethnicity results in my being evicted from my own family, then so be it. I'll deal with it. I'm just not giving up Amy.

"Daddy has something to say," my father says.

"I thought you might."

"You drop big bomb. Fourth year, first girlfriend."

"I know. I'm sorry."

"Daddy and Mommy are relieved," he says. "We thought for sure you gay."

DECEMBER.

Beverly Hills. Movie stars, pop icons, and miles and miles of work done on boobs, eyelids, lips, noses, tummies, and butts, much of it shaped, enlarged, reduced, and reconstructed by Dr. Romeo Bouley, PSS—Plastic Surgeon to the Stars.

I ease my rented Ford Escort onto Century Boulevard outside of LAX and hit the 405 on-ramp. Forty minutes later, I coax the Escort up the Pacific Coast Highway and head to the Malibu Beach Colony. Every car I pass is a Benz, BMW, Jag, Rolls, or Bentley. *Every* car. And every driver shoots me a look that says this guy's either lost or some-one's gardener.

Dr. Romeo Bouley's house sits along a beach as white as talcum powder, the house framed by two leaning palm trees embracing fronds like an elderly couple, darkening the front of a three-story Spanish mansion in shadow. Dr. Bouley has insisted I drive right from the airport to his house for a drink. He wants to get acquainted before we jump in first thing in the morning. I park my rented clunker in his driveway behind two Benzes and a Rolls. I walk up to his front door, pause to soak in the late-afternoon Southern California sun. Man. December, seventy degrees, and everyone owns a fifty-thousand-dollar car. I could get used to La La Land.

I step onto Dr. Bouley's Spanish-tiled front patio, aim my finger at his doorbell, and freeze. The cost of my three one-month electives suddenly whips into my head like a ripped cash-register tape. I'm beyond broke. Choosing My Own Adventure has emptied my bank account and forced me to take on new loans on top of my old loans. And I'm about to shell out even more money. Next month, I will begin traveling the country to interview for residencies in both plastic surgery and general surgery, my backup in case I get completely shut out of plastic surgery. It could happen. My sneak-attack interview with the chief resident in Springfield still stings. Since plastic surgery is so competitive, I figure I'll need to apply to at least fifty residencies. I crunch some quick numbers in my head and nearly choke. The moment I become a doctor, I will owe over $100,000. The number nearly sends me running straight back to my rented Escort. Screw it. No point worrying now. At least I'm saving a little money this trip because my brother has moved to Los Angeles and invited me to stay on the floor of his apartment. A big hello once again to Mom's Korean sleeping cushion.

Whap. The front door jerks open, knocks me back to reality. A large man, six-three at least, thick shoulders, trim waist, white hair sculpted into what looks like two sand dunes, an impressive sloping beak of a nose, sparkling gray eyes, glistening teeth, grips me in a handshake strong enough to bend iron. He wears dark blue scrubs with ROMEO BOULEY, MD embroidered on the pocket. The first time I've seen designer scrubs.

"Saw you out here, wondered why you didn't ring the bell. Tony, right?"

"Yes, Dr. Bouley—"

"Romeo. Come in, come in. Let's get you a drink. You look thirsty."

He slaps my back hard enough to dislodge a chicken bone. I step into his living room and stop dead in my tracks. It looks as if I've wandered into an antique store—Oriental rugs, ornate chests of drawers, end tables, dining room sets piled on top of each other, trumpets, tubas, clarinets, two accordions, violins, harps, and at least one lute. Most of all, scattered throughout the room on all of the furniture, on the mantelpiece, and stacked in every corner are lamps, hundreds of lamps—shaped and painted like naked women.

"Impressive, huh?"

"I've never seen anything like it. Like them. Like your collection."

"I know. I must have fifteen hundred naked-women lamps. I get 'em from all over the world. Some of the boobs light up. You can read by 'em. Use 'em for a night-light. What are you drinking?"

"Water is fine."

"No, no. I got a beauty from Sonoma breathing in the kitchen. I'm talking about a *wine*." He roars. "You want to see the rest of the house?"

"Yes, sure, love to."

I trail him through four thousand square feet, five bedrooms, six bathrooms filled with antiques and the other thousand naked-lady lamps. They're everywhere—on the kitchen counter, on the stairs, atop the refrigerator, on the back of toilets. We circle back to the living room. Romeo pushes aside a pile of crap on a velvet love seat, sinks down, and pats the seat next to him. I crunch into a velvet whoosh.

"How do you like Beverly Hills? Kinda reminds you of Springfield, doesn't it?" Head thrown back, another roar. A moment later, he socks back half his goblet of red wine, throws a long thick arm across the entire length of the love seat onto my shoulder. "So, what do you know about me?"

I actually do know something about Romeo Bouley, MD. I checked him out online. He carries the reputation as *the* go-to plastic surgeon among actresses, models, and strippers and has dated at least one A-list actress. Allegedly. He's also loaded. Allegedly.

"Nothing, really," I say.

"Oh yeah? Bullshit."

"Well, Dr. Kanner says you're the best."

He shrugs, drains the rest of his wine. I've barely touched mine.

"Another," he says.

"Oh, no, thank you, I'm fine."

"I was talking to myself." He laughs so hard the love seat shakes, then wriggles his butt, extracts himself from the divot he's made in the cushion, and propels himself into the kitchen.

"Everything you've heard about me is true," he says over his shoulder. He returns in five seconds, a meaty hand wrapped around a dusty wine bottle. "You're a smart kid. I assume you've done some research. Be disappointed if you haven't." He catches me in midsip. Before I can answer, he says, "I've done some research about *you*."

"Okay, I have read a little about you."

"Good. You're opening up. So you know. Now, look, starting tomorrow, you're gonna see some *shit*. So let's be straight with each other from now on, dig?"

"Yes. Sure. Dig."

"What do you want to know?"

I reach my wineglass over to the antique map chest Romeo uses as a coffee table. I set it down. "Have you ever dated a patient?"

"Never. I do date actresses and models, but they're never my patients. That's rule number one. Never date a patient. Rule number two, *never* date a patient. Don't go near a patient's boobs outside the operating room. Dig?"

"Not a problem. I have a girlfriend."

"I have a couple." Romeo plops back down on the love seat, landing like an anchor. "You're not in Kansas anymore, big guy. Or Grand Rapids. Or Springfield. We don't do a lot of Farmer Fred losing his pointer in the wood chipper. We do Miss September. Miss March. The Playmate of the Year. The star of a certain sitcom. The whole cast of a daytime soap. Vegas superstars. Most of the Nudes on Ice. They're all stunning, and most are available. We're the rock stars of medicine, Youner. We get all the tail, all the glory, and all the money. A lot of docs hate us. I get it. They're jealous. Most of them want to trade places with us."

I stare at him until he blinks. "What?"

"How did you know people call me Youner?"

Romeo Bouley, MD, once again lifts himself up from the love seat. "Told you. I did my research."

THIRD ELECTIVE. DAY one.

I stand outside the office of Romeo Bouley, MD, in Beverly Hills. I gape at the stained-glass windows in the burnished oak doors. I rub the stained glass lightly, shake my head, and step into the waiting room— leather couches, modern art, an Oriental rug, and twenty more naked-lady lamps. The receptionist, a former or potential centerfold, directs me to Romeo's office down the hall. An Oriental runner leads me to him. On the way, I pass framed covers of magazines that have featured Romeo—*People, Us Weekly, Playboy, Penthouse,* and a shocker, *The Saturday Evening Post.* I knock at his door frame; the door is open. He beckons me in, waves me to an armchair. His office? Leather, leather, leather, naked-lady lamps.

"You meet Heather?"

"The receptionist? She's very nice."

"Unbelievable, right? I did them. And no, I never did her. You cannot date your staff, either. That's another rule."

"For me, it's not an issue. I have a girlfriend—"

"Okay, listen. Lesson number one." He jabs a button on his desk. Behind me, the door whirs, rattles, and closes with a thwack. "Plastic surgery is like dating." He pauses to let this sink in. "Patient comes in for a consultation. Your first date. You make small talk, feel each other out, see if you're compatible. You have to look good, Youner. You look like shit, sloppy, whatever, she's outta there. She comes in because *she* wants to look good. How *you* look matters. Dig?"

"Yes." I sneak a look at what I'm wearing. White shirt, cords. I shaved. Showered. Applied deodorant. Combed my hair. Slapped on cologne. I think I'm all right.

He sees me checking myself out. "You pass. Now. While she's feeling you out on this first date, you're feeling her out, too. Main thing we're looking for is *crazy*. We want to avoid crazy. We see crazy, we run like hell. You know BDD?"

"I don't think so."

He whams back in his chair, links his hands behind his spectacular snowy-beach hairdo. "Body dysmorphic disorder. Affects about one percent of the population, about five percent of plastic-surgery patients. In Beverly Hills, ten percent, easy. Maybe twenty. Gum?"

"No, thanks."

He unwraps three sticks, pops them all in his mouth. He chews like a ballplayer, cheek puffed out as if working on a chaw. "This is a condition where a person looks in the mirror and sees something that doesn't exist. Or sees a distortion of the truth. You look in a mirror, you see a tiny bump on your nose. Mosquito bite, say. A person with BDD sees that same mosquito bite, and to her, it's the size of a big fleshy peach. I'm serious."

He chews violently for three more seconds, tears off a page from a prescription pad, spits the wad of gum into it. "Plastic-surgery patients with BDD see themselves as ugly and deformed. Doesn't matter how great the surgery turns out or how many times you perform a surgery to *correct* the first one, which they see as botched. In real life, they may look like Heather, but they look in the mirror and think they look like shit. And they blame you."

"Crazy," I say.

"A nightmare," Romeo says. "You can't always catch it, but you try. We get sued more than anyone. My lawyer loves me. Sends me on a cruise twice a year. Anyway, back to dating."

He taps out three more sticks of gum, unwraps them, jams them into his mouth. I've known Romeo Bouley, MD, for under a day, but based on his naked-lady lamp collection, the fact that he lives in the middle of *Antiques Roadshow*, the way he compares plastic-surgery consultations to dating, and how he chews a pack of gum every five minutes, I'm calling this guy quirky.

"So, okay, the consultation goes well, you agree to see each other again. Now we're talking Botox, collagen, that kind of thing. First base. That goes well, you move to second base. Lipo. Then you swing for the fences."

"Breast augmentation."

"Bingo. Start with a good-night kiss. Botox. Next you make out. Lipo. Then you do the deed. Boob job." He rips off another page from the prescription pad, wads up his gum. "I feel you, kid. You got a future."

DAYS TWO THROUGH twenty-nine.

A guy could get used to this.

Five, six, seven, a dozen gorgeous women a *day*. Professional women who act, pose, escort, strip, and screw for a living, all talented enough to appear on the cover of *Maxim* or in the pages of *Playboy*. The startling part is that if I'd ever met one of them in college, I'd have stammered, blanched, and launched into a monologue about my mother's cooking. Now, wearing a white coat in Dr. Romeo Bouley's office—even though I always identify myself as a medical student—I'm treated like another doctor. These women share with me their fear of surgery, explain why it's a curse having a beautiful face and gorgeous breasts, even confess their most intimate problems with husbands, boyfriends, parents. I listen sympathetically, and when they ask for my assurance—they always do—I promise I'll be right there with them throughout their procedure. Many grip my hand with heartfelt thanks. At times I feel like Romeo Junior.

"I tell you more than I tell *anyone*," a porn star, a favorite of Tim's, coos to me as Romeo begins her post-rhinoplasty follow-up visit. She has asked him to make her look more elegant, less trashy. She hopes to transition into mainstream acting at some point, which, from what I've seen, would be a blow to the porn industry.

"Everything looks good," Romeo says. "Healing nicely."

"I have a photo shoot tomorrow. Is that okay?"

"It's fine. You don't have to miss work."

"Can I hang from the ceiling by my wrists and ankles?"

"Just make sure they don't touch your nose."

"Can they put a cue ball in my mouth?"

I cough, mutter, "Warm in here."

Before she leaves, I get her autograph. I have her write, *To Tim, when I think of you, I touch myself. I seriously do.* He will *freak*. So will Jane.

"They tell us everything," I say to Romeo one afternoon.

"Oh, yeah," he says. "You know what they call us? Shrinks with knives."

No DOUBT ROMEO Bouley is quirky; he's also a talented surgeon and a gifted teacher. He's fast and steady with a scalpel, patient and generous with me. He allows me to suture more than anyone else has and even offers me a few incisions of my own. As I near the end of my month in Beverly Hills, Romeo invites me to return for a longer apprenticeship after I've established my residency. I accept his offer. I'm no longer hooked on plastic surgery. I'm obsessed. I've found my calling. I would love to work side by side with Romeo. Wouldn't mind living in Southern California, either, at least for a short time.

My last day. Our last procedure. Romeo will perform breast-implant surgery on Michelle, a stripper who's recently celebrated her fortieth birthday, a difficult birthday for many people, the end of the line for most strippers. For over twenty years, Michelle's stunningly over-size breasts have been her signature. Now they have literally become weights, causing her severe neck and back pain and brutal headaches. She has gone from performing at prime time in top Hollywood and Vegas clubs to stripping at noon in a dive by the airport. She wants to find a new line of work and needs her breasts reduced.

The anesthesiologist knocks Michelle out, we scrub up, gown up, prepare for surgery. Before Romeo makes his first cut, we ponder her pendulous breasts, the most imposing mountains of silicone I've ever seen.

"Gigantomastia," Romeo says. "Okay, I'm going in."

He makes a flawless incision around the areola of the right breast and starts cutting down to the implant.

"Grade-four capsular contracture," he says as he cuts. "I'll break down the grades for you. Grade one. Buttah. The way a breast should feel. Natural. Like you're back in high school. Grade two. Firmer than normal. Looks fine, feels a little firm. Most people can't tell the difference between one and two."

He pulls back, waits, allows the bleeding to stop. "Grade three. Too firm, appears abnormal. We're talking Nerf football. Not what you're looking for in a breast. And then there's this. Grade four. A bowling ball. The scar tissue is so severe it makes the breast round, hard, and cold. Here, feel."

He puts my hand on her left breast. Massive, rock-hard, cool to the touch. Forget stripping. How did she *walk* with these?

"Guys *like* these?" I say.

"You can take your hand off now, Tony."

I have already.

"I amuse myself," Romeo says. He chuckles, resumes cutting into the breast, going farther toward the implant. "I'm at the capsule," he says. "This scar tissue is *thick*. Knife, please."

The surgical technician passes him a scalpel. With immaculate precision, he works through the scar tissue down to the implant. Finally, sounding like an egg cracking, the implant pops through the scar tissue. Romeo puts aside the scalpel, grabs the edge of the implant, and yanks out a slice of clear silicone shaped like a discus, high as two Big Macs. He hands the implant to the surgical tech and peers inside the open breast pocket. "She's stacked," he says.

"She is huge," I say.

"No, Youner. She's *stacked*. There's another implant in there." He grunts and pulls a second implant out of the breast pocket. "You don't see this often. It's extreme. Anna Nicole Smith time. Only the truly insane plastic surgeons do stack jobs."

"You ever do one?"

"All right, now for the left side."

After Romeo removes the stacked implants in her left breast, he focuses on the scar tissue, which has progressed to such a severe state that it has turned the inside of both breasts into a chalky, calcified mess resembling the plaster of a cast. For over an hour, Romeo chips away meticulously, removing every bit of scar tissue, piece by piece, until all that's left of her breasts is a mass of stretched-out skin.

He then inserts temporary sizer implants that look like small inflatable balloons. On his count, we raise Michelle to a sitting position so Romeo can determine what size he should make the new implants. We lay her back down, and he begins to fill the sizer implants, inflating her breasts as if pumping up a tire.

"This looks good. Around a D cup. Two five-hundred cc implants, please."

The OR nurse opens two new breast implants and hands them to Romeo. He inserts one into each breast cavity. These implants will never fill out Michelle's breast in the same way as the stacked two-baggers, which is, of course, the point. Instead they settle into the bottom of each breast socket.

"Rock in a sock," Romeo says. "That's seriously what we call it. And now for the breast lift."

He begins suturing the nipples onto their new, higher location. He cuts off the excess breast skin and stitches the incisions back together, working with the concentration of a jeweler. The process takes over ninety minutes. At last he takes one step back. Before us lies Michelle and her new breasts, smaller, youthful, beautiful. Together, Romeo and I apply gauze dressings.

"Oh, shit," Romeo says.

"What?"

"Her nipples." He retreats another step. "*Shit*. Look. They're turning purple."

A moment ago her nipples were full and pink. They have darkened to the color of an eggplant. Romeo speaks faster than I have ever heard him. "Sometimes when you perform a breast lift on a woman with implants, the blood supply to the nipples becomes altered. Needle."

A small needle appears in a flash. He stabs the areola lightly, repeatedly. Dark red blood oozes out.

"Fuck. Her nipples are congested. Let's get some of these stitches out. We're looking for the nipples to turn pink."

We remove a few of the sutures that hold the nipples in place.

Still purple.

"Well, Anthony, we got a *situation*. Purple means there's blood flowing into the nipple but not going out. The blood is pooling up in there."

"Sorry, this means—?"

"Worst case? Her nipples will turn black and fall off. Instead of a nipple, she'll have a gaping hole."

"Shit," I say.

"Yep. Deep shit."

"What do we do?"

"Leeches."

I laugh. I can't help it. You have to love how Romeo keeps it loose even during a crisis.

"I'm serious," he says.

"Leeches?"

"Be fancy. Call it leech therapy. I've done it several times. We bring her to the hospital and attach a bunch of the bloodsuckers right there." He points to each of Michelle's nipples. "They suck the old blood out. In a few days, her body will create new blood vessels that will take over for the leeches. Hopefully." He turns to the OR nurse. "You know the drill. Call an ambulance."

"Wow," I say. "Leeches."

"New technology, my ass. We're going medieval."

. . . .

ROMEO ESCORTS MICHELLE to the hospital. I stay behind. I say good-bye to Heather and the rest of the staff, then I run an errand on Melrose Avenue in West Hollywood. By the time I head back toward Beverly Hills, the sun's starting to set. I drive into the hills, find a spot to park on Mulholland Drive, and watch the lights of the San Fernando Valley flicker on. It looks as if I'm peering down at a second night sky. At around seven, I head to the hospital to check on Michelle.

As I exit the elevator, I hear a scream. A woman stands in the middle of the hallway and points at the floor. She shrieks again and backs up slowly. I jog toward her and see a bloody trail coming out of Michelle's room. At the end of the trail sits a huge, bloated leech.

"It's nothing," I say. "Leech therapy."

The woman stares at me, horrified, her hands over her mouth.

I push open Michelle's door and find her lying in bed, sound asleep, the rest of the leeches locked up in a jar somewhere.

Beverly Hills.

Movie stars. Pop icons.

Leeches.

IN THE PARKING lot, still in his scrubs, Romeo leans against my rented Ford Escort. "I couldn't let you go without saying goodbye."

"I was going to find you, too. Thank you for everything."

"You got to see pretty much my whole bag of tricks. And I'm serious. Come back."

"I'd like that. Hey, I have something for you." I pop open the back of the Escort, reach in, and hand him a gift-wrapped box. "A little token of my thanks."

"Get outta town. What did you do?"

Like a kid at Christmas, he rips off the wrapping paper and flings off the cover of the box. He stares inside. His eyes begin to water. He shakes his head and pulls out my present.

A lamp shaped like a naked woman.

He bites his lip. "She's beautiful."

"The nipples flash the SOS distress signal."

He throws his arms around me, locks me in a bear hug. "You feel me."

"I feel you," I say, crushed in his embrace.

20

Monkey Time!

Fourth year. January.

And so it begins.

The end.

We interview for residency.

I've begun the process over the summer, filling out applications, gathering letters of recommendation, arranging for transcripts and scores. I send out applications in November. In late December I will hear where I've been invited to interview in January and February.

If I'm invited to interview.

I have chosen one of the most competitive fields in medicine. I'm told there are 60 openings for plastic-surgery residencies and 250 qualified candidates. Among those I envision a horde of gunners, ass kissers, and overachievers from Johns Hopkins, Stanford, and the Ivy League, causing me debilitating résumé envy. Not to mention frustration and bewilderment at some of the essay questions I have to write. One application—six pages of short-answer essays—closes with this 250-word doozy: *If you found Aladdin's lamp, what three wishes would you make?*

First, I would wish to get into your residency. Second, I would wish that you pay all of my expenses and pay off all of my loans. Third, I would wish that the residents and attending doctors I work with not be as stupid as this question.

I put this residency low on my list.

All told, I apply to thirty-five plastic-surgery residency programs and twenty general-surgery residencies as backups. In contrast, Tim applies to five residencies for psychiatry. Why the discrepancy? Two reasons. First, psychiatry is less competitive. Second, I'm paranoid.

Given the odds, a possibility exists that I may get shut out of every plastic-surgery residency. If that happens, I'll go to Plan B. I'm so determined to become a plastic surgeon that I'm willing to get there through the back door—complete six years of general-surgery hell and *then* reapply for a plastic-surgery residency. I dread having to go to Plan B.

In January, I receive fifteen interview invitations for general surgery and eight for plastic surgery. I prepare to spend the rest of January and much of February driving and flying around the country to meet the residency program directors and residents who will determine my fate. I take out another loan to cover my expenses. No big deal. Toss another $25,000 into the pot that someday I plan to pay back, hopefully before I move into my assisted-living apartment.

I start by driving to Toledo, Ohio, for a general-surgery interview. I have no interest in either general surgery or Toledo, Ohio, but it will give me an opportunity to practice interviewing. This will be a trial run. I'll probably schedule at least one more general surgery as a practice. I am all about preparation.

I spend the night before in my hotel room, asking myself dummy questions that I've obtained from Shelly the gunner, who's somehow obtained a list of sample questions that interviewers usually ask. The interview itself will make up only a fraction of a full day of tours, lunches, lectures, and possibly a second interview. I memorize the questions I'll be asked and prepare how to frame my answers. I work on my poker face as I practice such lies as "I find the field of general surgery absolutely fascinating" and "Why do I want to become a general surgeon? Oh, general surgery is by far the best fit for me. And I *love* doing trauma."

After Toledo, I hit Cleveland, spend another entire day pretending that I was born for general surgery. I drive back feeling like a fake. I still have thirteen more general-surgery residencies where I've been invited to interview, but I decide to put them off. I'm ready to take on plastic surgery. I've heard that some of the interviewers can be quirky—think Romeo Bouley, MD—but at least I won't be faking my passion.

INTERVIEW ONE.

Cincinnati.

I drive there the day before and again spend the evening in my motel room, grilling myself with questions. I'm more than ready.

I bomb the interview. A boring resident reads a bunch of boring questions off a sheet in front of him. I try to engage him, but he keeps his head buried in his canned questions, and we don't connect. After the interview, several other candidates and I go on a tour of the hospital where we'd be working. As we stroll down a corridor clustered behind our tour leader, an even more boring general-surgery resident droning on about their cutting-edge facilities, a young resident staggers out of the call room. He looks emaciated, his skin translucent and gray. He shields his eyes from the overhead lighting as if he's been hibernating and hasn't seen light in six months. He lurches toward a vending machine. I fall back from the group.

"Hey."

"Hey," he says in a reedy voice. "You got change for a five?"

"Allow me. My treat."

"You must be applying for residency."

"You saw through me. I'm trying to buy you off."

He smiles, points to a Snickers. The candy bar thunks into the metal tray.

"So, how do you like it here?" I ask.

"This place is hell." He chews, savors the taste. "The worst. It sucks."

"What sucks, exactly?"

"Everything. I haven't left the hospital in six days. You want me to take you through a typical day?"

"Please."

"You start rounding at five A.M. You finish by about eight. Then you round with the chief resident until nine. Then you do full rounds with the attending until eleven. Then you operate. By the time you're finished in the OR, it's four, sometimes five. Then you round again."

He swallows the rest of the Snickers in one bite. He looks at me with sunken, lifeless eyes. "Round, round, round. By the time I finish seeing patients, it's nearly midnight. Then I start all over again. Round and round. They won't let me leave. I'm a prisoner. They will not let me *leave*."

Okay, so we've established the bottom.

I still rank it ahead of all the general-surgery residencies.

THE CITIES, SURGERY centers, and hospitals begin to blur. I start to feel like I'm the ball in a pinball machine.

Then the interviews get weird.

Escape from New York

I spend two grand on an overnight trip to New York, which results in a one-minute interview after a two-hour wait in a hospital located in a burned-out section of the Bronx. Out of cash, I ride the subway from a sketchy subway stop in the North Bronx all the way back to JFK, an hour trip, my briefcase clutched between my clattering knees, my eyes fixed on the floor in fear, avoiding the eyes of the other riders on the car, who look like they're on their way to a Crips convention.

I put this residency low on my list.

Draw Me

In a midwestern medical center, an interviewer slides a sheet of paper across the desk. "Draw an ear."

"Sorry, did you say draw an *ear*?"

"Yes, Mr. Youn. The folds of an ear. And then I'm going to describe a deformity, and you're going to draw the procedure you would perform to correct it."

Hand shaking, I begin to sketch.

I put this residency one above Cincinnati on my list.

Tie One On

This interviewer smiles diabolically, waits for an eternity, and says, "Take off your tie."

I'm getting used to being ambushed, so I undo my tie and pull it off without question.

"Show me how you would do a muscle or a skin flap to re-create a nose. Do it with your tie."

He chuckles like Freddy Krueger.

I like the creativity this guy shows. I just don't like the guy. The way things are going, so far this one's my favorite.

See No Evil

Hands down, the craziest. In California.

An attending surgeon leads me into his office. He stands behind his desk and stares at me. I don't know whether to sit, so I don't. I face him, shifting my weight nervously, waiting for him to give me some indication of how to proceed. Finally, he points to a chair. We sit simultaneously. He reaches behind him and places on his desk a sculpture of three monkeys in "See no evil, hear no evil, speak no evil" pose.

He claps his hands. "IT'S MONKEY TIME!" he shouts.

I practically fly out of my chair.

"IT'S MONKEY TIME!" he screams again, then says quietly, "Discuss." He places a stopwatch next to the monkey sculpture. "You have thirty seconds to impress me . . . *Doctor*." He clicks on the stopwatch.

How do I get the hell out of here?

FINALLY, HOME.

Grand Rapids.

Where I began my adventure into plastic surgery six months ago, and where I discovered I wanted to be a plastic surgeon.

The moment I step into the surgery center, I'm greeted like a family member. My interviews feel relaxed, unhurried. The chief of plastic surgery asks me point-blank, no monkey business, "Why do you want to be a plastic surgeon?"

"I like the variety of surgeries that you do," I say. "I like doing reconstruction where you can really see changes." I pause. I've given this a lot of thought. "I love the immediate gratification," I say. "I love that you don't have to wait for lab reports or anything else to see the results of your work. And being a plastic surgeon is very creative, very artistic. I also believe that a plastic surgeon can change a patient's life."

I spend the whole day hanging out in Grand Rapids, getting reacquainted. Everyone treats me as if I'm already a resident. I leave with Grand Rapids locked as my top choice. Honestly, it's my first, second, and third choices.

I have to get in.

"IT'S GOING TO be tough."

Dr. Karr, a dean of our medical school in Grand Rapids and one of the three people who interviewed me, sighs at the other end of the phone. "They like you, Tony. They like you a lot. But they only have two spots."

"Really?"

"I know. What can I say? And—" He holds. "They already gave one of the spots to Garth Ellington."

My stomach flips over. I rub my forehead, lean against the wall in the kitchen on Flower Street. "Ellington, huh?"

"Do you blame them?"

I worked with Garth Ellington for one of the weeks I spent at Grand Rapids. Garth Ellington is thirty-one, married, has two adorable kids, has a black belt in kung fu, is a gourmet cook, does metal sculptures for fun—several of which have been displayed in a New York art gallery—scored off the charts on his Boards, and demonstrates the kind of natural skill as a surgeon that you can't teach. He's also one of the nicest guys I've ever met. I think of him as a real-life James Bond. No. I don't blame them.

"What about the other spot? Am I up against like two hundred others?"

"Not that many. Half that."

"Great."

"I'm pushing for you, Tony. I'm pushing hard."

"I appreciate that. Thank you. I really want this."

"I know you do."

"So, what do you think of my chances?"

Another pause.

"Touch and go."

21

Match Madness

Match Day.

The fifteenth of March.

The day we learn which residency program we will attend.

Everyone calls Match Day the single most important event in our four years of medical school. The hype doesn't do it justice. Match Day determines not just where we'll be but *who* we'll be.

After we complete our interviews (I attend all eight of my plastic-surgery interviews and almost all of my general-surgery interviews), we rank our residency programs in order of preference and submit the list to the National Resident Matching Program. The NRMP compares our list with the list the residency programs submit and then decides if there is a match. To me the process sounds like E-Harmony or JDate, but this is how it's done. I pray that our top choices match, because if none of our choices do match, we enter a nightmare—the dreaded Scramble. Through desperate phone calls, e-mails, faxes, and calling in every favor we can muster, we literally scramble to land in one of the few residency spots left somewhere—anywhere—across the country. We may enter the Scramble a dermatologist and exit a geriatrician. Or worse. We may find ourselves on the sidelines, an anomaly, an unemployed doctor.

I rank Grand Rapids first. I don't have a second choice. I rank the two places where I had my least objectionable interviews two and three. I rank Springfield, the hand clinic, fourth; Cincinnati, where I spoke to the zombie resident, second to last; the hospital in the North Bronx, last. While I'll be devastated if I don't land the one spot available in Grand Rapids, I'll understand and accept any of the other plastic-surgery residencies, as miserable as I'll be at some of them. That's how much I want to become a plastic surgeon.

The closer we get to Match Day, the less I sleep. The day before, I'm an ornery, fidgety, sleep-deprived wreck. All week Tim has appeared strangely calm and full of clichés, which makes the rest of us want to pummel him. He's ranked Cornell University first and has received every indication that he'll get in.

"It'll be what it'll be," he says. "Nothing we can do about it. You have to go with the flow."

"The ship has sailed," James says.

"It's out of our hands," I say.

"A penny saved is a penny earned," Ricky says.

"Screw you guys," Tim says.

The night before the rest of our lives, James abandons us to go to dinner with Daisy, Ricky disappears to destinations unknown, and Tim and I decide to take one last stroll across campus. It's a perfect spring night, brisk, breezy, the air smelling of lilacs. As we walk, images from the last four years blaze through my mind at warp speed, my collection of moments—the horrors of Owen Hall; riding my Huffy across campus, almost sailing over the handlebars after too many beers; orientation; our small group and catching our three-hundred-pound classmate, who has since dropped out; Clark the refrigerator repairman's unfortunate proposal at the USA Café to Daisy, who's now engaged to James; Youner, master of the shopping-cart dance; my first look into the bucket of hands; our first night at Flower Street and the ensuing ten thousand knocks on the head I received from the low ceiling leading into the basement; the endless days and nights in the Nerd

Room; Dr. Gaw and *gross* anatomy; clinical skills and my terrifying timed interviews with actor patients; the night I spent with the horrifyingly unfit mother whose pet raccoon feasted on her poor baby's face; the ten-hour Whipple surgery; *"I'M COMING HOME WITH YOU, PRETTY BOY!"*; the world of naked-lady lamps and leeches in a Malibu mansion; "Monkey time!" and my other ridiculous residency interviews; and Grand Rapids, the residency I long for, the place that feels like home.

And then I focus on the people, the ones who have touched my life forever—

Tim, Ricky, and James, my three dear friends who helped me resurrect my confidence and locate my true self. It has been my privilege to share my medical-school journey with them. And among my other privileges—I held a newborn baby as he first entered the world; I performed a perfect spinal tap on a small, ill child; I encouraged a man to face death and conquer it; I rocked a sick baby to sleep in my arms until the sun came up. And I felt honored and awed to have learned from the gifts of all the people who donated their bodies for my medical education. Last—and never least—I gazed into the eyes of a beautiful doctor-to-be who did not look away but was able to fall in love with someone as flawed as I.

"Four years, Youner," Tim says. "Gone in the blink of an eye."

"If you speak in one more cliché, I'm gonna throttle you."

"I can't help it. I speak in clichés when I'm nervous."

"You, nervous?"

"This calm, collected front? It's an act. I'm dying to get this over with. Not that anyone should wish time away. I can't stop myself."

I don't answer. I gaze at the sky and follow the murky shadow the moonlight casts over us. I feel as if I've drifted into a grainy 1930s black-and-white movie. After a moment Tim lays his hand gently on my forearm. "You all right?"

"I was just thinking. I can finally answer the question."

"What question?"

"Why I want to be a doctor." I hold for half a second. "I want to fix people," I say. "I want to make them look different if they need to, or even if they want to. Because maybe I can make them . . . *better*."

After a long silence, Tim says, "I guess I could say the same thing." He pauses again. "I didn't. But I could. And from now on, I will. And pretend that I was the one who said it first."

"You're such a jerk."

We crack up, laughing the way we did the first night we went to the USA Café. Finally, we stand silently, neither of us wanting to be anywhere but here. "Tim, seriously. I couldn't have gotten through these four years without you."

"Same here."

And then we hug, two brothers knowing that after tomorrow, nothing will be the same.

High noon.

An hour earlier, Tim, Jane, Amy, and I gather with the rest of our classmates in what swiftly becomes a hundred-person scrum in the lobby of the administration building. I see Shelly the gunner stationed in the very front. She probably slept here. Ricky huddles in a corner, alone, dressed in his lucky Hawaiian shirt. He blows us a kiss. James and Daisy occupy the opposite corner. They see us, wave, applaud. We applaud back.

For forty-five minutes we mingle, joke, make the lamest of small talk, my hand nervously clutching Amy's. At noon, the campus clock tolls its first of twelve booming chimes, and then a distant door opens, footsteps clack onto the buffed hall floor, the throng of us lift our voices, then lower them into a collective murmur. In a moment the tall, skeletal, white-haired dean who first spoke to us at orientation appears, walking in an even more exaggerated hunch than I remembered, holding in both scarecrow hands a stack of a hundred envelopes. We part for him like a human Red Sea. He stops in the center of us, says a few canned

words that not one of us hears, then slowly announces our names alpha-
betically, peering up after each one, waiting for us to come forward and
claim our envelope, which he offers with a thin grim smile.

Some students tear open their envelope on the spot. Some retreat
to a quiet corner and ease their letter out. Some of us shriek, some
curse, several wail in agony, joy, or surprise. Others grab their envelope and leave to open it privately. Around the fiftieth name, the dean
calls, "Tim O'Laughlin." Tim slouches forward, snatches his envelope, shakes the ancient dean's hand, and retreats. I, Youn, will have
to wait until the dean reads off almost every name in our class except
for two Youngs, a Yudelman, two Zees, and Zimmerman. Finally, the
dean croaks out, "*Youn,*" and presses an envelope into my outstretched,
trembling palm. I somehow manage to blurt, "Thank you, Dean," in
the voice of a soprano.

By prior arrangement, Tim, Jane, Amy, and I duck into the student
lounge, away from the madness. Amy drops my hand and plants herself
next to me, my spotter in case I read extreme news, good or bad, and
start to faint and keel over.

"You first," I say to Tim.

Calm no more, he tears open his envelope. We can all read the let-
terhead that he holds: *Cornell University.* He shouts, pumps a fist, and
throws his arms around Jane, who sneaks a Cornell baseball cap out of
her coat pocket and wriggles it onto his head. He screams again.

And then everyone turns to me.

Time stands still. I sway, light-headed. Then, as if I'm standing
to the side watching somebody else, I see myself open the envelope,
fumble with the letter, and read: *Grand Rapids Plastic Surgery.*

Shouting, screaming, wailing, some of it coming from me. Everything goes fuzzy, and then Amy and I are kissing while Tim hugs me.
I break away and scream at the top of my lungs. Tim and I link our
arms around each other, and we both scream at the top of our lungs. I
feel stupidly, lovingly, insanely high. I grab Amy's hand and we all bolt
out of the lounge and look for James and Ricky, but they've gone. I will

find them later and learn that both got into their top choices, meaning that Flower Street went four for four! We pour a round of champagne, and I call my parents. My mother sobs, and my father lets out a strange, unfamiliar grunt, and then I realize this is the second time I've heard him cry. We hang up, I start to pack, and as I do, I think about all the people I have to thank and the arrangements I have to make.

It—the Big *It*—doesn't happen until I'm on the road, driving away from campus, my four years of medical school behind me, so recently gone, already feeling like a filmy memory. I head home, my fingers clenched white on the steering wheel of my rickety Ford Tempo, which I've noticed recently has begun to lurch like an old man.

It may be time for a new car. My faithful old buddy has done its job, taken me where I want to go. I've finally gotten there. I have arrived.

And that's when it hits me for the first time.

I am a doctor.

Acknowledgments

TONY:

First and always foremost, thank you to God for all the blessings that have been bestowed on me. I know that I am not deserving of all the good fortune that has come my way. I am humbled by how good God has been, and continues to be, to me.

To Dad and Mom. Thank you for your unconditional love. While I didn't realize it at the time, having you as role models for determination, work ethic, and dedication to family have helped shape me into the person I am today. I am forever grateful to have you as my parents.

To Amy, my wife and companion. Meeting you is the best thing that's ever happened to me. Thank you for being so understanding and supportive with the time I took for this book. I love everything about you.

To my co-writer, Alan Eisenstock. You are a consummate professional, a fantastic writer, and a good friend. One of the best things about writing this book has been developing a friendship with you. It's been an honor working together on this book. Thank you for dedicating a year of your life to my story. I still owe you a beer!

To my agent, Wendy Sherman. Thank you for believing in this book and believing in me. You are the best agent in the U.S., period! Your advice has been so unbelievably helpful throughout this crazy process. Thank you for creating the perfect match with Alan and Kara.

To my editor, Kara Cesare. Thank you for being the biggest fan of my story. I know that I couldn't have sold this book without you, and am so grateful for your support and untiring dedication. I could not have asked for a better editor! The "Dream Team!"

To my editor-in-chief, Jen Bergstrom. Thank you for embracing me into the Gallery Books family and for all your kind words and encouragement. It's an honor to work with you. You are a gem.

To my publisher, Louise Burke, and the rest of the staff at Gallery Books. Being one of your authors is a dream come true. Thank you for all your support and guidance.

To Brian Smith. You are a creative talent and one of my best friends. I could not have survived medical school or written this book without you. We've come a long way, Smither!

To Mike and Lisa, Jim and Py. Thank you for being my closest family. Your love and support mean the world to me.

To Rachael Ray and the staff at *The Rachael Ray Show*. Thank you for allowing me to be a part of your show and making me look good. It's an honor to work with all of you.

To Nani Power. Thank you for taking the time to go over my manuscript and referring me to your agent.

To my family and friends who have supported me throughout my life and in the writing of this book. There are too many of you to name, and I fear that I will inadvertently leave someone out. You know who you are, from New Jersey to Grand Rapids to Chicago to L.A., and many places in between. Thank you for all the fun and laughs through the years. See you on Facebook!

To my employees and coworkers. Thank you for helping make me the physician I am. I could not do my job without your help. A doctor is only as good as the nurses, techs, PAs, and support staff around him.

To all the physicians who have graciously given their time to train and teach me. I have taken pieces of each of you to become the doctor I am today. I hope I make you proud.

To all the patients, past and present, who have allowed me to care for you, treat you, and, especially, learn from you. Thank you for bringing me into your lives and trusting in me to be your doctor.

Finally, to D and G—I hope that someday reading this story gives you comfort, pride, and guidance, even long after I am gone. I love you so much.

ALAN:

Thanks to Tony, the coolest, smartest, savviest, nicest, best collaborator ever, and now my friend. You even got me to blog.

Thanks to Brian Smith. Could not have done it without you.

Thanks to Wendy Sherman, agent supreme, who never gave up, and found us the perfect match with Gallery.

Thanks to everyone at Gallery, with enormous gratitude to Jen Bergstrom.

Thanks to Kara Cesare, our editor, simply the best. Without you, babe, *In Stitches* would not exist.

Thanks to the doctors in my life who had my literary back during the writing of *In Stitches*—Dr. Phil Schwarzman, Dr. Linda Nussbaum, and Dr. George Weinberger.

Thanks to Katie O'Laughlin and everyone at Village Books in Pacific Palisades, California, "my office," where Snickers and I hang out. And R.I.P. Top.

Thanks to David Ritz.

Thanks to all my dear friends and my family, especially my parents, Jimmy and Shirley Eisenstock.

And thanks, always, to Bobbie, Jonah, and Kiva, my heartbeats, and forever, Zachary.